CHINA'S ECONOMIC OPENING
TO THE OUTSIDE WORLD

CHINA'S ECONOMIC OPENING TO THE OUTSIDE WORLD

The Politics of Empowerment

Jonathan R. Woetzel

PRAEGER

New York
Westport, Connecticut
London

Library of Congress Cataloging-in-Publication Data

Woetzel, Jonathan R.
    China's economic opening to the outside world: the politics of
empowerment / Jonathan R. Woetzel.
        p.   cm.
    Bibliography: p.
    Includes index.
    ISBN 0-275-93163-3 (alk. paper)
        1. China—Economic conditions—1976-   2. China—Economic
policy—1976-   3. China—Foreign economic relations.   I. Title.
HC427.92.W654   1989
337.51—dc19   88-27577

Library of Congress Catalog Card Number: 88-27577
ISBN: 0-275-93163-3

First published in 1989

Praeger Publishers, One Madison Avenue, New York, NY 10010
A division of Greenwood Press, Inc.

Printed in the United States of America

The paper used in this book complies with the Permanent
Paper Standard issued by the National Information Standards
Organization (Z39.48—1984).

10 9 8 7 6 5 4 3 2 1

To my father,
always my best teacher.
Per aspera ad astra.

Contents

List of Illustrations

List of Abbreviations

BoC	Bank of China
CAAC	Civil Aviation Administration of China
CEIEC	China National Electronics Import-Export Corporation
CITIC	China International Trust and Investment Corporation
CPC	Communist Party of China
DFI	Direct Foreign Investment
FESCO	Foreign Enterprise Service Corporation
FTC	Foreign Trade Corporation
GNP	Gross National Product
GPCR	Great Proletarian Cultural Revolution
GSP	Gross Social Product
IEC	Import-Export Corporation
JV	Joint Venture
LDC	Less Developed Country
MEI	Ministry of Electronics Industry
MOFERT	Ministry of Foreign Economic Relations and Trade
NIC	Newly Industrializing Country
PLA	People's Liberation Army
PRC	People's Republic of China
RMB	Renminbi
SEC	State Economic Commission
SEZ	Special Economic Zone
SPC	State Planning Commission

Acknowledgments

Thanks are due to many individuals that this project reached its fruition, responsibility for it of course resting solely on myself. First and most importantly, my family's encouragement and support, especially Abdo Ballester, made a large and invaluable contribution to my research and writing. George O. Totten, Stanley Rosen, and James Rosenau all gave generously of their time, as did Li Daokui. Those who contributed in interviews, data gathering and discussions are too numerous to mention, but at a brief attempt I would like to especially thank Yao Nienqing, Wang Tieya, Tan Jian, Patricia Eyster, Liao Guocai, Ma Linghuan, Joshua Rottenberg, and Sabina Brady. I would also like to express my appreciation for the many comments and much good advice given to me by colleagues and fellow professionals, especially Terrey Arcus and David Willensky.

CHINA'S ECONOMIC OPENING TO THE OUTSIDE WORLD

Introduction: Thinking About China

The "China hand" is faced with at least three troubling issues. First and perhaps most important, is the persistent failure by both Chinese and foreigners to understand each other's motives and actions. The record of observers on both sides is dismal in predicting the great events of the last two centuries from the West's sacking of the Summer Palace in the early 1900s to the Chinese Cultural Revolution of the 1960s. Second, the current analytical approaches to Chinese politics, though many and varied, almost uniformly contradict each other's interpretations. Hence, it seems that proper "frameworks" for analyzing Chinese politics cannot be said to exist. Last, and significant, for the development of the field, the methodology of China research remains largely qualitative due to political pressures and socioeconomic constraints.

THE OBSERVERS' RECORD

In the 1800s, a common Chinese myth (dispelled during the Opium Wars) was that foreign soldiers could bend neither at the back nor the knees. Another held that without Chinese tea and rhubarb Westerners would sicken and perish.[1] The Neo-Confucianist orthodoxy relegated all foreigners to supplicant tributary roles. Even later "Westernizing" Chinese, such as the translator Yan Fu, flavored disdain with outright hostility following the end of the First World War as he wrote: "It seems to me that in three centuries of progress the peoples of the West have achieved four principles: to be selfish, to kill others, to have little integrity, and to feel little shame. How different are the principles of Confucius and

Mencius, as broad and deep as Heaven and Earth, designed to benefit man everywhere." Western scholar Herrlee Creel summarizes: "The Chinese had long considered themselves the most cultured, the most important, and indeed the only truly really important people on the face of the earth."[2] Western impressions of the Chinese on the other hand ranged from Rodney Gilbert's deceitful childish mandarin to Pearl Buck's idealized hardworking peasant. To quote Mr. Gilbert in *What's Wrong With China?*: "There are inferior races in the world, just as there are inferior men in every community. There are nations that cannot govern themselves but must have a master.... Races, like men, have their limitations.... [China is] the world's greatest contemporary burlesque."[3] Leading missionary A. H. Smith in his *Survey of Chinese Characteristics* of 1894 noted three traits of the Chinese mind obvious to him: disregard of accuracy; a talent for misunderstanding; and a propensity to be opaque.[4] Twentieth-century Western observers, lulled in part by these stereotypes, refused to accept the possibility of radical change in China.[5] Most held Bolshevism, the product of European discontent, could not take root in China. Chiang Kai-shek's tales of bandits were thus largely accepted until the publication of Edgar Snow's *Red Star Over China* in 1937.[6] To quote J.D. Whelpley in the *Fortnightly Review* in 1927: "The psychology and tradition of the Chinese render them less susceptible to Marxian doctrines than any people in the world. They are a nation of individualists, the entire social and economic system being founded upon the dignity and value to the community of the individual trader."[7]

On the other side, Mao Zedong and Zhou Enlai were equally bemused by the behavior of the American General Hurley on his visit to the Yan'an base camp in 1944. Colonel David Barratt describes the visit:

After the general had returned the salute of the officer commanding the company, he drew himself up to his full impressive height, swelled up like a poisoned pup, and let out an Indian warwhoop. I shall never forget the expressions on the faces of Mao and Zhou at this totally unexpected behaviour on the part of the distinguished visitor. After the review, Chairman Mao and the general climbed into the cab of the ancient truck and I squeezed in with them to act as interpreter. This was a task of some difficulty, due to the saltiness of the General's remarks, and the unusual language in which he expressed himself.... [It] required quick thinking and free translation on my part in order to give the chairman and Zhou Enlai some faint idea of what the talk was about.[8]

The communications gulf widened after the break of U.S.–China relations in 1949. Until the 1970s the major American and most Western media portrayed China as a monolithic yellow peril sweeping communism over Asia. Among the various popular images associated with this was that of the slave state, Russian control (until the obvious became apparent in the 1960s), mass starvation, and a China bent on precipitating a nuclear war as "there would be 300,000,000 left." The remark was actually made by Tito in 1958 when China and Yugoslavia were trading accusations. Walter Lippmann and Charles Mertz analyzed the *New York Times* coverage of the Soviet Union in 1920 and concluded that it was "nothing short of a disaster," the net effect "almost always misleading and misleading news is worse than none at all." Journalist Felix Greene likewise concluded in reviewing Western coverage of China from 1949 to 1964: "In many significant ways we are basing national policies on a concept of China that is unreal."[9] The official Chinese press, on the other hand, pictured China as a lone representative of the Third World fighting against superpower hegemonism. In reality, while both media images conflicted violently, neither was particularly accurate. China's opportunistic anti-Sovietism led it to do such not-communistic things as aid General Pinochet's Chile. Its territorial clashes with India and Vietnam belied its claims to Third World solidarity.

The gaps between images and reality of China were sharpest in periods of change. Foreigners seemed to encounter a particular poverty of explanation for China's major tilts from Soviet dependence to isolationism to Opening to the Outside World. No major Western scholar accurately forecast either the Great Leap Forward or the Cultural Revolution. Tai Chun-kuo and Ramon Myers have noted four major areas of misunderstanding among Western scholars: the effect of new political systems on the Chinese people; the extent of factionalism; the importance of ideas in political changes; and the existence of basic functional elements in the Chinese political system.[10] After the first few errors, few claimed to explain why China changed policy and how long the new one would last.

Put in perspective, the record may say more about logistics and observer biases than the reality of Chinese life. Many of the early visitors to China after 1949 especially during the Cultural Revolution, tended to be politically committed activists. For example, John Collier and his wife Elsie Collier, both English trade union activists, spent a year and a half in China from 1966 to 1968, after which they wrote a partial account entitled *China's Socialist Revolution*. To quote the Colliers, "I make no apology for the passages of social theorising appearing cheek-by-jowl with descriptions of ordinary events occurring in the factory, farm or college."[11] Their politically charged sentiments appealed to a segment of the Western community, especially disenchanted academics, but did not command universal assent.[12] Tom Englehart on the other hand rather poetically comments on long-time U.S. journalists leaving China in 1950: "Unwillingly, for the first time in a century, they left China to her own people. From the border at British-held Kowloon they looked back for some hint of movement in the peasant fields beyond, but for them night had descended on darkest China."[13]

Republic of China observers were also usually discounted by establishment Western observers for blatantly ideological assessments of Chinese current events, even when they were in fact correct.[14] Mainland Chinese sources such as *Renmin Ribao* and *China Daily* were considered propagandistic and had light foreign readership. The Chinese party-controlled press has indeed been unusually opaque by Western standards, tending to present Beijing official drafts as news accounts, giving little clue as to the actual source of change within the system. Events not in line with official foreign or domestic policy have gone unreported or twisted beyond recognition. For example, China's 1974–76 complete plant imports were a closely guarded state secret. In 1979, the overturning of the Bohai No. 2 Oil Rig was successfully covered up for months before discovery. This, however, is also an area where marked improvements have been made in the decade since 1976. In 1986, the Enterprise Bankruptcy Law debate in the National People's Congress was conducted publicly and televised. Reform has also brought a statistical renaissance. However, it is still difficult to understand how much weight to give many figures and what the margin of error is. Moreover, the 1986–87 expulsions of Western correspondents such as Lawrence McDonald of Agence France Press and John Burns of the *New York Times*, graphically illustrate official disregard for the sanctity of the press.

China's decentralization and secrecy have presented more problems for observers. The *neibu*, internal regulations with binding force, have been a potent weapon of the bureaucracy to keep outsiders, both domestic and foreign, in line. In one case, a Guangzhou joint venture discovered that the Bank of China took it upon itself to verify and inspect the work of a building contractor without informing the venture's management, withholding a foreign exchange payment until it had itself verified the work. Such secrecy combined with China's decentralized village economy has made it very difficult for foreign business to establish itself without enormous expenditures of time. In 1986 Wang Computer staffed its Guangzhou sales office with about five sales executives. These representatives made presentations in and around Guangdong provinces according to destinations given them by the Ministry of Electronics. Each trip took usually a few days at a time and most of the presentations did not result in sales. One salesman who had prior experience selling radios in China alone for three years, confided that those Wang sales he did make were on the average never larger than 1 to 10 machines, with peripherals, because of the small size of most village industries.

Personal relationships among factory managers have also prevented foreign business from entering Chinese markets. In 1986, a factory manager of a Guangdong electronic materials factory under the Ministry of Electronics noted that even though almost half of the ministry's factories had been reassigned to provincial authorities in Guangdong province, the factory managers remained the same. Hence, he was able to continue sales to them despite pressure from the Guangdong Foreign Trade Commission and foreign sales representatives.[15] Chinese prejudice in fact appears to be as responsible as Western prejudice for the communications gap.

For the West, though, the communications problem is not restricted to China. Public policy scholar Howard Wiarda notes: "At the root of our [United States] foreign policy dilemmas in these areas [the Third World] is a deeply ingrained American ethnocentrism, an insistence on viewing it through lenses of our own Western experience, and the condescending and patronizing attitudes that such ethnocentrism implies."[16] Unfortunately, many Chinese officials have likewise no comprehension of the basic principles of the Western experience. Vice Minister Li Lanqing of the Ministry of Foreign Economic Relations and Trade (MOFERT) for one has advocated importing Western managers to run Chinese factories thereby transferring management skills. However, Li has also noted that some foreign companies, especially Japanese, have found it difficult to communicate the problems they face so that he lacked conduits to effect positive changes in problem-plagued joint ventures.[17] Evidently, even with the best intentions, there are opportunities to improve communications on both sides.

AN INVENTORY OF APPROACHES

Tendency Politics

The second problem facing the observer of China is the multiplicity of apparently contradictory approaches. The major current of foreign analysis of Chinese politics from the 1950s to the 1980s has been based on the early "red" versus "expert" paradigm, of which Franz Schurmann's *Ideology and Organization in Communist China* is an influential example.[18] In the paradigm, the reds were usually identified as radical Maoists who took class struggle as the key link, and were dedicated to the infallible, dogmatic authority of the three red flags: socialism, the CPC, and Marxism Leninism Mao Zedong Thought. The experts, led by such politicians as Deng Xiaoping and Liu Shaoqi and economists like Sun Yefang, were perceived as being more pragmatic in their beliefs and rational in economic policy. Lowell Dittmer, for one, analyzed the split between Liu Shaoqi and Mao as a conflict between bureaucratic (expert) and charismatic (red) leaders, precipitated by a "premature succession crisis," that is, the 1959 elevation of Liu to chairmanship and Mao's retirement to the second line.[19] Such tendency analysis appeared to satisfactorily explain the major rifts in Chinese communism until the end of the Cultural Revolution in 1976.

These "tendency" perceptions were heightened by the extremes of the Cultural Revolution. An ideological struggle was being loudly waged in the Chinese press, mostly one-sided, against "capitalist-roaders." Possibly influenced by this, Western "red versus expert" analysis tended to discount the significance of geographic, economic and cultural factors in China's development strategy.[20] The bifurcated development priorities of a small leadership group were perceived as the prime movers in Chinese politics, as it was assumed or implied that the leadership had the ability to ensure their political priorities were implemented effectively and accurately, in the face of adverse economic conditions.[21] Of key importance, "red versus expert" analyses characterized Chinese elites "atemporally" divorced from dynamic changes in the societal base.

With the increasingly apparent flux in China's history, however, and the difficulty in tying key leaders to either the red or the expert camp in the post-Mao transition, critics have contended those two ideological tendencies alone became inadequate to provide a reliable and valid explanation of current political events. A decade previously, one had already noted acerbically that "what we have here is essentially a transplantation of early-day Kremlinology to the China field."[22] The issues behind the Cultural Revolution and the post-Mao transition were broader than the simple "two-line" or "three-line" explanation. As circumstantial evidence of this, the number of lines in present-day analysis of this type has proliferated.[23] The excessive focus on political line divorced from economic change as a determinant of Chinese politics appeared to be the mirror of the features of the Cultural Revolution in much Western analysis.[24] Essentially, some critics contended political line was and is a valid area of inquiry, but divorced from its socioeconomic context, the study became meaningless.

When put in socioeconomic context then, the political line discussion has evolved to a more sophisticated and relevant argument that there is a fundamental contradiction between modernization and what some have perceived as the Chinese totalitarian state.[25] For example, Richard Lowenthal in his seminal article "Development versus Utopia in Communist Policy" posited that Communist regimes faced an inevitable dilemma between the rising forces of spontaneous, self-generating change occasioned by economic growth and their own mandate as the vanguard of this development. In his words, the Communist state becomes "unable to continue its revolutionary offensive against society and unwilling to be reduced to a mere expression of the constellation of social forces at a given moment ... a guardian clinging to his role after his ward has reached adulthood."[26] The post–1978 experience of China would appear to test whether a vanguard party and economic growth are mutually exclusive.

Marxist Politics

The major body of writings on China is, of course, that of the Chinese. Unfortunately though, the Marxist concept of bureaucracy used by most Chinese scholars is clearly limiting. Bureaucracy, according to Marx, was only the manifestation of alienation in bourgeois society, the tool of the bourgeoisie to oppress the working class. Both Marx and Engels saw society without bureaucracy as the end of the communist revolution.[27] To attain the freedom of the species-being, the goal and the essence of Marxist human rights, the parasitic state apparatus must be smashed. To quote Engel's most famous statement on the elimination of the state:

The first act in which the state really comes forward as the representative of the society as a whole—the taking of possession of the means of production in the name of society—is at the same time its last independent act as a state. The interference of the state power in social relations becomes superfluous in one sphere after another, and then ceases of itself. The government of persons is replaced by the administration of things and the direction of the processes of production.[28]

Clearly in China, though, as in the Soviet Union and all other socialist countries, the government of persons remains a very tangible force. Nepotism is widespread in educational and work opportunities, cases of economic crimes among officials are frequently reported in the official press, and a range of material perquisites are available to bureaucrats.[29] Marx acknowledged the continuing role of the state, in the *Critique of the Gotha Programme*, to provide a distributive mechanism so long as resource scarcity exists.[30] Lenin's contribution of the vanguard theory emphasized the absolute necessity for an organized dictatorship of the proletariat to combat the capitalists. Neither, however, favored a bureaucracy unaccountable to its people, such as Stalin's became. To quote Lenin:

Under Socialism officials will cease to be "bureaucrats"; they will cease to be so in direct proportion as, in addition to the election of officials, the principle of recall at any time is introduced, and as salaries are reduced to the level of the wages of the average worker, and, too, as parliamentary institutions are superseded by working bodies, executive and legislative at the same time.[31]

Other twentieth century revolutionaries such as Rosa Luxemburg and Antonio Gramsci explicitly championed the rights of the individual in socialist society and the importance of ensuring accountability from the bottom up. The oft-quoted discussion of Lenin's dissolution of the Constituent Assembly in 1917 demonstrated Luxemburg's belief that political education could only be gained by personal experience, not handed down from the party. As she said: "The more democratic the institutions, the livelier and stronger the pulsebeat of the political life of the masses, the more direct and complete is their influence.... The whole mass of the people must take part in it [the socialist revolution]. Otherwise socialism will be decreed from behind a few official desks by a dozen intellectuals."[32] In reply, Lenin invoked necessity in *Proletarian Revolution* stating that the Assembly represented the interest of the counterrevolution and was composed of electors from a prerevolutionary canvass. To quote: "To say that the Constituent Assembly should not have been dispersed is tantamount to saying that the fight against the bourgeoisie should not have been fought to a finish, that the bourgeoisie should not have been overthrown and that the proletariat should have become reconciled with it."[33]

The existence and apparent intransigence of the bureaucracy in China, subjected to Marxist analysis, raises the question of a new class formation. Paul Sweezy comments in a 1967 essay *Lessons of Soviet Experience*: "Historically, property systems have been the most common institutional arrangement for ensuring the inheritability of privilege and blocking the upward movement of the unprivileged. But other devices such as caste and hereditary nobility have also served these purposes."[34] These other devices may be even more prominent in a society only recently from a "feudal" past such as China.

The essence of a Marxist concept of class is a common relationship to the means of production. While the abolition of private property has made a exploitative relationship formally impossible in socialist societies, a number of such disparate writers as Milovan Djilas, Leon Trotsky and Robert Michels have questioned whether a bureaucratic class can form on the ashes of the old society, not on the basis of ownership but appropriation. Trotsky would only go so far as to say that the bureaucracy represented a new stratum not class, as the preconditions for class relationships —a market for labor-power and for large means of production — were not present in Soviet society. Advocates of the "state capitalist" theory such as Djilas and Rizzi contended that the central bureaucracy did indeed form a class that extracted the surplus labor of the workers and used it to secure positions of privilege for themselves. Quoting Djilas: "The new ownership is not the same as the political government but is created and aided by that government. The use, enjoyment and distribution of property is the privilege of the party and the party's top men."[35] The growth of this bureaucracy was encouraged by the process of large-scale industrialization which itself created a class of interests specifically linked to the cause of production.[36] In the end, the de facto control of the means of production by a privileged class of bureaucrats and the frustration of workers' aspirations lead to a new revolution by a reborn party or by the workers themselves.[37]

The state capitalist theory can be criticized on a number of grounds—the bureaucracy may not be as economically motivated as a class definition would demand, party and state may not always constitute a monolithic entity, and the element of surplus-value exploitation necessary to establish class conflict may not be entirely present.[38] However, it raises essential questions. How unified is the bureaucracy by economic class interests? Richard Kraus states Chinese bureaucrats are a social group, a "class in formation" unified by common position.[39] If so, does the Opening to the Outside World encourage or retard the process of bureaucratic class formation?

The official Chinese position since 1978 states that all is well and the bureaucracy will serve the people. On the other hand, the ten years of the Cultural Revolution were predicated on the danger of a bureaucratic-capitalist restoration. Mao noted in one 1965 directive: "The class of the bureaucrats is a class in sharp opposition to the working class and the poor and lower-middle peasants. These people have already become or are in the process of becoming capitalist elements sucking the blood of the workers."[40] He was in the end unwilling to dismantle the party and state apparatus, however, as he demonstrated in ruthlessly suppressing the radical Shengwulian movement in 1968. Shengwulian claimed that 90 percent of the bureaucracy were capitalist-roaders and that Zhou Enlai was the number-one protector of parasitic, bureaucratic state-capitalism. After a period of activism lasting only a few months, they were declared a counter-revolutionary group and suppressed. Mao recognized that bureaucrats engendered contradictions in society, though not always antagonistic ones.

In the sphere of foreign economic relations, dependency theorists, such as Dos Santos, Cardoso, and Frank, have emphasized the possibility of parasitic linkages between domestic and external capitalist elites, though differing in the potential benefits to the host country of foreign investment and the best approach to trade-offs in using it.[41] The radical critique made by the Gang of Four attacked just such a "comprador capitulationist" policy as well. Zhang Chunqiao, the Gang of Four's leading theorist, often made the point that the struggle against counterrevolution would always be long and arduous. To quote him: "Even when all the landlords and capitalists of the old generation have died, such struggles will by no means come to a stop and a bourgeois restoration may still occur." According to the so-called Gang, Deng Xiaoping and others who sought to use Western technology were auctioning off China's sovereignty and tying the fate of China's industry to the belts of foreign capitalists.[42] For the Marxists then, the Opening's economic success or failure is irrelevant beside the larger question of political independence.

Bureaucratic Politics

Class analysis of these questions has been further developed by bureaucratic theorists. Max Weber, the foremost twentieth-century theorist of authority and legitimation, believed that the bureaucracy was technically the most efficient way of administering the affairs of man. To quote him: "It [bureaucracy] is superior to any other form in precision, in stability, in the stringency of its discipline, and in its reliability."[43] Moreover, Weber also held that the modern Western institutional system was specifically geared to realizing economies possible only with the organized control of knowledge within a bureaucracy. The development of bureaucracy was inevitable with the development of large-scale industry. Talcott Parsons and others have refined the Weberian concept of the bureaucratic state by pointing out Weber's tendency to overemphasize the coercive aspect of human relations in general. Weber did note the existence of collegiality in certain places such as medicine, college faculties and so forth, but believed the bureaucracy to be the juggernaut of modern society. Parsons noted in contrast that at least in the professional services field, a "company of equals" is the predominant association.[44]

Weber opposed rational-legal to traditional authority, the major alternative. Traditional authority, resting on the established belief in the sanctity of immemorial traditions, attaches legitimacy to a person who occupies a position of authority, not to rules. The commands of the ruler are legitimized by traditions or partly the chief's free personal decision. Traditional authority is both an older and a stabler form of organization than the rational-legal. The rational-legal bureaucracy by its very nature frustrates the individual desires of its subjects as it attempts to make them conform to a standard mold, more so than necessarily in the traditional state which may provide an effective sop to insecure modern individuals. When this frustration reaches a peak, both in traditional and rational-legal states, charismatic movements ensue, bringing violent changes. These movements, led by a visionary with moral authority, inevitably create their own attendant assemblage of staffs and institutions, and become routinized into either the bureaucratic or traditional molds.

In China, several previous studies of decision-making have focused on the remarkably long-lived charismatic nature of the Chinese state, as quintessentially invoked by the Cultural Revolution. Later scholars have, however, concluded for the most part that the revolution has been routinized and that this process began almost instantaneously with the Liberation in 1949. Weber said that in 1920 the ideals and material interests of the followers of the charismatic leader in continually activating and reactivating the community and in continuing their own relationship, led inevitably to the transformation of charismatic into traditional or rational-legal authority. In 1983, Richard Kraus noted: "In the absence of 'modern' Weberian legal-rational institutions, the ruler-subject bond [in China] has formed a basis for political activity that captures important aspects of a patrimonial model originally fashioned for a state with severely limited political participation."[45]

The Weberian concept of history is that of continual conflict between traditional and bureaucratic authority, between the chief and the rules. Because the struggle for power between administrative classes and the chief and the officials he depends on will determine educational opportunities and social strata within the state, this struggle is the most basic in forming a society's culture. Because the traditional state tends to obstruct development of rational economic activity through arbitrary actions by the chief and his staff and the absence of technical qualifications, while the bureaucratic state tends to promote the same, the conflict affects the basic allocative institutions of society as well.

In the Chinese case, Weberian methodology implies the precondition for the economic success demanded of the Opening would be the replacement of the traditional state with a rational-legal bureaucracy. Several analysts lay the failure of Confucian China to successfully meld modern technology to the inept bureaucratic state.[46] The existing conflict between patrimonial and rational-legal authority prompted by the Opening might itself create the opportunity for more social insecurity and the potential of a new charismatic movement. Applying Weber, Schurmann also contends that in Chinese socialism, the Party assumes the role of charismatic agent.[47] If true, the Opening could be seen as a bid by the Party to disrupt the established bureaucracy and increase its own influence.

Either way, the Opening is either an anomaly imposed by a leadership on the administrative structure or a sign of a far more pliable bureaucracy than many have suspected. Indeed, the evidence points to a greater flexibility on the part of Chinese decision-makers to make compromises than might be expected of a highly traditional-patrimonial state, for example, as illustrated in the Beijing Jeep rescue. The questions this in turn raises are—how did the Chinese leadership achieve this flexibility in the face of a 3,000 year old bureaucratic tradition and is this flexibility sustainable in the face of the pressures of complexity and incrementalism?

To help explain this, a further perspective on the relation of foreign policy to domestic structures is that of transnational scholars such as James Rosenau. Rosenau contends that the distinctions between domestic and foreign policy are increasingly blurred and that national entities are increasingly taking on adaptive characteristics on an issue-by-issue basis as transnational politics emerge.[48] Macro changes such as resource scarcities, spreading demands by the disadvantaged for a redistribution of wealth, and the growth of unofficial transnational affiliations based on common ties, hasten the authority crisis within and between nation-states. Domestic structures are inevitably losing time-tested authority as new and unfamiliar issues surface that they have neither competence nor authority to deal with.[49] If true, this would imply that more, not less, crisis is imminent in the Chinese bureaucracy and that bureaucrats would have an implicit interest in controlling the impact of the Opening to the greatest extent possible.

A last comment, and one that supports the hypothesis of a weakening bureaucracy, is the heritage of Confucian China and the overwhelming importance of factionalism in Chinese politics. To quote Deng Xiaoping on factionalism in 1975: "The leadership must be clear-cut and firm in its opposition to factionalism. How long can we wait for persons who have wrought havoc with the Party's cause to recognize their mistakes?"[50] Joseph Levenson has been one of the leading writers to compare modern and Confucian China, concluding that fragments of the old structure do indeed remain but to serve a modern purpose, not as traditional relics.[51] In this sense, the patrimonial rubric may explain the modern bureaucracy as well as it did the Confucian. Personal networks or *guanxi* based on common village, educational or occupational activities, then as now serve as informal channels by which the bureaucracy saves itself from sclerosis. As Herrlee Creel describes the "old" China: "The individual's strongest loyalty was to his family, which performed many functions that with us are performed by the state. Other bodies such as the village, or perhaps a guild, might be important to him. But the state was very remote from the ordinary Chinese."[52] Other parallels to yesterday are very evident, in Dengist key school educational and testing policies, the preference for moral suasion and rule by example, and the transmission of wisdom through texts. The distrust of commerce by officials is also a feature common to both old and new China. In 1892 Zheng Guanying editorialized the throne: "In recent days, although the court has advocated the governors-general and governors to develop commerce and open all kinds of manufacturing bureaus, and has authorized the inviting of merchants to manage them, yet the officials and merchants have habitually been unable to get along together and have distrusted each other for a long time." In 1984, the Central Committee officially stated: "If the state institutions were to directly administer and manage the various kinds of enterprises owned by the whole people, it would be very hard to avoid serious subjectivism and bureaucratism with a consequent suppression of enterprise vitality."[53] If these parallels hold true, one might expect a very decentralized kind of Opening, with bureaucratic winners and losers defined neither by markets nor rules, but instead by family ties and status.

METHODOLOGICAL ISSUES

At this point, it would be appropriate to summarize the difficult methodological issues that China presents to the researcher, many of which have already been noted. Generally speaking, the usual tools of the political researcher, such as opinion polls, voter profiles, and detailed population characteristics are both scarce and often unreliable when obtained. Government polls suffer from misleading questionnaire design and insufficient or nonrandom samplings. The *neibu* or classified nature of much of this information makes it unavailable to most foreign researchers as well. Statistical sources again are not necessarily accurate and in areas where ministries have conflicting authorities, almost never. For example, China publishes two separate trade figures, one from the Ministry of Foreign Economic Relations and Trade and one from Customs. Owing to differences in accounting standards, the trade balance varies by as much as one billion U.S. dollars between the two.

Primary research is also expensive and time consuming to conduct. Given the vastness of China and the lack of a developed telecommunications and transport infrastructure, it is difficult for the lone researcher to be assured of statistically reliable results in a survey or investigation. Government help again usually raises issues of accuracy and validity. The Western political scientist accustomed to the luxuries of information Europe, Japan and the United States provide, usually stands at a loss in China.

Within these constraints, however, China scholars have in the decade since 1976 gained access to more knowledge than ever before in the history of communist China. Although it may not be possible to survey the entire one billion people, it is much more feasible to investigate the facts in the major coastal and inland urban centers. With the Opening to the Outside World, informal interviews of Chinese subjects have become commonplace and China scholars are no longer restricted to refugee interviews in Hong Kong. In the field of foreign economic relations particularly, the expansion of foreign contact has encouraged a plethora of market research investigators and a growing corps of bilingual, bicultural Chinese businesspersons who can facilitate the researcher's efforts. Although, it still appears genuinely difficult to define the China field in terms of modernist, postmodern or similar methodological classification, the trend since 1976 is clearly towards that end.

For now, the combination of qualitative primary assessments through interviews with Chinese officials and managerial personnel, and the careful balanced use of official statistics verified by independent, external bodies such as the World Bank and the International Monetary Fund, appears to offer the best interpretive possibilities for the researcher. These statistics and interviews, moreover, have the further advantage that they can be relatively easily duplicated in other developing countries as well as in similarly closed societies such as the Eastern bloc. Again the favorite tools of opinion polls and demographic profiles are not and should not be used widely due to the fledgling state of the art in China as well as the not insignificant potential for political manipulation. Investment, imports, exports and even consumer expenditures are somewhat less easy to conceal.

NOTES

1. See Qian Lung's famous edict to King George III in 1793 and Commissioner Lin Zexu's letter to Queen Victoria in 1839, both included in Ssu-yu Teng and John K. Fairbank (eds.), *China's Response to the West: A Documentary Survey, 1839-1923* (Cambridge: Harvard University Press, 1979), pp. 6-28.
2. Herrlee G. Creel, *Chinese Thought: From Confucius to Mao Tse-tung* (Chicago: The University of Chicago Press, 1953), pp. 235-237.
3. Cited in Jerome Ch'en, *China and the West* (London: Hutchison Press, 1979), pp. 39-40.
4. Ibid., pp. 36-37.
5. Kay Knickrehm notes: "There is little doubt that the dominant popular view of China during the first 25 years of this century was influenced by racism and ethnocentrism." See Kay Knickrehm, "The Early Republican Period in China, 1900-1925," in Henry Myers (ed.), *Western Views of China and the Far East* (2 vols.) (Hong Kong: Asian Research Service, 1982), p. 103.
6. Scholar Jerome Ch'en succinctly summarizes: "Few observers had access to communist documents or other writings; few could have read them if they had; even fewer had any knowledge of the institutional arrangements or the ideological discussions which were held in the Soviet areas or in the Party." See Ch'en, *China and the West*, p. 57.
7. Cited in Ch'en, *China and the West*, p. 52.
8. Cited in Edward Rice, *Mao's Way* (Berkeley: University of California Press, 1972), pp. 111-112.
9. Felix Greene, *A Curtain of Ignorance* (New York: Doubleday & Co., 1964), p. xiii.
10. Tai Chun-kuo and Ramon Myers, *Understanding Communist China: Communist China Studies in the U.S. and the Republic of China, 1949-1978* (Stanford: Hoover Institute Press, 1986), p. 97.
11. See John and Elsie Collier, *China's Socialist Revolution* (New York: Monthly Review Press, 1973), pp. 9, 256-258.
12. See Michel Lindsay, "Foreign Views of the PRC in the 1970s," in Myers (ed.), *Western Views*, pp. 155-171.
13. Tom Englehart, "Long Day's Journey: American Observers in China," in Bruce Douglass and Ross Terrill (eds.), *China and Ourselves: Explorations and Revisions by a New Generation* (Boston: Beacon Press, 1970), p. 118. See also K.W. Watkins, "The Cultural Revolution through Western Eyes," in *China After the Cultural Revolution* (Brussels: Centre d'Etude du Sud-Est Asiatique et de l'Extreme-Orient, 1972).
14. To quote Tai and Myers: "The greater successes scored by ROC experts in understanding the general dynamics within the PRC owes much to their insiders' skills." Tai and Myers, *Understanding Communist China*, p. 125, 131.
15. Interview with the author, Guangzhou, 2 July 1986.
16. Howard Wiarda, *Ethnocentrism in Foreign Policy: Can We Understand the Third World?* (Washington D.C.: American Enterprise Institute for Public Policy Research, 1985), p. 3.
17. Interview with the author, Beijing, 14 January 1987.

18. See Franz Schurmann, *Ideology and Organization in Communist China* (Berkeley: University of California Press, 1966). Other analyses include Richard Lowenthal, "Development vs. Utopia in Communist Policy" in Chalmers Johnson (ed.), *Change in Communist Systems* (Stanford: Stanford University Press, 1970); Jack Gray, "The Two Roads: Alternative Strategies of Social Change and Economic Growth in China" in S. Schram (ed.), *Authority, Participation and Cultural Change in China* (London: Cambridge University Press, 1973).

19. See generally John Lewis, *Leadership in Communist China* (Ithaca: Cornell University Press, 1963), especially on contradictions in pp. 47-52; Lowell Dittmer, "Power and Personality in China: Mao Tse-tung, Liu Shao-ch'i, and the Politics of Charismatic Succession," *SICC* VII:1,2 (Spring/Summer 1974): 21-52.

20. Of the major examinations of Chinese Communist leadership, cultural explanations have been offered by Lucian Pye especially, bureaucratic ones by Harry Harding mostly in the context of post-Mao China, and interest group theories by an increasing number of scholars. See Lucian Pye, *The Dynamics of Chinese Politics* (Cambridge: Oelgeschlager, Gunn & Hain, 1981), and John Lewis, *Political Networks and the Chinese Policy Process* (Stanford: Northeast Asia-United States Forum on International Policy, 1986), on cultural/factional aspects; Harry Harding, *Organizing China: The Problem of Bureaucracy* (Stanford: Stanford University Press, 1981), on bureaucracy; and Andrew Nathan's seminal article, "A Factionalism Model for CCP Politics," *CQ* 53 (January-March 1973):34-66.

21. An updated version of the analysis is given in Edward Friedman, "Maoism, Titoism, Stalinism: Some Origins and Consequences of the Maoist Theory of Socialist Transition," in Mark Selden and Victor Lippit (eds.), *The Transition to Socialism in China* (Armonk, NY: M.E. Sharpe, 1981), pp. 159-214. See also Alfred D. Wilhelm Jr., "Chinese Elites and Comparative Elite Studies: A Progress Report," *SICC* XIII:1 (Spring 1980): 68-71; T. Tsou and M.H. Halperin, "Mao Tse-tung's Revolutionary Strategy and Peking's International Behaviour," *APSR* LIX:1 (March 1965): 80-99.

22. Yung Wei, "Elite Conflicts in Chinese Politics: A Comparative Note," *SICC* VII:1,2 (Spring/Summer 1974): 64-72.

23. Dorothy Solinger, *Chinese Business Under Socialism* (Berkeley: University of California Press, 1984); Carol Hamrin, "Competing 'Policy Packages' in Post-Mao China," *AS* XXIV:5 (May 1984): 487-518; and also edited by Dorothy Solinger, *Three Views of Chinese Socialism* (Boulder, CO: Westview Press, 1984).

24. For some relevant critiques see David Lampton, "Policy Arenas and the Study of Chinese Politics," *SICC*, VII:4 (Winter 1974): 409-413; Friedrich Wu, "Explanatory Approaches to Chinese Foreign Policy: A Critique of Western Literature," *SICC* XIII:1 (Spring 1980): 41-62; Chalmers Johnson, "Political Science and East Asian Studies," *World Politics* XXVI:4 (July 1974): 561-575; and Harry Harding, "Competing Models of the Chinese Communist Policy Process," *IS* (February 1984): 3-37.

25. See for example Richard Kraus, "China's Cultural 'Liberalization' and Con-

flict Over the Social Organization of the Arts," *MC* IX:2 (April 1983): 212-227; Jan Prybyla, *Issues in Socialist Economic Modernization* (New York: Praeger, 1980), pp. 39-69.

26. Lowenthal, "Development vs. Utopia," in Johnson (ed.), *Change in Communist Systems*, p. 115.

27. From the *Communist Manifesto*: "When, in the course of development, class distinctions have disappeared, and all production has been concentrated in the hands of a vast association of the whole nation, the public power will lose its political character. Political power, properly so-called, is merely the organized power of one class for suppressing another." Cited in John Elliott (ed.), *Marx and Engels on Economics, Politics and Society* (Santa Monica: Goodyear Publishing, 1981) p. 445.

28. *Anti-Duhring* in Elliott (ed.), *Marx and Engels*, pp. 497-498.

29. *Far East Economic Review* (18 September 1986), 46-59. See also Chalmers Johnson, "Comparing Communist Nations," in Johnson (ed.), *Change in Communist Systems*, pp. 1-32.

30. See Elliott (ed.), *Marx and Engels*, pp. 473-483.

31. V.I. Lenin, *Proletarian Revolution and the Renegade Kautsky*, in *Selected Works* (Moscow: Progress Publishers, 1952), Vol. 2 p. 130.

32. R. Luxemburg, *The Russian Revolution (and) Leninism or Marxism?* (Ann Arbor: Michigan University Press, 1961) p. 56

33. Lenin, *Proletarian Revolution*, p. 131.

34. See Paul Sweezy and Charles Bettelheim, *On the Transition to Socialism* (New York: Monthly Review Press, 1971), p. 88; David Lane, *The End of Social Inequality? Class, Status and Power under State Socialism* (London: George Allen & Unwin, 1982), p. 160.

35. Milovan Djilas, *The New Class, an Analysis of the Communist System* (London: Allen & Unwin, 1966), p. 65.

36. See J. Kuron and K. Modzelewski, *An Open Letter to the Party* (London: International Socialism Publications, 1968), p. 27.

37. See Leon Trotsky, *The Revolution Betrayed: The Soviet Union, What It Is and Where It is Going* (London: Pioneer, 1945); T. Cliff, *Russia: A Marxist Analysis* (London: Socialist Review Publishers, 1964).

38. See Lane, *The End of Social Inequality*, pp. 124-126.

39. Richard Kraus, "The Chinese State and Its Bureaucrats," in Victor Nee and David Mozingo (eds.), *State and Society in Contemporary China* (Ithaca: Cornell University Press, 1983), p. 141.

40. Cited in Andrew Nathan, *Chinese Democracy* (Berkeley: University of California Press, 1985), p. 73. See also Alan Liu, *Political Culture and Group Conflict in Communist China* (Santa Barbara: Clio Books, 1976), pp. 118-121.

41. Theotonio Dos Santos, "The Structure of Dependence," *American Economic Review*, (Spring 1970) 60:231-236; Robert Kautman, Harry Chernotsky and Daniel Geller, "A Preliminary Test of the Theory of Dependency," *Comparative Politics*, (April 1975), 23:303-330.

42. Cited in Maurice Meisner, "On the Dictatorship of the Proletariat in Chinese Thought," in Nee and Mozingo (eds.), *State and Society*, p. 127. See also "Criticism of Selected Passages of 'Certain Questions on Accelerating the

Development of Industry' " in Raymond Lotta (ed.), *And Mao Makes Five* (Chicago: Banner Books, 1978), pp. 287-300.

43. Max Weber, *The Theory of Social and Economic Organization* (New York: Free Press, 1964), p. 337. See pp. 329-334 for an enumeration of the characteristics of the rational-legal authority.

44. Ibid., p. 60.

45. See Mark Selden, *The Yenan Way in Revolutionary China* (Cambridge: Harvard University Press, 1971); Kraus, "The Chinese State," p. 143.

46. For example, Cheng Hung-sheng, "Historical Factors of China's Economic Underdevelopment," *JCS* (June 1984), pp. 221-234.

47. See Schurmann, *Ideology and Organization*, p. xiv, pp. 109-111. To quote: "In China, the Party has evolved as a mechanism to keep contradictions in organization alive, to prevent routinization and excessive bureaucratization."

48. See James N. Rosenau, *The Study of Global Interdependence* (London: Frances Pinter, 1980), pp. 53-72.

49. See James Rosenau, "A Pre-Theory Revisited: World Politics in an Era of Cascading Interdependence," *ISQ* 28 (1984): 245-305.

50. Deng Xiaoping, *Selected Works* (Beijing: Foreign Languages Press, 1984), p. 20. See also Jean Oi, "Communism and Clientelism: Rural Politics in China," *WP* (January 1985): 238-266.

51. See generally Joseph R. Levenson, *Confucian China and Its Modern Fate* (Berkeley: University of California Press, 1972).

52. Creel, *Chinese Thought*, p. 239. See also the work of Lucian Pye, especially *The Dynamics of Factions and Consensus in Chinese Politics: A Model and Some Propositions* (Santa Monica: The Rand Corporation, R-2566-AF, July 1980).

53. *Decision of the Central Committee of the CPC on Reform of the Economic Structure* (Beijing: Foreign Languages Press, 1984), p. 32; Teng and Fairbank (eds.), *China's Response to the West*, p. 113.

Part I

Strategy

1

The Opening in
Historical Perspective

The Opening to the Outside World, initiated in 1978, has greatly increased the significance of foreign trade within China's economy. As Chart 1 and Table 1 illustrate, by 1986, foreign trade was 13.7 percent of Gross Social Product (GSP) whereas in 1978 it was only 5.2 percent and had previously sunk to as low as 4.4 percent in 1965.[1] As early as 1975, Deng Xiaoping had called for a speed-up in exports to pay for increased technological imports. Later, in 1980 while drafting the Sixth Five-Year Plan, the State Council formally declared the Opening to the Outside World one of China's key tasks.[2] The Opening is unquestionably one of the most revolutionary events in the history of the People's Republic of China.

STAGNATION AND DEPENDENCY

Even prior to 1949 under Nationalist rule, foreign trade never reached the importance it has with the opening to the Outside World. In the 1920s the total value of China's foreign trade scarcely exceeded 1 percent of world trade and the trade itself took no more than 6 to 8 percent of China's gross national product.[3] In 1933, a year in which a relatively reliable estimate of national income is available, total external trade formed about 9 percent of the total.[4] Compared to other developing nations of the time, such as India, China had one of the lowest ratios.[5]

The pre-Liberation global insignificance of the China trade, in Western eyes could be laid to the passive forces of level of development, size of country and distance.[6] Or else, the inherent self-sufficiency of the Chinese

CHART 1
Trade as Percent of Gross Social Product, 1950–1986

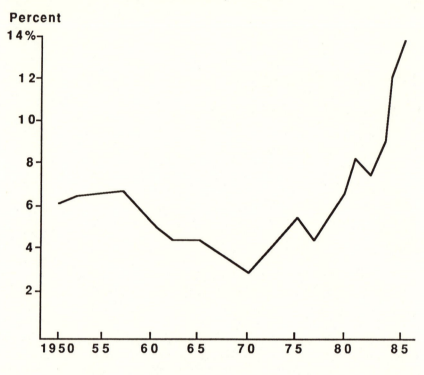

Percent

Source: <u>SYC</u> (1986), p.24, 481

economy that the early British traders commented on could be the root. European traders in the 1800s had considerable difficulty in finding a commodity that the Chinese wanted to buy before the introduction of opium, a product with the unique ability to create its own demand. China in fact enjoyed a positive balance of trade for more than two centuries under the old imperial system and the accompanying mercantilist trade. As Sir Robert Hart noted in 1900: "The Chinese have the best food in the world, rice; the best drink, tea; and the best clothing, cotton, silk, and fur. Possessing these staples and innumerable native adjuncts, they do not need to buy a penny's worth elsewhere."[7]

The fact that the major sources of national revenue — customs and salt tax revenues—were physically controlled by foreign interests which used them to service China's debt, accentuates the small size of the China trade.

TABLE 1
China's Foreign Trade, 1950-1986
(RMB Billions)

Year	GSP*	Trade	Imports	Exports	Trade as % GSP
1950	68.3	4.2	2.1	2.0	6.1%
1951	82.0	NA	NA	NA	NA
1952	101.5	6.5	3.8	2.7	6.4%
1953	124.1	NA	NA	NA	NA
1954	134.6	NA	NA	NA	NA
1955	141.5	NA	NA	NA	NA
1956	163.9	NA	NA	NA	NA
1957	160.6	10.5	5.0	5.5	6.5%
1958	213.8	NA	NA	NA	NA
1959	254.8	NA	NA	NA	NA
1960	267.9	NA	NA	NA	NA
1961	197.8	NA	NA	NA	NA
1962	180.0	8.1	3.4	4.7	4.5%
1963	195.6	NA	NA	NA	NA
1964	226.8	NA	NA	NA	NA
1965	269.5	11.8	5.5	6.3	4.4%
1966	306.2	NA	NA	NA	NA
1967	277.4	NA	NA	NA	NA
1968	264.8	NA	NA	NA	NA
1969	318.4	NA	NA	NA	NA
1970	380.0	11.3	5.6	5.7	3.0%
1971	420.3	NA	NA	NA	NA
1972	439.6	NA	NA	NA	NA
1973	477.6	NA	NA	NA	NA
1974	485.9	NA	NA	NA	NA
1975	537.9	29.0	14.7	14.3	5.4%
1976	543.3	26.4	12.9	13.5	4.9%
1977	600.3	27.3	13.3	14.0	4.5%
1978	684.6	35.5	18.7	16.8	5.2%
1979	764.2	45.5	24.3	21.2	5.9%
1980	853.1	57.0	29.9	27.1	6.7%
1981	907.1	73.5	36.8	36.8	8.1%
1982	996.3	77.2	35.8	41.4	7.7%
1983	1,112.5	86.0	42.2	43.8	7.7%
1984	1,314.7	120.1	62.1	58.1	9.1%
1985	1,624.2	206.7	125.8	80.9	12.7%
1986	1,877.4	258.1	149.9	108.2	13.7%

*GSP (global social product) refers to all products of agriculture, industry, construction, transport and commerce, net of non-productive services

Source: SYC (1986) p.24, 481

For 1925, Coons estimated payment on foreign debt took no less than 32.5 percent of budgetary revenue, and actual payment was 20.8 percent.[8] Similarly, Hou estimated that even excluding the Boxer indemnity, foreign debt service was 25.2 percent of budgetary revenue in 1914, and 36.3 percent of receipts in 1931.[9]

In this light, it is no wonder Louis Beale, a British commercial consul in Shanghai, noted in 1933 that China's trade was still "small and difficult." He, though, attributed this to "lawlessness and insecurity within the country."[10] Such "lawlessness" was not a new phenomenon; the foreign powers often complained of Chinese violation of treaties and antiforeign activities by the Chinese people, and often used such as excuses for imperialist intervention. The first Opium War began in 1839 as a consequence of Commissioner Lin Zexu's prohibition of opium imports and the public burning of twenty thousand chests in Canton. The Arrow War of 1856 originated as a retaliation for an alleged Chinese insult to the Union Jack. At about the same time, a French missionary was killed in Guangxi province, which the French used as a pretext to invade alongside Britain and capture Canton. The final phase of the Opium War in 1859 was occasioned by Chinese refusal to allow foreign ministers to proceed to Peking, the imperial seat, to ratify the treaties of 1858. The imperial French reaction to the 1870 Tianjin Massacre—precipitated by the French consul firing on a nationalistic demonstration—proved the impotence of the treaty system itself. Later, the successful Japanese invasion of 1894 and the various unequal treaties signed in pursuit of spheres of influence showed the adeptness of the foreign powers in putting to their advantage the central government's own weakness.[11]

After the Opium Wars from 1840 to 1860, foreigners became a (if not the) decisive political force in Chinese internal affairs. At first the Chinese authorities saw them as an equal threat with the rebellious peasants as, ironically, reactionary Chinese mandarins found allies in peasant protest movements such as the Taiping Heavenly Kingdom and the Boxers.[12] Both saw the foreigners corroding traditional Chinese culture and the status quo. Though the former were seeking to consolidate their rule, while the latter generally sought to gain economic advantages, sometimes at the former's expense, both representatives of "feudalism" were united against foreigners and Westernizing influences in the Chinese national bureaucracy.[13] For example, conservative Grand Secretary Wo-ren memorialized the throne in 1867 stating that the establishment of Tong Wen College for teaching astronomy and mathematics would "make the people proselytes of foreignism" and result in "the collapse of uprightness and the spread of wickedness." Likewise, the Boxer rebellion's major slogan was in fact: "Support the Qing Dynasty, exterminate the foreigners."

There were however, those who tried to steer a middle course between capitulation and conservatism. These early industrialists wanted to make the existing Confucian structure with its virtues of morality, its culture and its tradition, fit and absorb the Western influence, as it had so many other invasions, taking the best of the new technology and converting the conquerors. Li Hongzhang, who used foreign troops to suppress the Taipings and built China's first modern navy (the Beiyang squadron), and Zhang Zhidong, leader of the conservative reform movement in the early 1900s, advanced the so-called *ti/yong* formula, or "Chinese scholarship as the essence, Western scholarship for the application." However, with the growth of foreign influence in the Chinese state and the inability of the Qing court to deal with its own internal problems, these statesman and later warlords (including Yuan Shikai, Duan Qirui, and Cao Kun) came to be perceived by popular resistance as being under the influence of, and wielding state power for the benefit of, foreign interests. Moreover, rising Chinese nationalism began to lump Manchu and foreign interests together. As constitutional monarchist Liang Qichao wrote in 1922, the most fundamental achievement of the thirty years from 1892 was the "extermination of a government dominated by foreign people for more than one thousand years."[14]

In time, Chinese nationalism was supplemented by Marxist anti-imperialism in some protestors' minds. It evolved directly from the violent popular resistance to British entrance into Canton in 1847, to antimissionary activities in the late 1800s to the Boxer rebellion, the May 4th movement, the 1925 Hong Kong strike, and finally Mao's triumphant "Farewell, Leighton Stuart!"[15] This change from "feudal" to Marxist nationalism in the Chinese popular resistance contributed to the specific perception of trade as the root of Confucian China's decay—the tool of imperialist nations seeking only to divide and conquer.[16] The 1895 Treaty of Shimonoseki which explicitly recognized privileged rights for Japanese enterprises marked one turning point. Later, Yuan Shikai's government in 1912-1913 went on to guarantee explicitly the economic spheres of influence of the United States, Great Britain, and Russia among others. At the conclusion of World War I, China hoped that, as a participant in the war, it would be allowed the return of the concessions at Versailles. In the view of the victorious powers, however, China was, to use Metternich's term, "a mere geographic expression," and Germany's lost possessions were only turned over to Japan as it continued its expansion in Northern China.[17] In fact, it was not until 1930 that British officials handed back control of China's customs revenues to the nation. As late as 1926, British gunboats fired on striking Chinese.[18]

In the face of such imperialist tendencies, neither China's nascent capitalists and democratic reformers, such as Liang Qichao and Kang Youwei, nor the Nanjing government of Chiang Kai-shek and his bureaucratic-capitalist allies seemed able to help "feudal" China stand up for its rights. A frustrated Kang Youwei said in 1897: "The fact that a railway cannot be built without previous consultation with the German government [referring to Tianjin-Pukou railway in Shandong] and the fact that a magistrate can be kept in office or dismissed by others show that the emperor no longer has any power.[19] Chiang Kai-shek's own subservience to foreign influence in the interests of combatting the Communists after 1927 is well-documented.[20] As for the feudal "strong men," history records almost all were either pawns of foreign powers—especially Japan—or lacked authority.

The breakdown of national authority could not but have a larger, more deleterious effect on the development of native Chinese capitalist industry and trade. The facts are apparent in China's lack of industrialization relative to other developing countries—for example Japan, Russia, and even India. After seventy years of attempted industrialization, mechanized industries accounted for less than 4 percent of China's total industrial output and total industrial output for only 5.6 percent of total GNP.[21] The role of foreigners in this underdevelopment is still a matter of debate. Capital shortage, irrational management, foreign competition, and the resilience of traditional handicrafts can all be held responsible for China's arrested development. Foreign influence was certainly of little benefit in reducing any of these obstacles, and in some cases was a prime mover in their existence. Moreover, when compared to more successful examples of the time (such as Japan and Russia) the cumulative effects are not arguable—that is domestic wars, imperialist financial domination, foreign co-option of a corrupt elite, and the overwhelming advantages enjoyed by foreign firms participating in China's commerce, shipping, mining, and many factory manufacturing industries.[22]

ACHIEVEMENTS SINCE 1949

With such a past it is surprising that the Opening to the Outside World could have happened at all, let alone overnight. Apparently, several basic political achievements of independence and administrative unity were made after 1949. Without such, the China market would have remained a wistful foreign pipedream. The fact that the ideological Party was able to change significantly several key aspects of China's political economy is crucial to understanding the potential for the Opening. In delivering on some, but not all, of the promises they made when coming to power in 1949, China's socialist leaders set the stage for further changes.

Nationalism and Unification

Of the three "big mountains" of imperialism, feudalism, and bureau-crat-capitalism, which the Communists proclaimed overthrown in 1949, the first was the easiest to accomplish. As a poor, Third World nation with a history of imperialist domination, a policy of nationalist self-reliance came naturally to China. After the Opium War, China suffered a century of humiliation under corrupt puppets of Japanese and Western financial interests. *Hong Qi* noted in 1982 in the first publication of the *Almanac of China's Foreign Economic Relations and Trade*: "China has enough lessons to draw from.... There were people who worshipped all things foreign and surrendered the country's sovereign rights under humiliating terms. In contrast the other type of people acted arrogantly in dealing with foreigners and stuck to closed-doorism, thus landing themselves in isolation and ignorance. They also fell into oblivion."[23]

The collaboration between feeble Qing rulers and opportunistic imperialists against the peasants began with the Taiping rebellion in the 1860s. In 1861, Prince Gong submitted a memorial saying: "If we take this opportunity to reach an understanding with the foreign powers, if we unite with them to suppress the rebels, it will not be difficult gradually to wipe out the latter."[24] Foreign interests quickly obliged the throne but soon began to encroach on China's sovereignty. Foreigners took over key positions in China's Customs and administrative branches. While the Qing rulers effectively prolonged their own rule by some fifty years, their timidity and spineless collaboration turned China into a dependent nation. By 1937, foreign powers controlled 91 percent of China's railroads, 66 percent of its coal output, 97 percent of its iron, 64 percent of its cotton cloth and 55 percent of its electricity.[25] As Kang Youwei, the great Chinese reformer of 1898 noted: "Since we have been content to be weak and ignorant, how can we prevent the powers from attacking us and annexing our territory?"[26]

With Liberation in 1949, most foreign companies pulled out with the Nationalists. Those that remained were witnesses to an extraordinary turn in domestic policy. From a "feudal" society dominated by cliques of land-owning mandarins, Chinese development strategy turned to create a uniquely equal state, all the more remarkable for China's low level of economic development. To quote the World Bank in 1983: "China's past strategy and present system have created, on the whole, an extraordinarily equal society." According to their analysis, China's Gini coefficient of rural income inequality was 0.26 in 1979, substantially lower than other South Asian countries with Gini coefficients of 0.30 to 0.35. Much of this equality was achieved at a great, and ultimately unbearable, price. In fact, during the most intense years of the Cultural Revolution (1966–1968) income inequality declines were primarily due to average urban income declines attributable to politically induced violence rather than increases in rural incomes.[27]

One legacy of this egalitarian philosophy is that even with the Opening and the introduction of foreign-invested enterprises, wage differentials between production worker and factory chief have remained generally no more than 3 to 4 times. Pay-for-performance has also made it possible for some workers to earn more than top administrators. At Shanghai Volkswagen for example, average differentials in salary between worker and foreman have been only 10 to 12 percent.[28] At Beijing Jeep, the Chinese deputy general manager has refused raises because as he said: "I don't want to be alienated from the workers."[29]

A major reason for the success of the leadership in achieving the radical egalitarian restructuring of Chinese society in 1949 was the achievement of unprecedented administrative unity in China. The state bureaucracy constructed in 1949 was three-dimensional. A matrix of provincial, industrial and functional ministries shadowed by the Communist Party—it was unquestionably more efficient and powerful than any previously obtained in China.[30] The real redistribution of wealth it accomplished is ample evidence of its power.

At the formal top of the bureaucracy was the State Council, China's top administrative body, headed by the Premier. Reporting to the State Council have been two major staff bodies—the State Planning Commission (SPC) and the State Economic Commission (SEC). These bodies were since merged together at the 1988 National People's Congress. The SPC has been in charge of functional ministries such as Foreign Trade and Finance, while industrial ministries reported to the SEC. The SPC has also formulated most of the five-year and annual economic plans which the SEC in turn was responsible for implementing. At each level, there were, of course, also Party committees corresponding to the bureaucracy.

The third dimension of the matrix duplicated the entire structure at the provincial, county and lower levels. Local factory and bureau chiefs have wielded substantial power because of the decentralized welfare system.[31] Medical, educational and housing expenses were all taken care of by the enterprise to which the worker was assigned, leading to a great dependency on the part of the worker. Beijing's central economic planning has actually been confined to only a few key outputs such as steel and oil.[32] Integrated management still exists only within strict geographic limits. For example, one Swiss manufacturer's joint venture faced continuing problems from its inception in the early 1980s due to parochial rivalry between the Beijing and Shanghai factories of its Chinese partners. Neither would allow the other to distribute in its home market and both wanted the choice parts of the production process. When the venture once tried to put a Shanghai manager in the Beijing factory, a strike ensued.[33] In fact, most of the apparently "totalitarian" actions of the Chinese bureaucracy have only been implemented according to, and in deference to, local conditions. As a Chinese saying goes: "you have your policy, I have my way of doing things" [*Ni you nide zhengce, wo you wode banfa*].

In all three dimensions (industrial, functional, and geographic), much of whatever ability to govern the bureaucracy possessed resulted from transferring strict party discipline, nurtured during the long struggle, to the sphere of government. Cadres often did not even resign from their army posts as they took up new jobs as mayors, commissars, and industry chiefs all over China. In theory, the party was to be separate from the state. Its mandate was ideological, not administrative. In fact the Chinese Communist Party was a vanguard party built along Leninist, not Gramscite lines. Its primary task before 1949 was to lead the masses in struggle and to educate them in communist ideas, not to encourage them to educate themselves through unauthorized political struggle or the "mass line" of the Cultural Revolution.[34] Deng Xiaoping himself continued to emphasize the control function of Party cadres officially empowered to "play a guarantory and supervisory role and to see that the production tasks or operational tasks assigned to their own units are properly fulfilled."[35]

The political question became: where does supervision cease and actual control begin, especially with the relatively small percentage of cadres in the populace? Schurmann noted in 1961 that China's ratio of Party to population of 3 percent was among the lowest in Communist countries, East Germany's being 9.9 percent and Czechoslovakia's 11.6 percent.[36] The influence of the party on the economy has never been subtle.[37] Within the factory, the party secretary has often had more authority than the titular factory manager. Party-controlled trade unions have had exclusive control of welfare funds and a seat with veto power on the board of most enterprises. To quote a major joint venture's party secretary, also the head of the trade union: "Workers are the lords of the factory. The party's role is to protect the legal interests of Chinese workers."[38] In another instance reported in a party journal, an enterprising party secretary initially called a meeting to ask the question: Who has more power, the factory director or the secretary? Who is the No. 1 hand? When the secretary was voted down and handed a No. 2 badge, he refused it in a fit and took a reserve badge, saying he was a "supernumerary employee." He then began to argue over small points of status, all to the end of establishing himself as the No. 1 hand.[39]

The Importance of Ideology

As the cadres assumed control, Marxism Leninism Mao Zedong Thought was the banner under which independence and unification were achieved. *Webster's Dictionary* defines ideology as "a manner or the content of thinking characteristic of an individual, group, or culture."[40] In this sense there is no society that does not have competing ideologies, constrained only by the fertility of imagination and devotion. Ideology, though, can also be a powerful guide to action, accruing to organizations as well as to individuals.[41] The stronger the group support for an ideology, the greater its impact on policy. Conversely, the more policy a group is called on to make, the greater its need for a coherent ideology to govern its decisions. Hence, the desire of the cadres for a unifying ideology they could call their own.

The central importance of ideology to the cadres was also reinforced by the traditional emphasis on "moral rule" in Chinese society.[42] Neo-Confucianist rulers exemplified not only technical merit but also were "spiritually superior" to their subjects. Ruling through *li*, (literally, ceremony) meaning a complex of social conventions endowed with moral connotations, they served as both moral examples and responsible administrators of the people's welfare.[43] Some cadres coming with rifle in hand after overthrowing the corrupt Kuomintang regime may have taken advantage of the "mandate of heaven" mentality of the feudal Chinese peasantry to install themselves as local chieftains, their ideology as the "mandate."

Given this "feudal" grounding, some Western analysts have now hypothesized that with modernization the ideological party state is inherently untenable and must deteriorate into a personality cult or irrelevant dogmatism.[44] Chinese spokesmen both before and after 1976 have meanwhile continued to affirm the importance of ideology in the conduct of political affairs and in daily life as well. At the landmark 1978 Eleventh Plenum of the CPC, Deng Xiaoping's call to "emancipate the mind and seek truth from facts" was in fact a signal for renewed attention to the practical consequences of ideological work, not for its abolition.[45] Deng has stood his Four Cardinal Principles alongside the Four Modernizations, as well as his occasional support of campaigns against capitalist thinking and "bourgeois liberalism."[46] Ideology and the raising of proletariat consciousness have remained the key work of the political leadership. Democratization, the legal system, distribution of exchange power, and the organization and leadership of party and state, have all fallen within the sphere of ideology."[47] Even those who have sought political reform have implicitly acknowledged the place of ideology. As Su Shaozhi, the liberal 1985-86 director of the Marxism Leninism Mao Zedong Thought Institute, said: "The Four Modernizations are the material aspects of modernization. Modernization should also include political, social, cultural and ideological modernization."[48]

Rather than attack ideology then, the reformers have argued that during the Cultural Revolution the proponents of class struggle mistakenly emphasized Marxist ideology's destructive and abolishing power. In contrast, they would rather emphasize its importance in promoting growth. Both views acknowledge Marxism as the centerpiece of policy and the freedom of the species-being as the ultimate object. Both oppose alienation and exploitation. The key difference appears to be the Cultural Revolution's reflexive identification of the freedom of the species-being with class struggle and its equally reflexive identification with economic growth made by some of the reformers. Where the proponents of the Cultural Revolution saw revisionism in the superstructure as the major danger, the reformers have seen "feudal" habits rooted in the economic base.

The implicit tension of making such a complete reversal since 1976, appears on the surface to threaten the unified ideological front so often officially invoked by the Chinese press. If ideology is a set of values shared by a group, some ideology will be part of Chinese politics by definition. With so much change, however, it is hard to say that the unified doctrine of Marxism Leninism Mao Zedong Thought is still a valid criteria to measure China's policies. It seems to be the bounden determination of China's veteran revolutionaries but whether their successors will think so is another question. As the late conservative Chen Yun has noted there are already, and will continue to be, "ideological" and "nonideological" factions within and outside of the Party.

CULTURAL REVOLUTION AND SELF-RELIANCE

The achievements of 1949 were evidently not enough though to prevent China's isolation and stagnation from 1966 to 1976. Economic growth slowed and political freedoms were stifled. While Marxism Leninism Mao Zedong Thought ostensibly was a force for change, the class struggle theory turned commerce (both domestic and foreign) from a lever of growth into an instrument of politics. Was this also Marxist ideology?

A Marxist Digression

Marx was quite often critical of specifically "political" movements which he saw as divorced from the real concerns of the workers. In the *Communist Manifesto*, he scathingly indicted the utopian socialists St.

Simon, Fourier and Owens for their ignorance of the laws of history, their lack of theoretical rigor and the necessary failure of their appeal to the ruling classes to spontaneously change their ways.[49] However, he also criticized revolutionaries without beliefs, those "democratic bohemians," as equally likely to lead to a minority coup instead of a genuine revolution of the whole. To quote from one of his editorials in the *Neue Rheinische Zeitung*: "They have no other aim than to overthrow the next government; and have the deepest contempt for the theoretical elucidation of the working class and its interests."[50]

Marx's deep-rooted skepticism of both types of political struggles hinged on his belief in the fundamental prerequisite of economic emancipation for successful revolution. He saw political movements as only the outgrowth of class struggle, the dynamic world history.[51] Revolts occurred as the contradictions increased between mass production and the concentration of its fruits in the hands of a few. Revolutions transpired only with the replacement of one mode of production by another.

Nonetheless, Marx was first and foremost a revolutionary and as such engaged in political efforts. At his graveside, Engels eulogized Marx saying: "His real mission in life was to contribute in one way or another, to the overthrow of capitalist society and of the state institutions which it had brought into being, to contribute to the liberation of the modern proletariat, which he was the first to make conscious of its own position and its needs, conscious of the conditions of its emancipation. Fighting was his element."[52] Marx began his investigation of politics and economics with a fierce determination to find a way to eliminate misery. His analysis of capital followed the critique of Hegel, both philosophically and logically. Marx was interested not in a theory of price but in social relations; he focused on the political relationship between worker and boss, not the superficial phenomena of circulation.[53]

Marx reconciled the vision of historic economic process and the desire for political change in ideology. As he saw it, ideology expressed the existing contradictions between economic base and "political" superstructure. In the Marxist sense, it covered the whole range of beliefs and values that surrounded the class relationship. Yet it could be used by one class to overthrow another, even to the point of accelerating the historical dynamic.

Under capitalism, the capitalist ideology of "commodity fetishism" attempted to obscure the real social relationships between boss and worker with "mystifications" such as land, labor and capital. It attributed real, social qualities to the "products" of individual labor as well as the labor itself. Thus the rich explained to the poor that commodities had inherent, natural values found through the "free" interplay of supply and demand of the market, independent of the value of the labor involved. This interplay of course was actually fundamentally subject to constraints rooted in labor relations. Value can only be created in production, not exchange. Capitalist exploitation could not be explained as equitable, without the "mystical" attribution of value to objects and vice versa. Thus the ideological phenomenon of "reification" or commodity fetishism was at the heart of capitalism.[54]

Communism was the workers' ideological negation of commodity fetishism. Specifically, it identified the key capitalist evils as alienation and exploitation. In capitalist labor relations, workers were alienated from the products of their labor which appeared as objects arrayed against them. They were alienated from their own life activity as their work did not belong to them but was only an activity forced on them by the owners to extract surplus profits. Workers were alienated from their "species-life," their common bond as workers, because their productive activity was not their own. Finally, because they were alienated both from their product and the productive activity, workers were actually alienated from the social relation that was capital itself.[55]

Exploitation was the other hallmark of capitalist production. In the first chapter of *Capital* Marx wrote: "Capitalist production is not merely the production of commodities, it is essentially the production of surplus-value."[56] Surplus income would be created in any society where output was greater than that which was necessary to sustain reproduction. In a capitalist society, however, a propertied class on the basis of its ownership of the means of production directed the surplus to its own pockets.[57] Moreover, only in a capitalist society, where both labor power and physical products were commodities subject to exchange, did surplus value take the financial forms of profits, rents and interests. These profits, rents and interests were all expressions of the basic robbery of the workers' time that took place in the sphere of production. Exploitation was fundamentally a sociopolitical phenomenon, not an economic debate on exchange value.

Given the pernicious effects of commodity fetishism in hiding alienation and exploitation, Marx saw raising the workers' consciousness of communist ideology as his and every dedicated Communist's life work. By explaining things as they were (not as commodity fetishism would make them appear) the Marxist had the power to change the world. Based on this commitment, the Marxist actively exposed the real social relationships of alienation and exploitation around him, continually integrating theory with practice.[58] The Marxist ideologue set a personal example, exercising authority on the basis of persuasion and explanation, not myth or traditional authority. There was no line between practical and pure ideology as ideology itself was a spur to action, to seizing the means of production.[59] As a general theory, communism had to conform to the concrete conditions of society around it, while actively promoting progressive change as well.[60]

The Stagnation in Chinese Thought

Up until the Great Proletarian Cultural Revolution (GPCR), the development of China's version of Marxism (Marxism Leninism Mao Zedong Thought) had been fairly regular with the exception of the short and oddly named Great Leap Forward. As China's ideologues recognized the Stalinist thesis that the law of value continued to operate in the socialist society because of society's economic base of commodity production and exchange, wage distribution according to work performed, circumscribed free markets, and pricing fluctuation reappeared in the recovery period from 1962 to 1966. The contradiction between base and superstructure was acknowledged but the change would have to be made in the base, not the superstructure.

The GPCR changed that. At the time, it promised the dawn of a new age of advanced socialist democracy. In retrospect, it signalled a giant leap backward towards isolationism. The so-called Gang of Four stressed that only if the revolution in the ownership system could be consummated, would socialist society materialize. In Marxist terms, the superstructure took priority over the base in a drastic revision of classical theory. The criteria of class struggle was the key link in Chinese society.

The consensus on class struggle led inevitably to the downgrading of international trade as China projected its internal political conflicts onto the stage of the world economy. Prior to the GPCR, Chinese foreign policy reflecting the U.S. blockade and the Sino-Soviet split had been oriented to generally promoting revolutionary movements in as broad an anti-imperialist front as possible. During at least the height of the period from 1966 to 1968, however, the focus changed from "making revolution" to the problem of China's own "post-revolutionary" political development and the struggle against revisionism. As a result, Chinese anti-Soviet activities intensified, global anti-imperialist "united front" activities diminished, and the propagation of Mao Zedong Thought moved to the forefront of China's international agenda. Compare the united-front Third World perspective of Lin Biao's 1965 essay "Long Live the Victory of People's War" to this 1967 *Beijing Review* comment reflective of the personality cult: "The rapid and extensive dissemination of the great, all-conquering thought of Mao Zedong is the most important feature of the excellent international situation today."[61]

According to GPCR thought, just as the revolution in the relations of production could boost production within China, so could a socialist China overtake the capitalist countries' production in the world economy. GPCR partisans went so far as to attack the Ministry of Petroleum in 1975, just as it was beginning to export oil, as a "nest of national capitulationists." As one slogan ran: "Management is absolutely not a question of production and business operation. It is a question of the political line."

In 1976, at the last Guangzhou Trade Fair held under the so-called Gang of Four, rather than slogans on Chinese exports or economic themes, visitors were greeted by a huge poster across the entrance proclaiming; "Denounce Indignantly the Crimes of Unrepentant Capitalist-Roader Former Vice Premier Deng Xiaoping."

GPCR foreign relations placed a higher value on partners' political credentials vis-à-vis Mao Zedong Thought, China's new official credo, than on the economic content or political goal of the relationship in general. In the view of some, China as the Middle Kingdom had the luxury to ignore the strategic considerations of the outside world, in favor of the self-evident superiority of the Chinese way.[62] Instead, as a political instrument, GPCR foreign relations functioned in two ways: as aid to the spreading of Mao Zedong Thought in fraternal socialist countries; and to balance those absolutely necessary imports (e.g., grain). Necessary imports were politically curtailed to the bare minimum whenever possible.[63] The former, more important, cause was known in the slogans of the time as: "mutual support and cooperation in the economic sphere with fraternal socialist countries."[64] One example of such "mutual support and cooperation" was the effort in 1966 to swing Cuba to its side of the Sino-Soviet conflict by cutting its rice supply. Castro, unfortunately accused China of joining American imperialism in economically blockading Cuba.[65]

The roots of the self-reliance sentiment may be partially traced to the drastic impact of the Sino-Soviet split. Confronted by the U.S. blockade in 1949, China had little choice but to turn for massive amounts of aid to the Soviet Union, its historical enemy but ideological ally. Soviet technicians built the backbone of the Chinese economy over the decade from 1949 to 1959 as well as rebuilding the educational, political and cultural apparatus on their model. Although, as the Soviets were fellow socialists, exploitation could not be said to exist, much of the Chinese leadership never felt comfortable with the arrangement while it lasted. As early as April 1949, Zhou Enlai said: "If foreign aid holds benefits for China, of course we want it, but we cannot be dependent on it. We should not be dependent even on the Soviet Union and the New Democracies. . . . One of the main causes for Chiang Kai-shek's defeat is that he relied on foreign aid for everything."[66]

The dispute that ultimately led to the tearing-up of contracts amply illustrated the unwillingness of the Chinese leadership to follow Soviet policies even to the detriment of China's own economic interest.[67] In November 1957, Mao travelled to Moscow on the occasion of the fortieth anniversary of the Russian revolution. While there Mao first disputed Khrushchev's thesis of peaceful transition, asserting that at some stage in the transition to world socialism, imperialist resistance would be encountered which would make it necessary to resort to armed force. The reactions of the Soviet leadership which had just signed agreements to give

China the atomic bomb are not known but no major military aid commitments were made as had been expected. Following his return, despite this unfavorable response, Mao immediately upped the ante as the Taiwan Straits crises ensued. China shelled Quemoy and Matsu Islands and U.S. armed forces entered the region to escort Nationalist ships and planes. Khrushchev shortly thereafter sent a note to both China and the United States urging a ban on nuclear weapons before additional countries, including China, received them. In October 1959, Khrushchev visited Beijing and lectured Mao on endangering world peace, having shortly before withdrawn his offer of nuclear weaponry. Mao in response began to engage in open polemics with the Soviets, especially in a series of articles in April 1960 on the ninetieth anniversary of the birth of Lenin. The Soviet leadership in turn issued a secret letter indicting Chinese policies which was distributed at a 1960 Bucharest Party conference where Peng Zhen and Khrushchev shared an acrimonious exchange on the subject of world peace and coexistence with capitalism. Thereafter, the Soviet press issued hints about China's excommunication from the socialist bloc to which the official Chinese reply was that the Soviets would only succeed in cutting themselves off and that the self-reliant Chinese people would respond with rage and heroism. Both sides fulfilled their promises in August of 1960 and more than 1,000 Soviet technicians picked up their blueprints and went home.

With the split, the policy of "standing with one camp" gave way to "walking on both legs" from 1960 to 1966. Self-reliance now entailed a broader mix of partners but with a far lesser degree of dependence than in the relationship with the Soviets. Trade with market economies expanded rapidly while that with centrally-planned economies dropped. In 1961, China took on its first credit arrangement with capitalist countries, agreeing to buy grain from Australia and Canada. From 1963 to 1966, contracts were signed with Europe and Japan for over fifty plants worth more than $200 million.[68] The total remained small, however, compared to the larger Chinese economy, especially with the aftermath of the Great Leap Forward in 1960–1962.[69]

In large part, this was because it was deemed better to ensure balanced trade by curbing imports rather than expanding exports. The harsh lesson of Soviet withdrawal pushed self-reliance in the 1960s to become a conservative posture, encouraging an inward-looking trade stance far removed from the socialist internationalism of the 1950s. For example, prior to 1964 Renminbi (RMB) exchange rates were set at very high levels resulting in losses on many export items. At the same time prices on imports were fixed on a strictly controlled cost-plus basis, although domestic prices on imported materials such as steel and fertilizers were considerably higher. Thus the foreign trade corporations ran continual deficits. In response, instead of lowering the RMB exchange rate to encourage exports, the Price Committee resolved to set import prices at the same level as domestic goods, thereby allowing the foreign trade corporations more profitable operations but restricting imports and thus total trade volume.[70]

The fiscal conservatism of the early 1960s soon became the "closed-door" policy of the Cultural Revolution from 1966 to 1976. To achieve the domestic political objective of class struggle, the so-called Gang raised the spector of a capitalist restoration and closed off relations with the outside world. To quote Wang Hong-wen: "Had Liu Shaoqi or Lin Biao come to power, capitalism would have come back, the Chinese society would have returned to a semi-feudal and semi-colonial society or become the colony of Soviet social-imperialism."[71] He and others in the leadership capitalized on traditional Chinese ethnocentrism, resentment of foreign domination, and a notion of socialism in one country to effectively shut China off from both the Soviet and the capitalist bloc. One 1976 *Hong Qi* article noted: "As a socialist country, we must have an independent economic system and can only take our own road of industrial development. Innumerable facts prove that the Chinese people are entirely capable of catching up with and surpassing the world's advanced standards in the field of science and technology."[72] Albania became China's sole ally in international circles. Foreign trade played a minimal role in the Chinese economy and almost no debate on economic issues is recorded in Chinese journals. Thus, isolated from outside influences, the Cultural Revolution played out the class struggle until Mao's death in 1976. While such a position may generally be termed autarkic and "closed-door," the limits placed on economic relations during the Cultural Revolution precluded discussion of competing economic policies. Only with the fall of the so-called Gang of Four, and the decline of "politics in command," did thorough discussions of the political economy of trade occur.

As the policy of self-reliance evolved from expansionary socialist internationalism in the 1950s to conservative "slow growth" policies to a "closed-door," the range of partners and the avenues for China to achieve mutual benefit shifted and narrowed. Foreign trade increasingly took a back seat, first to domestic economic problems after the Great Leap and then to political problems during the Cultural Revolution. By 1976, while China's leadership still professed solidarity with the Third World, the realization of the freedom of the species-being had become exclusively a domestic affair.

NOTES

1. Gross Social Product as defined by the State Statistical Bureau (SSB) differs from GNP in two respects: (1) it excludes net income from services provided by nonmaterial sectors such as culture, education and public services (barbers, hotels, etc.); and (2) it includes consumption of raw materials, fuel and

power used in the process of material production, which is excluded in GNP. Net, these differences tend to make GSP underestimate GNP by as much as 20 to 30 percent.

2. See Deng Xiaoping, *Selected Works*, p. 44; Zhao Ziyang, "Report on the Sixth Five Year Plan," in *Fifth Session of the Fifth National People's Congress (Main Documents)* (Beijing: Foreign Languages Press, 1983), pp. 130-132.

3. Ch'en, *China and the West* p. 335.

4. Hou Chi-ming, *Foreign Investment and Economic Development in China, 1840-1937* (Cambridge: Harvard University Press, 1965), p. 189. Hou also notes that the ratio was larger than this in the 1920s or about 12 percent of national income, which contradicts Ch'en's estimates. See also Albert Feuerwerker, *China's Early Industrialization: Sheng Hsuan-Huai (1844-1916) and Mandarin Enterprise* (Cambridge: Harvard University Press, 1958), pp. 42-43, 264.

5. See Charles Kindleberger, *Economic Development* (New York: MacMillan, 1958), for a graphic representation of trade-income ratios.

6. See John K. Fairbank and Ernest R. May (eds.), *America's China Trade in Historical Perspective: The Chinese and American Performance* (Cambridge: Harvard University Press, 1986).

7. Except, of course, opium and, later, weapons. Cited in Ch'en, *China and the West*, p. 27.

8. A.G. Coons, *The Foreign Public Debt of China* (Philadelphia: Lippincott, 1930), p. 15, 60.

9. Hou, *Foreign Investment*, pp. 23-49.

10. Louis Beale, G. Pelham, and J. Hutchison, *Trade and Economic Conditions in China, 1931-33* (London: H.M. Stationery Office, 1933, reprint San Francisco: Chinese Materials Center, 1975), p. 7.

11. See Hou, *Foreign Investment*, pp. 103-111; Beale, Pelham and Hutchinson, *Trade and Economic Conditions*, pp. 91-92.

12. On peasant protest see H.F. MacNair, *Modern Chinese History: Selected Readings* (Shanghai: Commercial Press, 1927), pp. 346-357; Ho Ping-ti, *Studies on the Population of China, 1368-1953* (Cambridge: Harvard University Press, 1959), Chapter 10.

13. Citations from Hu Sheng, *Imperialism and Chinese Politics* (Beijing: Foreign Languages Press, 1981), p. 96.

14. Cited in Teng and Fairbank (eds.), *China's Response to the West*, p. 273.

15. See Mao Zedong, *Selected Works* (Beijing: Foreign Languages Press, 1956), Vol. IV, pp. 443-459.

16. Hu Sheng, *Imperialism and Chinese Politics*, pp. 172-185.

17. Wunsz King (ed.), *V.K. Wellington Koo's Foreign Policy: Some Selected Documents* (Shanghai: Kelly and Walsh, 1931, University Publications of America reprint, 1976), pp. 1-37.

18. Jurgen Osterhammel, "Imperialism in Transition: British Business and the Chinese Authorities, 1931-1937," *CQ* 98 (June 1984): 260-287.

19. Cited in Hu Sheng, *Imperialism and Chinese Politics*, pp. 126-128.

20. Ch'en, *China and the West*, pp. 268-270, 277-282.

21. Ibid., p. 362.

22. Ch'en, *China and the West*, pp. 362-379; Hou, *Foreign Investment*, pp. 125-165, 189-194; John K. Fairbank, Alexander Eckstein, and L.S. Yang, "Economic

Change in Early Modern China: An Analytic Framework," *Economic Development and Cultural Change* IX:1 (October 1960): pp. 1-26.

23. *ACFERT* (1984), pp. 379-380.
24. Cited in Hu Sheng, *Imperialism and Chinese Politics*, p. 45.
25. Ch'en, *China and the West*, pp. 359-361.
26. Cited in Hu Sheng, *Imperialism in Chinese Politics*, p. 128.
27. See World Bank, *China: Long-Term Development Issues and Options* (Baltimore: John Hopkins University Press, 1985), pp. 29-31; Alexander Eckstein, *China's Economic Development* (Cambridge: Cambridge University Press, 1977), pp. 204-205.
28. Interviews at Shanghai Volkswagen, Shanghai, April 1987.
29. Interviews at Beijing Jeep, Beijing, April 1987.
30. For a detailed report see Janet Cady (ed.), *Economic Reform in China: Report of the American Economists Study Team to the PRC* (Washington D.C.: National Committee on U.S.-China Relations, 1985).
31. Andrew Walder, "Some Ironies of the Maoist Legacy in Industry" in Selden and Lippit (eds.), *The Transition to Socialism*, p. 218; Andrew Walder, "Organized Dependency and Cultures of Authority in Chinese Industry," *JAS* (November 1983): 51-76.
32. Barry Naughton, "Summary of Findings," in Cady (ed.), *Economic Reform in China*, p. 8.
33. Interview with the author, Shanghai, August 1986.
34. "Constitution of the Communist Party of China" in *The Twelfth National Congress of the CPC* (Beijing: Foreign Languages Press, 1982), p. 97.
35. Ibid.
36. Schurmann, *Ideology and Organization*, pp. 138-139.
37. For the Soviet context see Paul Cocks, "The Rationalization of Party Control" in Johnson (ed.), *Change in Communist Systems*, pp. 153-190. See also *Dushu* in JPRS-CPC (19 March 1987), pp. 25-30.
38. Interview with the author, Beijing, 9 June 1986.
39. *Sixiang Zhengzhi Gongzuo Yanjiu* in JPRS-CPS (12 March 1987), pp. 24-27.
40. *Webster's Ninth New Collegiate Dictionary* (Springfield: Merriam Webster Inc., 1984), p. 597.
41. Schurmann, *Ideology and Organization*, pp. 18-23.
42. Tang Tsou, "Back from the Brink of Revolutionary-'Feudal' Totalitarianism," in Nee and Mozingo (eds.), *State and Society*, p. 62.
43. See Creel, *Chinese Thought*, pp. 25-46.
44. Notably Lowenthal, "Development vs. Utopia," in Johnson (ed.), *Change in Communist Systems*, pp. 33-116.
45. To quote: "Seeking truth from facts is the basis of the proletarian world outlook as well as the *ideological* basis of Marxism [italics added]." Deng Xiaoping , *Selected Works*, pp. 151-165.
46. The Four Cardinal Principles are the socialist road, the dictatorship of the proletariat, the leadership of the Communist Party and Marxism, Leninism, Mao Zedong Thought. The essence of the Four Principles is to critize both leftist and rightist trends that threaten either to derail China's economic growth or introduce political challenges to the socialist consensus. Ibid., pp. 166-191.

47. *The Twelfth National Congress of the CPC* (Beijing: Foreign Languages Press, 1982). p. 10.
48. Cited in JPRS-CPS, 17 March 1987, 25-30.
49. "Communist Manifesto" in Elliott (ed.), *Marx and Engels*, pp. 356-357.
50. "Neue Rheinische Zeitung" in Elliott (ed.), *Marx and Engels*, pp. 357-359.
51 "Communist Manifesto" in Elliott (ed.), *Marx and Engels*, pp. 370-371.
52. "Speech at the Graveside of Marx," in Elliott (ed.), *Marx and Engels*, p. 334.
53. See F. Perlman, "Introduction: Commodity Fetishism," in I.I. Rubin, *Essays on Marx's Theory of Value* (Detroit: Black & Red, 1972), pp. ix-xxxviii.
54. "Capital" in Elliott (ed.), *Marx and Engels*, pp. 124-128; Rubin, *Essays on Marx*, pp. 5-13, 31-45.
55. "Manuscripts" in Elliott (ed.), *Marx and Engels*, pp. 136-139.
56. "Capital I" in Elliott (ed.), *Marx and Engels*, pp. 189-190.
57. "Capital I" in Elliott (ed.), *Marx and Engels*, p. 182.
58. "Communist Manifesto" in Elliott (ed.), *Marx and Engels*, p. 371.
59. See also Johnson, "Comparing Communist Nations," in Johnson (ed.), *Change in Communist Systems*, pp. 15-26.
60. Dankwart Rustow, "Communism and Change," in Johnson (ed.), *Change in Communist Systems*, pp. 343-361; D.S. Zagoria, "Ideology and Chinese Foreign Policy" in G. Schwab (ed.), *Ideology and Foreign Policy: A Global Perspective* (New York: Cyrco, 1978), pp. 103-116.
61. *BR* 43 (1967): 26-28. See Peter Van Ness, *Revolution and Chinese Foreign Policy* (Berkeley: University of California Press, 1970), pp. 201-252, for a detailed analysis.
62. See Mark Mancall, *China at the Center, 300 Years of Foreign Policy* (New York: Free Press, 1986), especially Chapter 6.
63. See Allen Whiting, *Chinese Domestic Politics and Foreign Policy in the 1970s* (Ann Arbor: University of Michigan Papers in Chinese Studies, 1979), pp. 74-75.
64. *China's Foreign Trade* I:1 (1974): 24.
65. Union Research Institute, *Communist China 1966* (Hong Kong: Union Research Institute, 1966), p. 190.
66. Cited in Zheng Weizhi, "Independence is the Basic Canon," in Zhou Guo (ed.), *China and the World* (7) (Beijing: Beijing Review, 1986), p. 9.
67. The following is drawn from Rice, *Mao's Way*, pp. 152-158, 177-179.
68. Colina MacDougall, "Policy Changes in Foreign Trade," in Gray and White (eds.), *China's New Development Strategy*, p. 143.
69. *ACE* (1981): 621.
70. Xue Muqiao: "Readjustments in Prices and Exchange Rates Deemed Essential," *Intertrade* (March 1986): 19-21.
71. Cited in Lotta (ed.), *And Mao Makes Five*, p. 59.
72. Cited in Lotta (ed.), *And Mao Makes Five*, p. 289.

2

The Feudal Problem

The Opening to the Outside World arrived as China awoke from the feudal nightmare of the Cultural Revolution's later years. The decision itself came triggered by a recognition of and consensus on the feudal state of China's economy. It was generally agreed that the feudal "small-producer" mentality and structural exchange restrictions were China's major economic problems. This consensus on the key task in the years ahead was instrumental in creating the impetus for change that the Opening required.

POLITICAL DISSATISFACTION

The Fall of the So-called Gang of Four

In 1975, the doughty Sichuanese Deng Xiaoping was restored from his second internal banishment to manage the day-to-day work of the Central Committee as Premier Zhou Enlai lay ill. Deng and Zhou concentrated on economic issues, announced the Four Modernizations programs, and set about rectifying what they saw as years of industrial and agricultural decay. However, Deng's restoration was to be short. Mao and the so-called Gang of Four launched a mass movement in November 1975, to "criticize Deng and counter the Right deviationist trend." Capitalist-roaders within the Party were accused of trying to "reverse the correct verdicts" of the Cultural Revolution. The movement intensified with mass rallies and frequent newspaper attacks throughout the spring.

As the campaign mounted, Premier Zhou died on January 8, 1976. One of the founders of the People's Republic, Zhou symbolized to many the caring qualities of a Confucian ruler. The so-called Gang, however, saw Zhou as a Confucianist in both style and substance, as well as a major political obstacle. Their advocates maintained Zhou had always been opposed to worker control of factories and had been instrumental in establishing a Party bureaucratic class that threatened to take China back to capitalism. Mourning services were forbidden and the public campaign against Deng and Confucianism continued. With the mounting tension in early April, millions turned out unofficially at Tiananmen Square in Beijing to pay their respects to the late Premier in a direct challenge to the authority of the so-called Gang. The event culminated on April 5, after several days of gathering crowds, public security forces moved in to disperse the crowds and remove wreaths laid around the Monument to the People's Heroes. A tape recorded message was played from Wu De, the mayor of Beijing, ordering dispersal and a riot ensued in which thousands were arrested and numerous casualties occurred.[1] Two days later, on April 7, a Central Committee bulletin ordered the dismissal of Deng Xiaoping from all of his posts and appointed Hua Guofeng Premier. Deng retreated in disgrace to south China where he remained under the protection of General Xu Shiyu, an old friend and commander of the Central China region.

After the Tiananmen Square incident, unrest continued to mount as on July 28 the massive Tangshan earthquake shook east central China from Tianjin to Beijing. Over 242,000 people were killed and 164,000 badly wounded according to official counts. Relief work was slow in coming, delayed in part at least by the ongoing efforts of the so-called Gang of Four to press their anti-Deng campaign. Tianjin itself was not rebuilt until 1979. The threats of Yellow River floods continued to render the economic situation perilous. Soon in Guangzhou, wall-posters appeared saying: "Rally behind Chairman Mao; pay tribute to Premier Zhou; commemorate Yang Kaihui and down with Wu Zetian!"[2] In Shanghai, the publication by *Wen Hui Bao* of an article critical of Zhou Enlai led to a wave of protests. Trains running from Shanghai to other cities were covered with poster criticizing *Wen Hui Bao* and praising the late Zhou. Increasingly, the protests became bitingly critical of the deterioration in living standards during the Cultural Revolution and nostalgic for Zhou's efforts to improve the lot of the peasant's life. As some said, the U.S.S.R. put a "satellite up in the sky and the red flag dropped to the ground," while China "put a red flag up but the trains are late."[3]

On September 9, public questioning of authority appeared to be reaching crisis proportions as all over China people began mourning for the passing of Chairman Mao. With the loss of the Great Helmsman factional infighting at the top intensified by an order of magnitude. On September

16, two days before Mao's funeral, the so-called Gang of Four published an editorial in *Renmin Ribao* without submitting it for Politburo discussion. In it they transmitted a falsified version of Mao's last testament, saying "act according to the principles laid down," implying according to some that heretofore unrevealed principles were in their possession. In Shanghai, wall posters appeared calling for "support of Zhang Chunqiao for Premier." On September 29, Jiang Qing came to Qinghua University where in introducing her, a follower said: "Comrade Jiang Qing repressing her own grief and bearing herself like a true leader, has come to the University to talk to us." Wang Hongwen allegedly ordered automatic rifles and machine guns distributed to 100,000 Shanghai militia and a train made available to transport the militia to Beijing.

On the other side, meanwhile, General Xu Shiyu, Deng's ally, returned to Beijing. There, he and Ye Jianying, Li Xiannian and several close political and military allies plotted the overthrow of the so-called Gang. In the first week of October a Dengist ally, Chen Xilian, military commander of the Beijing military region, reportedly ordered troops under Mao Yuanxin, Mao's nephew and an ally of the so-called Gang, not to come to Beijing but to remain stationed at Shanhaiguan. It became apparent why as on October 6, Wang Dongxing, Mao's former bodyguard, led the elite 8341 Unit in arresting Jiang Qing, Wang Hongwen, Zhang Chunqiao, Yao Wenyuan and seven underlings on the orders of the Central Committee as represented by Hua Guofeng. Six days later the first newspaper reports trickled out that the Great Proletarian Cultural Revolution (GPCR) had come to an end.

The Decision to Open

The unseemly transition of power led to revelations of many serious deficiencies in China's economy and government. Slow response to natural disasters was laid to the "natural" economy with its feudal "self-reliant" development policy of overly rigid controls, lack of specialization, limited authority and responsibility mechanisms, and a general lack of attention to economic results. GPCR partisans who had contended that China would help the capitalists by trading with them were accused of holding to a mythical conception of China as a developed economy, capable of implementing at will a "product" economy, heedless of the crude barter-based reality of China's commerce.[4] The GPCR partisans had maintained China's experience would show to the world that one-sided revolution can boost production. The crises of 1976 dictated to the contrary that improving economic work was also necessary to address the stagnant "self-reliant" economic legacy of feudalism. Moreover, in the eyes of the leadership, there were few places with problems more acute than the sphere of foreign economic relations. The threat from internal discord now clearly exceeded that of foreign domination, and the benefits to be derived from opening up far outweighed the dangers of remaining in a semi-feudal self-reliant small-scale mode of production.[5]

The so-called Gang of Four had always emphasized the threats and not the benefits to China from external relations. The Soviet "social-imperialists" threatened China's territorial integrity by stationing troops on the border. Capitalist-roaders within the country could always be counted on to collaborate with foreign enemies. As they said: "Under China's historical conditions those who stubbornly choose to take the capitalist road are in fact 'ready to capitulate to imperialism, feudalism and bureaucrat-capitalism.'"[6] Deng and his cohorts in the Ministry of Foreign Trade were accused of entering into long-term contracts with foreign countries to despoil China of its natural resources. External political threats were clearly more important than the potential economic benefits of trade.

By 1976, however, the political threat from internal stagnation had sharply escalated. After the overthrow of the so-called Gang in October, new Chairman Hua Guofeng attacked them for a "vicious political purpose in using cunning tactics to blur the distinction between learning from other countries and the philosophy of servility to things foreign."[7] Numerous industrial organizations including the Ministry of Coal and the All-China Marketing Cooperative made urgent calls for immediate imports of needed materials. The Fifth Five-Year Plan would be revised, it was announced, because of "sabotage."

Temporary measures prevailed and debate continued through the National Conference on Learning from Da Qing in Industry from April 20 to May 13, 1977. During the Cultural Revolution, Da Qing oil field had been praised as a showpiece of self-reliance. Hua Guofeng took a more moderate path, noting that it had "assimilated some of the science and technology of foreign countries, but did not simply follow the beaten path."[8] At the conference, however, Hua appeared in the majority of speakers as he held to "taking class struggle as the key link" against those like Ji Dengkui who gave the closing speech and only spoke of "grasping the work well." Hua's speech in many ways indicated his fundamental closeness to the Cultural Revolution and its accomplishments. He endorsed the theory that a two-line struggle still existed, as well as the theory of "continuing the revolution under the dictatorship of the proletariat," and he urgently called for war preparation. Hua still believed that the problem in China's modernization was a lack of sufficient revolutionary fervor to go ahead with the work regardless of whether the conditions were available. To this, however, he added the need to pay attention to economic results in an attempt to use ideological fervor to solve economic problems.

Hua's economic plan came out shortly after the Da Qing conference and unfortunately reflected more fervor than practicality. An overly optimistic forecast, it called for the largest expansion of foreign trade in China's history in order to finance projects on the scale of mechanized agriculture by 1980. In the press, the so-called Gang of Four's opposition to trade was branded as "typical idealism and metaphysics." Cadres in the Ministry of Foreign Trade reportedly paraded through the streets on the occasion of the communique of the Third Plenum, adopting the slogan: "We must do our best to mobilize all positive factors, both at home and abroad, both direct and indirect, and build China into a powerful socialist country."[9] In July, at another national conference, Vice Premier Li Xiannian and Yu Qiuli clarified that while still maintaining the posture of self-reliance, "self-reliance has nothing to do with a 'closed-door' policy. It does not mean refusing to learn good things from other countries."[10] The ideological shift gave foreign trade professionals legitimacy once again; however, it did not guarantee success.

The distinguishing characteristic of Hua's plan of readjustment was speed. Annual growth targets proposed by Hua reflected his ambition; over 10 percent annually in industry and over 4 percent in agriculture. Contracts for whole plants and technology imports soared to $8.5 billion in 1978/79. However, the economy responded sluggishly to the campaign of exhortation and by the end of 1977 agriculture had lagged behind population growth for the second consecutive year. In mid-1978 Hua realized that more might be needed to handle the contradictions between the planned economy at home and the "anarchistic situation" in the international market. In line with his emphasis on politics in command, Hua phrased the issue politically, calling for a "great emancipation of our minds" and a "clearing away of ideological obstructions." These obstructions included the belief that foreign trade was of little account in the economy, that it was a losing business, that it was ideologically dangerous. Rather, Hua called on the Chinese people to increase trade as a patriotic act to consolidate the dictatorship of the proletariat and seek national honor.[11]

The presentation of Hua's Ten-Year Plan for National Development dominated 1978. Again its distinguishing characteristic was the size and speed of its ambitions. Under the plan, 120 major industrial projects were to be completed including 10 steel mills, 9 nonferrous metal complexes, 8 coal mines, 10 oil and gas fields, 30 power stations, 6 railways, 5 harbors, petrochemical plants and a variety of manufacturing facilities for producing machinery and electronics.[12] Even so, Hua was already finding it difficult to earn enough foreign exchange to finance the already large imports. With the growth of a $1.1 billion cumulative trade deficit from 1977 to 1979, the Central Committee Work Conference met in December. There Hua's plan was reevaluated, "politics in command" definitively criticized, and a new policy of "readjustment, reform, consolidation and improvement" adopted. As Deng Xiaoping would later say: "Revolutionary spirit is a treasure beyond price .... But revolution takes place on the basis of the need for material benefit. It would be idealism to emphasize the spirit of sacrifice to the neglect of material benefit."[13]

The Opening to the Outside World, officially launched by Hua Guofeng's overambitious round of complete plant imports in 1977–1978, hit its stride in 1980 after a brief consolidation period. China's total foreign trade accelerated annually at 14.5 percent in the decade since 1976, an 8 percent increase over the previous growth rate since 1952. Committed foreign investment in the Chinese economy grew to over $19 billion at the end of 1986. By any criteria, China abandoned the "closed-door" policy of the Cultural Revolution. While its leadership maintained the official policy of self-reliance, the meaning changed radically.[14]

THE "FEUDAL" MENTALITY

As a student of economic history, Marx might have called the decision to open inevitable. He often praised the revolutionary effects of the commodity economy on feudal production relations. To quote his description of India: "These idyllic villages, inoffensive though they may appear, had always been the solid foundation of Oriental despotism ... they restrained the human mind within the smallest possible compass, making it the unresisting tool of superstition, enslaving it beneath traditional rules, depriving it of all grandeur and historical energies."[15] Marx in all likelihood would have had the greatest skepticism of any nation's ability to achieve revolutionary development while cut off from the outside world and the process of exchange. Both the commodity and the socialist economies are fundamentally characterized by the existence of a developed sphere of exchange.[16] Finally, he might also suspect the motive as exploitation, the reaping of surplus profits, cannot be rooted in the sphere of exchange, i.e., international trade.

Marxist analysis, however, gives little insight into the nature and basis of Chinese interest groups. These groups control the day-to-day implementation of whatever strategies the leadership decides on. Unlike American interest groups which operate through the mass media, ballots and the legal system, traditional Chinese interest groups are distinctively small-scale leadership-oriented and family-based. Mao once said on the eve of the Cultural Revolution that the Chinese peasant was poor and blank. Poor he may be but his mind is filled with the accumulation of a three-thousand year heritage. Most Chinese interest groups are based on and cater to this heritage, a heritage on which China's reformers squarely place the blame for China's failure to modernize since the first Open Door policy.

The Politics of Guanxi

The personality cult, blind obedience to a patrimonial superior, and the "conservative mentality" [baoshou sixiang] are at the heart of the feudal heritage. According to reformers, these obstacles have prevented the expansion of individual creative energies and the spread of ideas. To quote leading establishment economist Xue Muqiao: "The vestiges of feudal autocracy left over from history cannot be eliminated in a short time."[17]

Guanxi, the original social "glue," have always played a key role in Chinese society. These networks start in the village of birth. The decentralized nature of the Chinese economy has encouraged over centuries a clannishness not unlike that of feudal Europe. Cadres who have grown up together in the same locality always have the opportunity if not the duty to call on and assist each other whenever possible.[18] Links within the village are often far stronger than between village and center, which contributes in turn to extensive collaboration between local party, state and enterprise leaders to cover up misdeeds. According to one report, one such "understanding" occurred in the Guangxi provincial municipality of Luizhou in 1984. There some local cadres kept back a portion of state taxes levied, in order to reinvest the money at the local level by putting it in local banks which would then lend it to enterprises. In another instance, one company got away without paying tax in exchange for selling its products to the local authorities at lower prices.[19] These informal village-based networks however not only contribute to illegal activities such as smuggling and tax evasion but also become the only way to pull strings when bureaucratic means stall. For example, much of the success of the rural Guangdong economy is due to small-scale village industries (such as textiles and electronics assembly) manufacturing directly to their Hong Kong family member's specifications, thereby avoiding the hassle, taxation and higher cost involved with the Special Economic Zones.

Informal networks can also be based on a common job or place of work.[20] Some of the strongest of these exist among fellow army comrades, only the most famous being that of the Long March veterans.[21] In the 1800s the compradores of Canton and Shanghai working for Swire and Jardines also developed networks of their own.[22] A century later, with the adoption of the Soviet economic model in the early 1950s and the development of giant industrial plants, many of the new Chinese elite came to know each other at one of a relatively few major enterprises in steel, automotive, coal, electric and other industries such as the Changchun Automotive Works. Among those who worked in that enterprise in the

1950s were to name a few Jiang Zemin, the Mayor of Shanghai; a vice minister of the Ministry of Foreign Trade Economic Relations and Trade; the director of a major state financial institution; and a senior management counsellor.

Likewise, in the Ministry of Electronics Industries (MEI), factories "passed down" [xiafang] to the provinces in the 1984 decentralization reforms still maintained close personal relationships with, their former bosses. In this way they received the benefits of the Ministry's R&D funds and sales contacts with other large user ministries. The MEI in turn received foreign exchange from those independent factories without accounts at the Bank of China.[23] To quote one Guangdong Ministry official: "*Guanxi* determines who gets the order to import for factories around here."[24] Much as the large heavy industrial enterprises were the places to be in the 1950s, trade organizations such as those within the MEI are the chosen occupations of the aspiring Chinese elite in the 1980s. An "insider's" report from Hong Kong noted on children of cadres in business: "Their chief means is still a network of connections, and serving as middlemen in reselling commodities."[25]

The third major source of informal ties is a common education. Overseas schooling was one of the key bonds of some of the original Communists—for example, the so-called 28 Bolsheviks who studied in the Soviet Union.[26] The key school system reestablished by Deng Xiaoping also channelled the best and brightest of Chinese youth into special schools where they were rigorously trained and tested. At the top of the pyramid, the graduates of the Institutes of Foreign Trade in Beijing and Guangzhou all have become a tightknit group headed for the top management of the foreign trade corporations. Even at the high school and junior high level though, educational affiliations can follow a manager throughout his career. Among the most prestigious middle schools in Beijing are the No. 101, the No. 4, and the Middle School attached to Normal University. Quoting a Hong Kong journal's account of them: "During the Cultural Revolution, this kind of school was regarded by the 'gang of four' as a 'breeding ground for aristocrats,' a 'thorn in the flesh,' and 'a mote in the eye.'"[27]

Baoshou Sixiang

Three thousand years of *guanxi* produced a way of thinking peculiar to its own limited horizons—the conservative mentality [*baoshou sixiang*]. Among the core beliefs of *baoshou sixiang* were the sanctity of the local patriarch, tradition as legitimation, the importance of family background for power, and the resort to force or the "rule of man" rather than the rule of law to resolve disputes. According to the reformers, these beliefs buttressed feudal authority in the past and have encouraged corruption and inefficiency in the present.

Baoshou sixiang was particularly suited to the realities of the peasant's life. Little contact with the outside world allowed him no unfavorable comparisons. The local landlord was one of only a few land-holding families that dominated rural life. Traditional family life was an extended unit, male-dominated and subject to strict generational hierarchy.[28] The pressures of unending attendance to harvest submerged the peasant's individual importance to that of the group, emphasizing unity of purpose. As the individual peasant could usually never produce enough to break out of feudal dependency, the patterns became deeply engrained. Those who were successful in climbing the ladder were soon coopted by marriage into the landholding elite.[29] The elite in turn maintained a vested interest in keeping the boundaries of each family's terrain small and those of the clan's territory secure and well-guarded.

Feudal *baoshou sixiang* also inhibited democracy in the Western sense. Freedom of expression was not called for or necessary. Dissent only threatened the patriarchal state and never strengthened it. Traditionally, a dissenting minister expressed himself by committing suicide rather than disturbing the Confucian hierarchy. Superiors infused with such moral authority could by definition not be questioned. Thus their vested interests tended to preclude the development of rational-legal authority.[30]

An historical reference helps to illustrate this. Over 2,000 years ago, the Legalist school of philosophers had first introduced the concept of law to China.[31] According to Han Feizi, the chief Legalist scholar, law was a tool of the emperor to dictate with and thus subject to his desires.[32] As such it proved to be an effective administrative device as the Emperor Qin Shihuang unified China for the first time. The Qin dynasty lasted for only a few years after his death, however, and the Legalist decrees were scrapped as soon as they had been created. In contrast, in the twelfth century, the neo-Confucianist orthodoxy of Chu Hsi, which combined traditional Confucian moralistic rule by example with a Legalist flavor of strict punishments according to law, enjoyed a tenure of centuries. To quote the great statesman and leader of the Neo-Confucianist revival Wang An-shih: "The cause of the distress is that we ignore the law.... Nevertheless, there has not been a single case in history, from ancient times to the present, which shows that it is possible to obtain good government merely by relying on the effectiveness of the law, without having the right man in power."[33]

After 1949 and the unification of China under communist rule, the harmful effects of *baoshou sixiang* appeared first as military-based factionalism. Chen Yun, conservative Politburo Standing Committee member, explained candidly in 1979: "No one alone will be able to secure power. Only by forming factions can people secure power and positions.

As a result there are naturally parties outside the Party and factions within the Party."[34] Factionalism carried too far endangered the unity of China itself. After 1949, for example, Gao Gang, political commissar for Northeast China, began to act with a large degree of independence in Manchuria, even negotiating agreements with the Soviets on the disposition of Japanese war material as if Manchuria were a separate state. Both he and Shanghai boss Rao Shushi were arrested in 1954, accused of establishing an independent power base, disrespect for Chairman Mao, and plotting to secede. Later in early 1955, it was announced that both had been deprived of their posts and expelled from the party. Gao Gang it was alleged had committed suicide upon arrest. Thirty odd years later, Deng Xiaoping would criticize Party Secretary Hu Yaobang for the same crime of political factionalism with his Communist Youth League colleagues.

Throughout the long struggle in the border areas, factions formed in some degree because many Communist Party of China (CPC) military leaders had the opportunity and sometimes the necessity to form "mountain strongholds."[35] From these redoubts they expanded their influence and built deep links to the local populace. In outlying areas such as Xinjiang, Inner Mongolia, and parts of Sichuan, the influence of leaders such as Wang Enmao, Ulanfu, and Li Qingchuan grew especially strong. By 1966 all had held power for over twenty years and both Ulanfu and Wang held the three posts of military commander, political commissar and party secretary.[36] All three were gradually purged during the Cultural Revolution, but their subordinates remained and, aided by "closed-door" policies, the *baoshou sixiang* phenomena of factionalism and the "rule by man" ran unchecked throughout the Cultural Revolution. The legal system suffered grievous damage from 1966 to 1976. Law faculties and courts were closed. People's tribunals carried out Mao's own preference for summary trials. Ideology served as a proxy for morality eliminating any middle ground for participatory discussion to take place. Mao assumed almost god-like characteristics, while the "capitalist-roaders" became "ghosts and monsters" and had to be cured of their "sickness" through reeducation.[37] Without legal safeguards, lack of planning, favoritism in appointments, overworked government organs, protection of criminals, and corruption, all symptoms of the "rule of man," reappeared to stifle potential gains in the economy.

The harmful effects of this lawless legacy especially in foreign relations were still visible in 1986, a decade later. In Guangdong and Fujian provinces as a whole some 20 percent of all economic crimes investigated in 1985 involved foreign businesses. Of these, over 80 percent were expatriates who had left China for Hong Kong since 1979. In one 1984 case in Fujian, a total of 170 million yuan was discovered to have been acquired through "speculation and profiteering," 60 million by fraud, and 20 million by smuggling. Of the 20 defendants, more than half were government cadres.[38] The entrenched power of these party cadres—the political, administrative and economic chiefs of their areas since 1949—and their *guanxi*-based networks was not yet broken in 1986. Only in 1984 did some say party leadership should be primarily in the political and ideological sphere, not the economic. By 1986 even Deng Liqun, the conservative former chief of the CPC Propaganda Bureau, admitted that party officials have to pay more attention to party work in the ideological sphere and not get bogged down in production affairs.[39] Breaking up the unofficial networks and removing the *baoshou sixiang* that stifles growth remains a major task of the reformers.

Baoshou Sixiang and the Bureaucracy

The bureaucrats represent a special case of "conservative" thinking. In the aborted 1898 Reforms, leading industrialist Viceroy Zhang Zhidong attacked the bureaucrats calling them: "Vulgar officials who like to take improper ease ... those who are confused and lazy, and who like to shirk work, to be influenced by favoritism, or to take the easiest tasks."[40] Bureaucracy is not unique to China and inefficiency exists in even the most advanced economies yet China's problem is of singular proportion.

Much of China's bureaucratic inefficiency is rooted in the issue of personnel union at all levels. With Liberation, the modern cadre was supposed to both monopolize political power and administrate.[41] During the Cultural Revolution, the so-called Gang of Four asserted the superiority of the former "red" quality over the latter, claiming that the overeducated intellectuals had become "white and expert." One widely-praised student allegedly handed in a blank exam paper as a protest against intellectualism. Later reformers would criticize the Cultural Revolution for ignoring education entirely and especially training for production. To quote one *Renmin Ribao* editorial: "For quite some time, some people considered education as an item of consumption that had no connection with production. When they thought of expanding production, they considered building factories, buying machines, constructing irrigation works. They seldom considered, or simply did not consider, the question of training people."[42] Between 1966 and 1978, there were a total of 1.4 million graduates from institutions of higher learning, a 10 percent drop from the period from 1949 to 1965. In 1976, there were a mere 50,000 engineering graduates in all of China.[43]

With the Party's monopoly on political power, however, cadres with or without education had assumed control of administrative and management functions since 1949.[44] In communes and factories, the party secretaries usurped the general managers' role. Regular cadre participation in manual labor, the policy of "sending down" cadres to the provinces to experience local realities, and constant ideological education were all directed at mitigating the danger of personnel union.[45] Only during the Cultural Revolution, however, especially in 1967 and 1968, did "power seizures" by student and Red Guard groups sometimes disrupt the local authority cultures. Even then, leading cadres declared sham seizures in the hopes of being overlooked in the general turmoil.[46] In the end, managerial authority remained concentrated in the hands of the same institution that had held it before—the Party.[47]

Personnel union also developed between party and government, especially at the local level.[48] With the effective dissolution of the legal system during the Cultural Revolution, provincial and village party committees functioned on the basis of personal relationships and patrimonial authority.[49] In the bureaucracy, loyalty to party superiors replaced legal or meritocratic criteria. Party leaders made administrative decisions on the basis of partisan, political objectives.[50] Mass participation in government, at first encouraged in the mass campaigns [yundong] of the Cultural Revolution, was reduced after 1968 to include only expressions of support for prevailing authority.

In time, personnel union among party, enterprise, and management functions created a monolithic political bureaucracy at the local level against which the individual Chinese had no institutional avenue of appeal. Mao foresaw just such a development and launched the Cultural Revolution precisely to avoid it. He identified the problem as stemming from the top capitalist-roaders in the Party down, however, and not in the feudal economy and the grassroots structure of the Party. With the use of yundong to "pull out" the capitalist-roaders within the party, chaos ensued in the economic base. Factionalism spread, law deteriorated, economic production slowed and violent clashes grew. After the Wuhan mutiny in 1968 and the seizure of the minister of Public Security and his entourage by rebellious troops, Mao had to abandon the mass mobilization strategy and the army assumed control of many governmental and administrative tasks in cooperation with local powerholders. Ironically, the movement to stop personnel union resulted in its intensification.

Since 1976, the Opening to the Outside World has revealed that bureaucratic Party penetration of economic affairs remains substantial. According to one source, Party and government organizations started more than 27,000 enterprises in the years from 1982 to 1986, and over 67,000 functionaries were involved in these. Of these, 15,000 had been separated from their original units and were being operated independently, 3,000 others were under investigation by mid-1986. In 1985 alone, more than 8,700 enterprises run by Party and government departments were disbanded.[51] Laws and regulations were vague and full of loopholes that presented economic incentives for cadres to exploit their traditional authority through speculation in pricing, raw materials, loans, and tax evasion. According to one report, over 90 percent of the major crimes prosecuted by the Jilin provincial procuratorate were the result of gaps and loopholes in the reform process.[52] Worse, in 1985, of all economic crimes investigated in China, 58 percent involved government employees on official duties.[53]

AN ECONOMY OF RESTRICTED EXCHANGE

Given the obstacles of *baoshou sixiang* and personnel union, it may not be surprising that by 1976, the so-called Gang of Four's self-reliance had achieved a mixed record. China had not rejoined the ranks of Third World commodity suppliers exploited by the superpowers. Moreover, self-reliance did coincide to an extent with the furthering of some of China's other policy goals such as industrialization and the growth of native technological expertise. It failed, however, to achieve agricultural self-sufficiency and production efficiency. More importantly, domestic production relations remained under "feudal," small-scale conditions; the freedom of the species-being remained fettered by the lack of exchange.

Lack of Coordination

China's isolated pursuit of economic and political development was characterized by spurts of unbalanced growth and decline. After the initial achievement of agricultural self-sufficiency in the late 1950s, acute grain shortages followed the Great Leap Forward and China was forced to import large quantities of fertilizers and grain. Native technological expertise did develop in certain areas such as space and aircraft but in general Chinese technology failed to produce major advances.[54] Per capita Gross Social Product (GSP) actually fell 18 percent from 1966 to 1968 and only in 1970 did it recover to a still paltry 458 RMB, barely surpassing the 1966 level of 411 RMB. In 1976, per capita GSP remained stagnant at only 484 RMB. In contrast under Hua Guofeng, per capita GSP rose to 784 RMB in 1979. In 1985, it stood at 1554 RMB.[55] The period from 1978 to 1986 is also the only time in post-war history that inequality has been reduced by raising peasant incomes as opposed to lowering those of urban workers.[56]

China's isolation from the world, as evidenced by its low trade-income ratio relative to other large countries and lack of diplomatic recognition prior to 1972, reflected the lack of horizontal coordination within China. The villages of China were as "complete" [*xiao er quan da er quan*] as possible, just as China was in the global village. Net domestic purchases by state-owned commercial departments dropped from 81 billion RMB in

1966 to 73 billion RMB in 1968—the only drop ever experienced by China outside the Great Leap Forward. Likewise, total foreign trade fell from 13 billion RMB to 11 billion RMB in the same period.[57]

The organizational drawbacks serve to illustrate the broader problems of the self-reliant development policy. The Ministry of Foreign Economic Relations and Trade (MOFERT) began as the Ministry of Foreign Trade in 1949. Reorganized in 1958 just prior to the Great Leap Forward, it was joined in 1960 by the Commission on Foreign Economic Relations, established to handle expanding trade with non-Communist countries following the Sino-Soviet split.[58] In 1978 the Foreign Investment Commission was established with the passage of the Joint Venture Law. In 1982 these organs and the State Import-Export Commission were amalgamated into what is now MOFERT.[59] MOFERT's subsidiary Foreign Trade Corporations (FTCs) were themselves large bureaucracies importing billions of dollars of goods annually. In addition, a number of Import-Export Corporations (IECs) directly linked to industrial Ministries were created in the early 1980s.[60] These IECs were encouraged to link industry and trade but to do so at the bureau, not the enterprise, level. Together the FTCs and the IECs controlled the bulk of China's foreign trade but with decentralizing reforms, provincial authorities have also taken over a certain small portion of the trade. Finally, a number of export-oriented factories have received a still experimental status as independent traders.[61]

Under the prereform bureaucracy at the enterprise level—because the FTCs monopolized trading resources and connections—factory managers could not make independent decisions to import necessary equipment or export to the world market. Instead, the relevant FTC through its local bureau linked to the department-in-charge of the factory would form a decision-making system above the enterprise level. One enterprise sourced raw material, sent it to another ministerial enterprise for processing, which sent it to another for distribution and finally to the FTC for export. This ministerial monopoly of decision-making in turn resulted in a shortage of qualified general managers at the enterprise level.

The lack of coordination between ministries has become one of the prime causes of wasted resources with the Opening to the Outside World. China's economic organization after 1949 had established strong vertical relationships but weak horizontal communications across geographic, industry or functional borders. Information flow was restricted through the use of internal regulations [neibu]. Ministries sought to become independent of outside supply, even self-sufficient for the most part. Rural funds were still largely kept at home and in village cooperatives rather than in faraway banks. With the Opening many provinces lobbied for foreign investment in their protected local industries where economies of scale appeared hopeless. Of those enterprises that did import technology a number were in fact unable to "reverse engineer" because production departments were separated from the importing departments.[62] Bureaucrats in charge of these departments claimed collective responsibility prevented any one from being held to blame. Products failed to get to market, producers did not receive needed supplies and decisions were not made.

In another example, many large foreign companies have been hard-pressed to develop countertrade. Although willing to partially forego payment in foreign exchange for badly needed heavy industrial equipment and other machinery, Siemens, for example, found it difficult to buy Chinese coal as the Ministry of Coal generally sees little incentive to cooperate with the importing ministry. Several pharmaceuticals joint ventures have also tried to obtain tetracycline as a partial solution to their foreign exchange issue, yet the exporting ministry sensing the loss of a foreign exchange source has charged at least one firm upwards of a 50 percent commission.

Lack of Scale

Lack of horizontal coordination by itself would not be such a problem except for the largely uneconomic scale of the local economies. Self-reliance exaggerated these already-present effects by increasing the ability of local authorities to delay change by maintaining "cellular" economies.[63] Instead of one China, 40,000 Chinas existed during the GPCR, each self-sufficient in jobs, economy, and authority. In 1980, for example, at the Shenyang Engine Factory, China's major engine manufacturer, toolshops made the cutting tools needed to design production technology and to cut metal. The factory also made all of its screw machine parts, cutters, reamers, engine elements, and other basic tools needed in the metalworking process that precedes the build-up of subassemblies and final assemblies.[64]

The small size of these local economies did not provide the incentive or rationale for mass production techniques that export markets might. As of 1986, one of the largest and most prestigious of the industrial joint ventures still had difficulties using its Western marketing manager effectively because he could not understand the Chinese supply system. When Western managers further attempted to introduce modern inventory control methods, production came to a halt because 80 percent of the factory's domestic materials were in-plan and were allocated at biannual nationwide meetings. Localization was difficult because suppliers used to small geographic fiefdoms had no economies of scale and could not provide large quantities. The factory did no marketing itself as almost all of its output was allocated. Of the 22,000 units produced in one year, the large majority were allocated in the state plan. Of the rest, half went to the provincial Department-in-Charge to barter for steel, and only 4 percent were sold by the factory itself for a total income of $3,000,000 of hard foreign exchange. Capital budgeting including investment in construction, material supply and staffing remained entirely within the government planning mechanism and the approval procedure was arduous and complicated. The Deputy General Manager had only one wish: "Once we've done our own feasibility study, just let us alone!"[65]

The persistence of exchange restriction fostered alienation among Chinese workers even at the height of the Cultural Revolution. The so-called Gang held that the Cultural Revolution would spur technical development because workers would feel a sense of self-fulfillment in working self-reliantly.[66] Management was not simply a question of production but primarily of political line. Yet without a developed exchange market, the enterprise manager became responsible for the workers' health, education, welfare, political outlook, housing and medicine, as well as his occupational situation.[67] Andrew Walder's research has noted the feudal authority patterns in Chinese factories, patterns that were actually encouraged by the centralization of authority in the hands of the factory manager over all aspects of the worker's life. Local party secretaries functioned as feudal protectors, dispensing jobs, welfare benefits, and physical protection in exchange for the production of agricultural and industrial goods.[68] These goods in turn generally accumulated with the village or region, rather than circulating in a way that would create a national market.[69] The problem was fundamentally that without separating the roles of factory manager, party secretary and government administrator, local cellular economies lacked the economic scale and flexibility to profit economically from trade. The party secretary's time was fully occupied by day-to-day administrative tasks.[70] The factory managers and local administrators lacked the independence to seek trade opportunities. In 1985, for instance, the Da Bao Shan iron mine's annual output was still fixed by the Guangdong provincial planning commission, its profit and taxes by the provincial finance department, energy supply by the provincial economic commission, senior staff appointments by the Guangdong Metallurgical Industry Corporation, and sales handled by a unit of the same corporation.[71] Under these circumstances, turf fights and personalities have become the most important factors in making economic decisions by default. The Chinese worker remained alienated from both his fellow worker and his work over which he had little to no control.

Chinese industry failed to keep pace with world advances in industrial productivity and the contradiction that exchange restriction perpetrated between the weak economic base and the claim to socialist production relations became clear. As all resources lay in the hands of the local boss, the system itself restricted the worker's choices to stagnation and decline, or power-seizure and anarchy. Cultural Revolution authorities in fact realized the grave consequences of lower production and the threat of chaos and always pushed noisily for "greater and higher production." However, small-scale production could not and did not respond. Instead a number of insider accounts ironically point out factional efforts by the so-called Gang to protect their own Shanghai power base as well as general economic mismanagement. Reportedly, in Wenzhou the collective economy was so neglected that 80 percent of the land had to be unofficially divided among the peasants to farm individually.[72] Overall, national income fell from 14.7 percent annual growth from 1963 to 1965, to a low of 5.5 percent growth between 1971 and 1975. By 1976, the combination of restricted exchange and a "conservative mentality" had led China's economy to a halt and appeared to force a serious rethinking by both the people and leadership.

NOTES

1. For an account from the perspective of the so-called Gang of Four, see Lotta (ed.), *And Mao Makes Five*, pp. 265–269.
2. Yang Kaihui was Mao's first wife. Wu Zetian was China's only female emperor, ruling from 790 to 805 in the Tang Dynasty. By attacking Wu, the posters criticized Jiang Qing who also sought to make herself empress. See Chi Hsin, "The Rise and Fall of the Gang of Four," in Chi Hsin (ed.), *The Case of the Gang of Four* (Hong Kong: Cosmos Books, 1978), p. 32.
3. Cited in Ibid., p. 139.
4. See Rensselaer W. Lee III, "Political Absorption of Western Technology: The Soviet and Chinese Cases," *SICC* XV:1 & 2 (Spring/Summer 1982): 9-33.
5. See JPRS-CEA (3 September 1985): 53-55. To quote: "The reform of the foreign trade system relies on the same theoretical foundation as the reform of the economic system."
6. Cited in Lotta (ed.), *And Mao Makes Five*, p. 305
7. Cited in FBIS (24 January 1977), p. E8.
8. *The National Conference on Learning from Da Qing in Industry* (Beijing: Foreign Languages Press, 1977), p. 11.
9. Cited in FBIS, (25 July 1977), p. E1.
10. Cited in FBIS (1 August 1977), pp. E24-26.
11. Cited in FBIS (12 July 1978), pp. E7-9.
12. U.S. Congress, Joint Economic Committee, *China Under the Four Modernizations*, U.S. 97th Congress, 2d session (Washington D.C.: GPO, 1982), p. 24.
13. Deng Xiaoping, *Selected Works*, p. 157.
14. See Friedrich Wu, "Socialist Development of Self-Reliance Within the Capitalist World Economy: The Chinese View in the Post-Mao Era," in Harish Kapur (ed.), *The End of Isolation: China After Mao* (The Hague: Martinus Nijhoff Publishers, 1985), pp. 234-263.
15. "Articles on India" in Elliott (ed.), *Marx and Engels*, pp. 322-325.
16. To quote: "The mass of propertyless workers ... presupposes the world market

through competition," in "The German Ideology," in Elliott (ed.), *Marx and Engels*, pp. 441-447.

17. See Xue Muqiao, *China's Socialist Economy* (Beijing: Foreign Languages Press, 1986), pp. 259-279; FBIS (19 August 1986), pp. K22-33.

18. Victor Nee, "Between Center and Locality," in Nee and Mozingo (eds.), *State and Society*, p. 243; JPRS-CPS (7 April 1987), pp. 30-33.

19. See *SCMP* (9 November 1985), p. 5.

20. See Schurmann, *Ideology and Organization*, pp. 228-231.

21. See for example George Sung's quantitative analysis of personal ties during the Cultural Revolution: *A Biographical Approach to Chinese Political Analysis* (Santa Monica: Rand Corporation, 1975).

22. See generally Yen-p'ing Hao, *The Commercial Revolution in Nineteenth-Century China* (Berkeley: University of California Press, 1986).

23. Interview at Ministry of Electronics Industries, Beijing, June 1986.

24. Interview at China National Electronics Import-Export Corporation, Guangzhou, May 1986.

25. Cited in FBIS (8 April 1986), p. W4.

26. See *CBR* (May-June 1987), pp. 25-27.

27. *Chiu-Shih Nien-Tai* in JPRS-CPS (25 April 1986), pp. 26-27.

28. See Andrew J. Watson, "A Revolution to Touch Men's Souls," in Stuart Schram (ed.), *Authority, Participation and Cultural Change in China* (London: Cambridge University Press, 1972), p. 294. See also generally M. Freedman, *Lineage and Society: Fukien and Kwangtung* (New York: Athlone Press, 1966).

29. See generally C.K. Yang, *The Chinese Family in the Communist Revolution* (Cambridge: M.I.T. Press, 1959).

30. See Nathan, *Chinese Democracy*, pp. 224-232.

31. See *Shehui Kexue* in JPRS-CPC (12 March 1987), pp. 42-47.

32. See Creel, *Chinese Thought*, pp. 135-159.

33. Cited in Theodore de Bary (ed.), *Sources of Chinese Tradition*, Vol. 1 (New York: Columbia University Press, 1960), pp. 414-419.

34. Cited in *IS* (16 April 1980), p. 83.

35. Deng Xiaoping, *Selected Works*, p. 28.

36. Rice, *Mao's Way*, pp. 384-412.

37. See Lotta (ed.), *And Mao Makes Five*, pp. 261-264.

38. *Zhongguo Faxue* in JPRS-CPS (24 March 1987), pp. 59-64.

39. *Sixiang Zhengzhi Gongzuo Yanjiu* in JPRS-CPS (12 March 1987), pp. 19-23.

40. Cited in Teng and Fairbank (eds.), *China's Response to the West*, p. 173.

41. See Schurmann, *Ideology and Organization*, pp. 162-172; and generally Lewis, *Leadership in Communist China* (Ithaca: Cornell University Press, 1963).

42. Cited in *World Executive's Digest* (March 1986), pp. 35-41.

43. *SYC* (1985): 591.

44. See Schurmann, *Ideology and Organization*, pp. 284-308.

45. See Benedict Stavis, "The Dilemmas of State Power," in Nee and Mozingo (eds.), *State and Society*, pp. 189-193; Lotta (ed.), *And Mao Makes Five*, pp. 309-317.

46. Rice, *Mao's Way*, pp. 388-432; Stuart Schram, "The Cultural Revolution in Historical Perspective," in Schram (ed.), *Authority, Participation and Cultural Change*, pp. 100-108.

47. See Lotta (ed.), *And Mao Makes Five*, p. 292.
48. Tang Tsou, "Back from the Brink," in Nee and Mozingo (eds.), *State and Society*, p. 77.
49. See Paul and Rosemarie Tong, "The Chinese Legal Reform and Its Limitation," *JCS* (February 1981), pp. 111-118.
50. Parris Chang, "Evolution of the Party Since 1949," in Yu-Ming Shaw (ed.), *Power and Policy in the People's Republic of China* (Boulder, CO: Westview Press, 1985), pp. 45-69.
51. Cited in FBIS (30 April 1986), p. K1.
52. See *Shehui Kexue* in JPRS-CPS (12 March 1987), pp. 42-47.
53. *Zhongguo Faxue* in JPRS-CPS (12 April 1987), pp. 59-64.
54. See *Defense Electronics* (May 1986), pp. 125-135; *NYT* (18 May 1986), p. B3.
55. *SYC* (1985), p. 20, 185.
56. Irma Adelman and David Sunding, "Economic Policy and Income Distribution in China," paper presented at Regional Symposium on Chinese Politics, UCLA (Los Angeles: UCLA, November 1986), p. 29.
57. See Kuang-sheng Liao, *Anti-foreignism and Modernization in China, 1860-1980* (New York: St. Martins Press, 1984), pp. 169-210. China's GPCR experience in self-reliance is comparable in some aspects to present-day Burma and Sri Lanka until 1976. See David Morawetz, "Economic Lessons from Some Small Socialist Developing Countries," *World Development* VIII (1980), pp. 337-369.
58. See Schurmann, *Ideology and Organization*, pp. 182-186.
59. See Jamie Horsley, "The Regulation of China's Foreign Trade," in Michael Moser (ed.), *Foreign Trade, Investment and the Law* (Hong Kong: Oxford University Press, 1984), pp. 9-13.
60. See *ACFERT* (1985), pp. 418-421.
61. For example China Silk, Shanghai Handkerchief, Anshan Iron and Steel, Changzhou Agricultural Machinery, Qingdao Textile, and Guangda. See *Guoji Maoyi* in JPRS-CEA (9 July 1985), pp. 78-82.
62. *Fujian Luntan* in JPRS-CEA (24 October 1985), p. 54.
63. See Audrey Donnithorne, *Centre-Provincial Economic Relations in China* (Canberra: Australia National University, 1981); Victor Nee, "Between Center and Locality," in Nee and Mozingo (eds.), *State and Society*, pp. 223-243; Schurmann, *Ideology and Organizations*, pp. 216-220, 438-443.
64. *Aviation Week and Space Technology* (9 June 1980), pp. 18-22.
65. Interviews with the author, Beijing, 19-20 June 1986.
66. See Lotta (ed.), *And Mao Makes Five*, p. 136.
67. Walder, "Some Ironies of the Maoist Legacy in Industry," in Selden and Lippit (eds.), *The Transition to Socialism*, pp. 215-236.
68. Walder, "Organized Dependency and Cultures of Authority," p. 71.
69. See generally Solinger, *Chinese Business Under Socialism*.
70. See XINHUA in JPRS-CEA (16 July 1985), pp. 3-4; *Dushu* in JPRS-CPS (16 March 1987), p. 28.
71. *AWSJW* (21 April 1986), p. 1, 23.
72. See Chi Hsin (ed.), *The Case of the Gang of Four*, pp. 97-98.

3

The Opening as a Change Agent

The Third Plenum of the 11th Congress of the Communist Party of China (CPC) in December 1978 was a major turning point in contemporary Chinese history. Reformers entered, as typified by Deng Xiaoping, Hu Yaobang and Zhao Ziyang, all veteran CPC members and comprising three-fifths of the CPC Standing Committee of the Political Bureau in 1986. These reformers put their political legitimacy in the slogan: "truth from facts."[1] They redefined the leading criteria of socialist progress from defeat of bourgeois right to the realization of the Law of Value, and moved the "touchstone of legitimacy" from class struggle to development.[2] In so doing, the Opening to the Outside World was proposed as part and parcel of a larger set of reforms designed to attack the feudal problem, primarily in the domestic economy, and expand the horizons of the individual Chinese producer.

TO LEARN FOREIGNERS' SKILLS

From the historical perspective, China's Opening to the Outside World is only one in a lengthy series of attempts at resolving the fundamental discontinuity of China's stagnation since the Ming Dynasty. In this sense it has been part of a lengthy pattern of introducing and largely failing to apply new ideas constructively to Chinese conditions. The difference is that at no time in China's history since the expansionary and conflict-ridden days of the Han and Tang Dynasties has there been so much trade in China's economy. Neither has there been such a political consensus on developing effective, goal-oriented foreign economic relations.[3]

Confucian Reformers

Wei Yuan, a progressive politician at the end of the Qing dynasty published the influential work *Haiguo Tuzhi* in 1842. He stressed that in order to "check" the foreigners, China had to catch up with them in military skill, and the only way to do that was to "learn foreigners' skills." A member of the lower gentry, Wei was Commissioner Lin Zexu's assistant during the Opium Wars. These men, being in much more frequent and regular contact with the foreigners were the earliest to realize how much China stood to learn from the West. The *Haiguo Tuzhi* was the first serious Chinese effort to describe the foreigners. It was soon followed by a work by Xu Jishe, the governor of Fujian Province, *A Brief Survey of the Maritime Circuit* [*Yinghuan Zhilue*], a more comprehensive synthesis of current information accompanied by up-to-date maps. These visionaries, however, paid the price of China's own backwardness. The conservative Manchu court dismissed Lin Zexu in 1840 as the scapegoat for failure in the Opium War, and Xu Jishe was purged for excessive contact with foreigners, though he was later reinstated in 1865.[4]

Later, the self-strengthening [*ziqiang*] movement of the 1860s began to put into practice some of Wei Yuan's and others' ideas. Viceroy Zhang Zhidong along with Minister Li Hongzhang played key roles in the movement. Viceroy of Nanking, Zhang, in an 1898 joint memorial with Liu Kunyi, proposed the *ti/yong* [essence/application] policy, specifically in the context that manufacturing be made the *ti* of China's economy, trade its *yong*. Li was the architect of China's foreign policy of "using one foreigner against another," as well as being the builder of China's first modern navy and the initiator of the telegraph and railways in China. Both Li and Zhang who led foreign troops in the suppression of the Taiping Rebellion were among the most respected Chinese officials of the late 19th century and both acknowledged the necessity of reform,. They and others had imported Western technology to help in the development of China's industry, constructing major Western-style enterprises such as the Foochow shipyard and the Kiangnan manufacturing bureau and focusing on boosting iron and steel production.

Li Hongzhang along with Zeng Guofan, another influential statesman, instituted a number of programs to send Chinese students overseas starting in the early 1870s. Democratic reformer Liang Qichao hoped in 1902: "The 'returned' students, . . . having been civilized and influenced by the commendable tradition of a foreign country, possessing both patriotism and youthful capabilities, are the masters and rulers of the future of China." Viceroy Zhang Zhidong, noted in his 1898 essay *On Learning*: "Three years at a foreign school is better than three years at a Chinese school."[5] Within China, several leading institutions, notable among then Tongji University (Sino-German) and Qinghua University (Sino-U.S.), were established with foreign help. As Ruth Hayhoe notes: "The contribution of Western scholarly values and patterns to China's cultural modernization was . . . real and enduring, expressed both in the establishment of specific educational institutions and in a broader influence over notions of how a modern Chinese education system should be organized."[6]

However, the Confucianist reforms remained mired in a corrupt and unresponsive bureaucracy. Jerome Ch'en penetratingly comments: "In the absence of popular participation and supervision of the political process, an unreliable civil service like that of China in the second half of the nineteenth century could distort, weaken and/or tear to shreds any edict, any decision, any programme."[7] None of the "self-strengtheners" would forsake the Confucian system for the only alternative as they saw it—"complete Westernization" [quanpan xihua]. For the most part the early overseas educational programs were small and unsuccessful, and the returned students easy targets for writers such as Lu Xun who labelled them "cultural compradores." None achieved high rank in the Manchu government. Only the Work Study Scheme established in 1912 produced a number of future Chinese leaders, and most of these became Communists who appeared to have learned more working in French factories than studying in French schools. Eventually, the crisis occasioned by the disastrous Sino-Japanese War of 1895 made it clear that the *ziqiang* movement had not fulfilled its targets. Moreover, in its wake, the xenophobic residue of the failed Boxer rebellion signalled a fresh round of stagnation.[8]

The failure of the *ziqiang* movement in China was particularly apparent when compared to its Japanese counterpart—the 1868 Meiji Restoration. By the turn of the century, following the humiliating Treaty of Shimonoseki signed after the 1895 Sino-Japanese War, it became obvious that Japan had outstripped China in "learning foreigners' skills." Chinese observers laid this to both the development of a Western style political system and a "rational" economic system. In economic matters, Japan's adoption of large scale production and the encouragement of commercial production compared favorably to Chinese small-scale feudalism. Zheng Guanying, a Chinese industrialist of the late 1890s, noted: "The [Japanese] authorities have ordered their local officials to do their best to imitate the production of all foreign goods."[9]

Politically, Japan introduced real constitutional reforms where Kang Youwei's relatively mild 1898 reforms premised on Western ideas of constitutional monarchy were suppressed by the Dowager Empress and Yuan Shikai in China. Comparing China to Japan, Feng Guifen, a modernization advocate, noted: "The ruling and the ruled are not so separated; in this aspect, China is falling behind." Wei Yuan, the original advocate of "learning foreigners' skills" professed admiration for the American democratic system, saying that "it will pass from one generation to another doing no harm." Zheng Guanying demanded: "It is imperative to set up a parliament if China is to become prosperous."[10]

Based on these observations, a large movement to learn from Japan ensued and by the turn of the century it is estimated the number of Chinese students studying in Japan exceeded 10,000. Sun Yat-sen was a leading exhorter of the movement to learn from Japan. Speaking to a group of Chinese students in Japan in 1905, he said: "The purpose of your coming to Japan is to absorb its civilization. . . . If China is capable of applying its own civilization, it will not be surprising for it to surpass Japan."[11] Yet China did not surpass Japan, despite Sun's desires. And at the same time that many of the best and brightest students were attempting to bring Western civilization to China, another group adopted more radical policies.

The Communists

Much of the leadership of this group studied in France under the Work-study Program. To name just a few of those who went abroad in the early part of the twentieth century reads like a Who's Who of the future Communist elite—for example, Zhou Enlai, Deng Xiaoping, Zhu De, Chen Yi, and Nie Rongzhen. They all rejected the previous Westernizing *ti/yong* formula as well as the liberal democratic philosophies of Dewey and Bertrand Russell. As Chen Duxiu, a pioneer Marxist, noted in "The Basis for the Realization of Democracy" in December 1919: "Dr. Dewey's explanation of socio-economic democracy can be regarded as a belief shared by all schools of socialism."[12] When they returned to China, they found themselves in the midst of the aborted 1911 revolution, Yuan Shikai's takeover, and the anti-Japanese, pro-"science" May Fourth Movement. Thence, many of them applied themselves to the task of social revolution. To quote Chen Duxiu again: "Since the revolutionary situation of the world and the domestic conditions of China indicated so clearly, my change of view was inevitable."[13]

Of the three major groups of Chinese students in France, the first left after the Lyons protest strike in 1921.[14] The second group, including Zhou Enlai, left after occupying the Chinese embassy in Paris in 1924. Rice comments that the persuasive ability of Zhou was so great that he persuaded General Zhu De, a man twice his age, to join the Communists at this time. The third group included Deng Xiaoping, nicknamed the "Doctor" of mimeography for his skill with a copying machine. This group left in 1926 or thereafter and a number of its members also proceeded to the Soviet Union for further study. In time, many of these came to be known as the "Returned Student Faction" and the key leaders as the "Twenty-eight Bolsheviks." Upon their return to China with Comintern backing, they dominated the CPC off and on from 1930 until Mao settled accounts in the 1942–44 Rectification [*zhengfeng*] campaign. Prominent among them were Wang Ming and Qin Pangxian, who in January 1931 replaced the over-ambitious Li Lisan with the aid of Pavel Mif, Comintern representative.[15] Concerning them, Stuart Schram notes: "The Russians had spent a lot of money sending the 'Returned Students' back to China, and therefore felt that these young men had a *prima facie* right to leadership over the Chinese Communist Party."[16]

Mao Zedong was the great exception to the trend to learn foreign skills. He criticized the early Westernizers, noting that the Western and Japanese "teachers" were always committing aggression against their Chinese pupils. The pupils, moreover, were chronically unsuccessful in realizing their ideals.[17] When Zhou Enlai and other young radicals went to Paris under the Work-study Program, Mao stayed in Hunan, editing socialist newspapers in the provinces and developing the basic cells of the nascent Party. Later, in struggles with the Moscow-dominated faction, Mao would criticize the Soviet students for leftist dogmatism and an inability to grasp the essential Chinese characteristics of revolution. In his own words: "For the past few decades many returned students have been making this mistake. They return from Europe, America or Japan and all they know how to do is to recite a stock of undigested foreign phrases. They function as phonographs but forget their own responsibility to create something new."[18] This is not to say that Mao rejected out of hand all foreign skills. Mao acknowledged the efforts of the early modernizers to learn from the West, though critically, and later in the 1950s he grudgingly assumed the role of student to the Soviet Union. To quote him then: "We must overcome difficulties, we must learn what we do not know. We must learn how to do economic work, from all who know, no matter who they are . . . . The Communist Party of the Soviet Union is our best teacher and we must learn from it."[19]

As far as the Chinese revolution was concerned, however, Mao was determined to see that it would be led by and for the Chinese. He told Edgar Snow in 1936: "We are certainly not fighting for an emancipated China in order to turn the country over to Moscow!" Essentially, Mao believed that the purpose in studying foreign skills was to foster the growth of Chinese things—not to mechanically adopt the fundamentally Western theory of Marxism but to adapt it to specific Chinese characteristics. Again in Stuart Schram's words: "By postulating that Leninism, in order to play its proper role in China, must be transmuted to such an extent that it lost its foreign essence—and thereby perhaps its identity—Mao was proposing, in effect to use the Leninist heritage primarily as a storehouse of techniques . . . to overcome the evils inherited from the past but to do so in original and specifically Chinese terms."[20]

During the first Five-year Plan from 1953 to 1957, despite Mao's dedication to self-reliance and distaste for the foreign-educated students, some 15,000 Chinese students travelled to study in the Soviet Union. They returned, steeped in the Soviet bureaucratic planning process to take up positions in the functional and industrial bureaucracy. Throughout the coming years these Soviet-educated students of the 1950s ascended into the universities, the ministries and industry. Despite the communal, mass line workstyle developed in the CCP's guerrilla war, wholesale transfer of Soviet institutions occurred from 1949 to the mid 1950s. Renmin University, founded in 1950 on the Soviet model, would later be described in the Cultural Revolution as a "beehive of doctrinairism," precisely Mao's earlier criticism of the Twenty-eight Bolsheviks.[21] This influence was minimized by the self-reliant efforts of Mao during the Cultural Revolution and earlier the Great Leap Forward. These, combined with the "cellular" structure of China's economy, ensured that the planning process introduced by the Soviets and managed by their students never grew to rival that of the Soviet Union's. To quote a visiting American economist in 1985: "Planners confirmed in striking fashion the relative crudeness of central planning as practiced in China."[22]

Nonetheless, in specific industries Soviet management practices have had a lasting impact on China's modernization efforts. For example, the electronics field was almost carbon-copied from the Soviet model.[23] A small number of prestigious, largely autonomous research institutes dominated the industry. Highly centralized planning allocated research funds and facilities. Theoretical and applied research remained largely separated as were hardware and software. Basic research outweighed consumer applications and the military took up one-half to three-quarters of total electronics production by the mid-1970s. More generally, by 1986 the Soviet-educated students formed a key part of the state-planning apparatus (for example Premier Li Peng) and it would appear that their formative education in the Soviet Union had to play a key role in their outlook.

The second great wave of students abroad arrived in 1976 after ten years of Cultural Revolution isolation. In 1986, most educated Chinese in their forties speak some Russian, but teenagers will likely speak English. It is estimated that at least 30,000 Chinese students are currently abroad, the vast majority in the United States or Europe.[24] These students have come to the West, as did those earlier to the Soviet Union, to learn the practice of production. It is most likely that the two groups will find much to debate about each others' management ability. Yet it is exactly the previous impact of the Soviet students that indicates the potential for change the new students will bring. With their return, the process of learning foreigners' skills has at least the opportunity to begin again.

EXPANDING EXCHANGE

As the history of "learning foreigners' skills" implies, a modernized China appears to be integrally tied to the expansion of China's foreign relations. Senior economist Xu Dixin put it succinctly: "China has not much of a foundation to speak of, being a semi-colonial and semi-feudal society in the past. If we should start from scratch in everything we would lose much time.... [In] making the Four Modernizations faster and better, Opening to the Outside World is inevitable."[25] Expanding development is seen to be impossible without expanding the trade and vice versa.[26] To quote Ma Hong, senior academician and Director General of the Research Center for Political, Economic and Social Affairs of the State Council: "Economic reforms and the open door policy nurture each other."[27]

A Marxist Comment

Aside from the forecast of increased exchange, there was relatively little said by Marx and Engels on the subject of foreign economic relations and their ideological significance. They did note in the *Manifesto* that the working class has no country, only its own class-consciousness.[28] Marx's analysis of capitalist expansion predicts the increase of interlocking relationships throughout the world, alliances between corporations, the linkage of foreign policies to domestic events in other countries, and the global spread of information technologies.[29] As the proletariat exercised its supremacy, national boundaries would continue to disappear with the forces of commoditization and universalization and the growth of a socialist political superstructure. The future socialist world would be universal as nation-states were replaced by one vast cooperative workshop. Socialism in one country was by definition a transitory phenomenon as isolationism was not the historic trend in the Marxist dialectic.

Marx's further writings on foreign trade were mostly confined to an analysis of imperialism, in itself contradictory. He warned against the painful effects of the growth of world capitalism and worker immiserization, developing the prototype of dependency theory in observing Ireland, England's oldest colony.[30] Lenin's *Imperialism: The Highest Stage of Capitalism* further developed the dependency theses which Andre Gunder Frank and others have since put forward.[31] Yet in the case of India, Marx saw imperialism as a historically necessary force, a bloody scourge to erase feudalism. Moreover, he made a central criticism of the theory of unequal exchange, which is at the root of much modern dependency theory.[32] Unequal exchange of value cannot be exploitation in Marxist terms, because value is only created in the sphere of production and not in exchange. Mere participation in the world economy is not equivalent to joining the capitalist mode of production, as exploitation must always take place between classes, not nations.[33] It is regrettable that Marx died before writing the next volume of *Capital*, which was to have dealt with international trade. Even so, China's 1978 reformers have claimed that China faced conditions never envisioned by the Marx and Engels of 19th century industrial Europe.[34]

Expanding Trade

As already noted, according to the reformers, the key economic obstacle to modernization was China's economy of restricted exchange. They contended that the GPCR had strayed from objective appraisals in favor of a "self-reliant" utopian strategem, hence China fell off the Marxist path away from feudalism. Specifically, in attacking the GPCR, reformist economists created the concepts of "natural" (feudal/self-reliant), "commodity" (market) and "product" (planned) economies as Marxian stages in economic development. According to the reformers, the "leftist" trend prematurely attempted to introduce advanced collective or "product" forms of production unsuited to China's means of production. Instead, China slipped backwards towards a "natural" or self-reliant feudal economy. The GPCR represented a "trend in which ideology surpassed the development of the objective process."[35] The disruptions this "rash advance" caused made it necessary in 1978 to reemphasize the priority of economic growth, of moving China from "natural" to "commodity" socialism. Equity, though still a cardinal socialist value, receded as China compared itself unfavorably to other rapidly industrializing countries.

Specifically, the reformers hoped that growth would be spurred by opening up to the outside world. This was nothing short of a sea change in leadership thinking. For example, the explanation many modern Chinese economists offered to the slow growth in the industrialization of China's exports was the long-time feudal, physiocratic habit of regarding foreign trade only as a means of "balancing surplus and shortage." Reining in imports versus increasing exports, avoiding the use of foreign capital, self-reliance versus the use of foreigners' skills, were all examples of this thinking. Qing Dynasty China exported solely to cover costs of necessary imports, first opium and later military technology. Exchange in the foreign market was based not on a comparative cost advantage, but as an exchange of use values, or more often one-way tribute, without regard to the material benefits and economies possible. Not until the Opening to the Outside World did prevailing Chinese economic thought evince a shift away from the "surplus and shortage" school.[36]

At that point in 1978, the reformers contended that growth could be promoted if China efficiently saved scarce capital investment resources and foreign exchange by making use of China's comparative advantages in world trade. They noted that abstract, socially necessary labor could be economized in the sphere of circulation on the basis of comparative costs.[37] China should import where its domestic needs were urgent and its comparative social labor position was weak and export where its position was strong, for example, export textiles and import airplanes. Thus, if China saved social labor, productivity would rise and more resources would be available for modernization. In one analysis, economist Sun Xiangjian even calculated a set of formulas to derive value-based foreign exchange profit targets for imports and exports by stage of production, that is whether it is more profitable in any given industry to export raw, semi-finished or finished materials.[38]

Opposition to the policy of growth through comparative advantage was muted at the leadership level. There were those who at the same time wished to create powerful economic leverage that the state's central authorities could use. However, no one said this leverage should prevent the overall development of China's trade. In fact, proponents noted this leverage could be used to promote the development of comparative advantage through tax, credit, and wage policies, more effectively than had the direct planning methods. Because of, *not* in spite of, the fact that China had a "planned" economy, the normally slow and painful process of economic development might be accelerated by the judicious use of foreign economic relations. State planning in the past served only to maintain a balance of international payments. Now it would be called on to encourage growth by expanding exports. In an even larger sense, foreign trade would be an "economic lever" by which technology and management skills would transfer, hence modernization could take place.[39] To quote economist Teng Weizao: "Reforms must ensure that the function of state planning as a regulator in foreign trade is combined with that of the market and that our export potential is properly realized."[40]

New "Forms of Production"

Having decided to expand exports, reformers found it necessary to follow through on their other promises of new "forms of production." Loosely defined, the term referred to ways to link producing ability to economic interest, or pay for performance. In theory then, the individual or organization would strive to become an efficient producer, maximizing benefits while minimizing costs. One reformist discussion of efficiency noted: "Not only must we treasure every small unit of time in every move of economic activity, but we must also give thoughtful consideration to the time objectives in every item of our economic construction within our socialist modernization."[41]

One theoretical forum in mid-1986 concluded: "The present excessively centralized management system should be changed and the change of government functions is one of the vital factors in the [economic] structural reform."[42] As this quote implies, one of the first steps reformers took was to review the dominant role of state production. They contended that public ownership was only a facade concealing a stagnant "cellular" economy. Economist Liu Guoguang rebuked unified state ownership in favor of "market coordination under the guidance of planning and with macroeconomic control," this being dialectically more appropriate for China's present stage of economic development.[43] To achieve socialized production, it might be necessary to abandon structures which had monopolized the guarantee of the dignity of labor and socialist relations of production in China since 1949.[44] To quote the editors of the influential Chinese economic theory journal *Jingji Yanjiu* in 1985: "We have broken with the traditional view that in a socialist society, we can only implement a unified form of public ownership."[45] This was not to deny the importance of stable leadership by the socialist system in the economy. Indeed as early as 1956, Chen Yun, Vice Premier and senior economic planner, who was generally regarded as a conservative by Western analysts, outlined a centrally-dominated design for an economic system with "free production in accordance with market changes and within the limits permitted by the state plan."[46] On the other hand, at one Shanghai symposium on the economy in 1984, two researchers quoted Marx to the effect that "the developed countries have only shown the comparatively underdeveloped their future."[47]

Also implicit in the strategy was a tendency to move those parts of the national economy that were unprofitable to a more economically efficient local scale of production. According to some reformers, provinces and localities could run more efficiently than Beijing most of China's small-scale industries such as textiles. The center, however, played a crucial role in large-scale, capital-intensive sectors such as power, communications and transport infrastructure. Senior Chinese finance officials noted in one conversation in January 1987: "Centralization against decentralization is too general a phrase. What is more important is economic scale and the fostering of horizontal coordination."[48] Horizontal coordination between local enterprises [*hengxiang lianxi*] is to be encouraged over vertical integration within ministries [*shuxiang lianxi*] in key industries such as the automotive, electric power, and high technology in over 30,000 major enterprises. Vertical integration had in the past resulted in managers building up small-scale enterprises doing everything from nuts and bolts to final assembly, at very uneconomic scales. The Hubei and Changchun automotive groups are two examples. They were created in 1986 as two of seven major automotive groups, amalgamated from 137 "small but complete" plants. Before, small volumes made economies of scale infeasible as the plants produced between 100 and 1000 cars each per year. Even with the reform, however, Shanghai Volkswagen sourced wheels in 1987 from four separate factories at uneconomic volumes. In the automotive industry at least, decentralization would be only a return to the feudal economy.

Given this history, reformers have hypothesized that expanding foreign trade would not only directly promote economic growth but would also encourage appropriately efficient economic scale of production. The expansion of demand it represented could eventually break down the uneconomic village walls. On this basis, the China Export Bases Development Corporation invested a total of 300 million yuan between 1981 and 1985 and pledged to further invest 400 million yuan in the next four years to develop China's export bases crossing regional, sectoral and departmental boundaries. The Special Economic Zones (SEZ) were likewise supposed to act as "windows" for the interior—from 1979 to 1984 the Shenzhen SEZ generated total revenue of 519 million yuan for the mainland while the mainland generated 313 million yuan for the SEZ.[49] At one 1984 conference on world economics, it was also proposed that "while industrial structure of a closed system relies on its domestic mineral resources, as production develops to a certain point, demand will inevitably shift to international science and technology resources."[50] As defined in the authoritative *Guoji Maoyi*, such technical trade referred to the "selling and buying of the knowledge of industrial production as well as the buying and selling of hardware like machinery and equipment."[51] This trade in science and technology and "advanced management techniques," it was hoped, could break down feudal regional barriers as well.

So far, opposition to direct foreign economic involvement and the breaking up of village economies has been greater than to increasing trade. Breaking up industries has led to the problem of finding jobs for dispossessed workers. Some have even gone so far as to claim that the Special Economic Zones are "capitalist dumping grounds" or as political scholar Zheng Baoyin noted: "In China SEZs are new entities that have emerged in the last few years ... some people ... maintain that special zones are a 'revival' of the concessions of old China." Economist Tan Si wrote likewise: "The logic of these people is ... modern capitalism is unable to free itself of periodic economic crises. Its decadent and moribund nature has become more obvious than ever .... To import foreign capital at this point is tantamount to making things convenient for capitalism, which is desperately seeking a way out for its surplus capital."[52] Behind the economic criticism though may lurk a more basic fear of "complete Westernization" [*quanpan xihua*] reminiscent of the early Qing conservatives. While perhaps inevitable, the conflict between the hard-line nationalists and more pragmatic developers has appeared to be manageable in other societies. For example, restrictions on foreign domestic involvement have existed until recently in Japan and still do in Korea. Yet growth has remained high in both, implying that domestic exchange can be improved, though perhaps more expensively, without foreign involvement.

THE SKILLS FOR CHANGE

To encourage expanded exchange, some reformers have also realized that in addition to economic issues they needed to change China's basic political organization. No strategy would work unless the required governing skills and structure existed. Only with a government that encouraged individuals to broaden their horizons through the free flow of information and legal reform would the Opening reach its economic goals. Building these governing skills though, reaped fewer immediate economic benefits and encountered greater political resistance.

The Rule of Law

How the government governed—or the character of authority relations—was one of the key skills the reformers initially focused on. During the GPCR, personal directives and mass campaigns [*yundong*] dominated to the exclusion of laws. Almost all aspects of daily life underwent politicizing. Reformers on the other hand seemed intent on depoliticizing many aspects of day-to-day life and introducing formal legal structures, while preserving the essence of the communist voluntarist spirit.

Specifically, between 1979 and 1985, China drew up over 300 administrative laws, including administrative statutes and regulations. Of these, over 50 percent concerned foreign economic relations. In 1985 China had economic relations with 177 countries and regions, and had signed protocols with 96 countries and the European Economic Community.[53] As of 1983, China's bar expanded from virtually nil in 1976 to over 18,500 lawyers.[54]

In the aftermath of the Cultural Revolution it was Hua Guofeng who had first noted it is "essential to strengthen the socialist legal system if we are to bring about great order across the land." Two years later, Deng Xiaoping stated: "To ensure people's democracy, we must strengthen our legal system. Democracy has to be institutionalized and written into law, so as to make sure that institutions and laws do not change whenever the leadership changes."[55] And in 1986, an article in China's leading legal newspaper, *Zhongguo Fazhi Bao* noted: "The party has its party discipline;

the government has its administrative discipline, the state has its laws . . . political structure reform requires that law as a clear and universal norm act as a means for promoting overall decision-making."[56]

One of the key issues in managing legal reform was "spiritual civilization." Many conservatives saw the emphasis on law detracting from the selfless communist model. To quote Peng Zhen reporting on the 1982 Constitution: "Now that we have established the socialist system, we should and can strengthen nationwide education in communism among the cadres and the people. Only in this way will it be possible to keep the socialist orientation in our modernization drive and to ensure that our social development keeps heading for the correct goal and retains its ethical motivation."[57] Even reformers placed importance on building "spiritual civilization" while opening to the outside world, to strengthen resistance to "corrosive bourgeois ideology." Deng Xiaoping noted in 1985: "In recent years production has gone up but the pernicious influence of capitalism and feudalism has not been reduced to a minimum. Instead some evil things that had long been extinct after liberation have come to life again. We must be determined to change this situation as soon as possible."[58]

In one of those ironic twists common to Chinese politics, though, reformist legality was itself proposed by reformers as a bolster to spiritual civilization. To quote the journal *Outlook*: "Reforms have not only directly propelled the construction of spiritual civilization but are favorable to preventing the unhealthy tendencies of sabotaging the construction of spiritual civilization."[59] The 1986 Party Congress further restressed the importance of simultaneously building spiritual and material civilizations, affirming that the revolutionary tradition of socialist ideals was basic to the Party's authority.

Aside from "spiritual civilization" the major conflict in the legal reform was the relationship between the Party and the law. Party members themselves were not immune from civil prosecution, although within the party, Party discipline was a rule apart from the law.[60] The creation of a legal system was not intended to supercede the Party's basic authority and introduce Western bourgeois democracy. Rather, it was supposed to universalize and formalize the process by which the people's government ruled. Yet legislating morality was a tricky thing. If the leadership was free to decide what constituted revolutionary behavior, the legal reform could resemble more classical Chinese Legalism than a social contract. On the other hand, the very vagueness of Chinese laws, so often decried by foreign businessmen, coupled with the repeated invocation of socialist principles, also provided the basis for a differentiated yet legal approach.[61] As Yu Haocheng, a noted democratic reformer, stated: "If it is said that political issues can be discussed, what if people air counterrevolutionary views? My reply is that one violates the criminal law by airing counter-

revolutionary views. One who does this must be punished by the law. . . .
Democracy and the legal system are in fact the two sides of a coin."[62]

"Democratic Construction"

To achieve economic expansion, the reformers also found it necessary
to call for "democratic construction." Specifically, building Chinese
democracy entailed a program of gradual official press and public speech
liberalization, strengthening of the People's Congress, the introduction of
law, deemphasis of the personality cult around leaders, and other reforms
to be carried out under the ethical aegis of the Party. American scholar
Brantly Womack astutely foresaw the move as he remarked in 1984: "Despite the ambiguities in the regime's commitment to democratic institu-
tionalization, modernization can be expected to provide a continuing
pressure to resolve ambiguities in favor of democracy."[63]
The reformers claimed that the Cultural Revolution had hindered
development by restricting the creative inquiries of the people.[64] To quote
from the *Resolution on CPC History*: "A fundamental task of the socialist
revolution is to gradually realize direct popular participation in the
democratic process. . . . Inadequate attention was paid to this matter after
the founding of the People's Republic, and this was one of the major factors contributing to the initiation of the 'cultural revolution.'"[65] Political
reform had to be linked with economic progress though. To quote Ni
Zhifu, member of the Politburo: "Economic construction is inseparable
from ideological, cultural, democratic, and legal construction as they are
closely related to each other and are regarded as a whole."[66] Tan Jian, a
senior research fellow in the Institute of Politics, spelled out further how
political reform or "democratic construction" was necessary for economic
progress. He proposed five major policies: "democratization" [*minzhuhua*]
or the extension of individual rights in many respects; freeing up information flow [*gongkaihua*]; legal reforms [*fazhihua*]; scientific decision-
making [*jueci kexuehua*]; and economic levers [*diandu tixihua*]. These he
believed would preserve stability while promoting growth.
Tan Jian also maintained that standing politically still was the only way
to ensure instability given the rapidly changing international political
economy.[67] China should learn from the experiences of others though it
would not apply wholesale, foreign political institutions unsuited to
China's low-income, agricultural, Confucian, industrializing society. Hu
Sheng put it: "We must not close ourselves to the different schools of
thought abroad and instead, what we should do is to conscientiously dis-
cuss, study and criticize them."[68] One of the main strengths of the Opening
to the Outside World as a political catalyst for change lay in its ability to
provide reference points. By making horizontal comparisons against

others rather than vertically against themselves, the Chinese people and leadership would perceive more accurately their successes and failures. Such a perception was key to pushing the national institutions and interests towards change. The Opening to the Outside World in the realm of thought was a concomitant of economic progress. As Li Lanqing, Vice Minister of MOFERT, has noted: "the single most important factor holding back foreign investment in China is the lack of trained Chinese management personnel."[69]

By 1986, the Chinese leadership appeared to be taking some specific lessons from their "foreign studies." For example, while numerous articles on the Hungarian and Yugoslav reforms were the early topic of conversation in late 1970s and were generally used to justify already taken decisions by the Chinese leaders, in 1984, talk shifted to the specific debt and wage problems of Poland and Hungary and the positive examples of the Newly Industrializing Countries. Nina Halpern has concluded that, at least until early 1980, a distorted view existed, a "constraint imposed by the need to support current domestic policies." Since 1980, however, articles on economic affairs abroad have focused more on the problems of economic reform and how they can be overcome, rather than mere cheerleading, although a considerable amount of that still exists.[70] Goh Keng Swee, Singapore's economic *eminence grise*, has been retained as an advisor for the SEZs. Many SEZ boosters have called for the creation of a "separatist" offshore financial center on the Singapore model where relationships between residents and foreigners are restricted.[71] The much-touted Joint Ventures are increasingly becoming more visible as "windows" for learning new management skills or "demonstration effects" in the World Bank's phrase.[72] Even the experience of foreigners in political development, in fact political science, has been held to a long-term lever for modernization. As one commentator noted in the *Beijing Review*: "Not only is it impossible to uphold Marxism behind closed doors, it is also impossible to develop socialist culture and ethics in a closed society."[73]

In urging individual initiatives and grassroots participation in government, though, the "democratic constructionists" were deemed by the top leadership to differ substantially from the 1978-79 so-called Democracy Wall activists. Those earlier reformers either had argued very close to abolishing Party leadership or had used the Wall to put up very personal grievances for redress. Both were quickly suppressed by a disturbed elite and an apathetic mainstream.[74] To quote senior minister Wan Li: "The so-called democratic policy decision-making must be scientific.... Otherwise it is only democratic in form and not in reality."[75] Neither Deng nor the conservatives was willing to allow disorder, subversive ideas, or Party indiscipline to endanger the economic gains made since 1949.[76] The later 1986 activists instead argued more wisely that democracy directly promoted economic progress, and thus was tolerated. To quote Shanghai's

Wenhui Bao: "The reform of the economic structure calls for the reform of the political system. At the same time the political system guarantees economic structural reform."[77] Reformers were also flexible enough to accommodate some conservative demands. For example, while reformers urged expert ability should receive new emphasis as a requirement for participation in government, they acknowledged good political character and the willingness to accept party authority would remain prerequisites.[78] Moreover, those who practiced "democracy without centralism" and "personal freedom of expression without party unity of will" could be proseuted as economic criminals and corrupt officials.[79]

To many Western scholars such political reforms have appeared closer to what some have characterized as "institutional revisionism" as opposed to systemic change. Lowell Dittmer, for one, has argued that revisionism is a construal of Marxism that emphasizes scientific materialism at the expense of "romantic, voluntarist, dialectical aspects."[80] One reason for much of this controversy among foreign observers may be the strong debate within the Chinese leadership on the value of Western political ideas for Chinese people. Arguments against their relevance exist. Socially conservative leaders note prostitution, gambling, and drugs have all had minor resurgences in Chinese society. Taxi drivers in Guangzhou play Lionel Richie tapes incessantly. The Shanghai Seaman's Club back of the old Blood Alley has returned to its seedy glory.[81] More factually, some are disturbed by student unrest over "democracy" and see the repercussions possibly spreading to the industrial sector. Deng Xiaoping, the chief reformer, was responsible for launching the 1983 Campaign Against Spiritual Pollution. The later campaigns against bourgeois liberalism have reemphasized the leadership's interest in maintaining socialist ethics. The very name of the policy, the "opening to the outside world" [*kaifang zhengce*], explicitly sets it apart from the previous "open door policy" [*kaimen zhengce*].

Observers' concern over the leadership's advocacy of Western political concepts may, however, be misplaced. Given the entrenched opposition to some of the reform proposals, success ultimately appears to depend more on the reformers' ability to develop a grassroots core of agents for change. This may not necessarily contradict Western ideas of free speech and individual rights. To many Chinese in 1986, however, free speech may sound much like the "big character" [*dazibao*] rabble-rousing of the Cultural Revolution's early years from 1966 to 1968.

To prevent chaos and to implement change relatively quickly, just as in the Yanan period of "penetrating the natural village," the use of grassroots change agents appears to be inevitable. These agents from party members to entrepreneurs are to advance at the grassroots the reformist concepts of expanded trade, efficient scale, legal reform and democratic construction against "feudal" political and economic interests. In developing these agents though, the leadership must recognize that they come from all social strata, not just bureaucrats and politicians. This would be a key difference between the Opening and the failed Confucian reform movements of the past. To quote a 1984 article by a Chinese sociologist: "The challenge of the New Technological Revolution tells us that in the development of science and technology it is necessary to bring into play the creative capacities of the people. To this end it is necessary to enlarge the self-conscious external participation of the people."[82]

NOTES

1. To quote Zhao Ziyang in 1985: "It is not good either to overestimate or to underestimate them [facts]. The general principle should be to seek truth from facts and make accurate assessments." See Communist Party of China, *Uphold Reform*, p. 66.
2. The phrase is Lowell Dittmer's.
3. See Sheng Guangyao, *Foreign Trade in Ancient China* (Guangdong: Guangdong Renmin Chubanshe, 1986), (in Chinese); Mancall, *China at the Center*; and Hao, *The Commercial Revolution in Nineteenth-Century China*, pp. 14-34, 163-212.
4. Mancall, *China at the Center*, pp. 176-178; Ch'en, *China and the West*, p. 61; FBIS (14 February 1986) pp. K20-24.
5. Ch'en, *China and the West*, pp. 153-174; Teng and Fairbank (eds.), *China's Response to the West*, pp. 197-209.
6. Ruth Hayhoe, "A Comparative Approach to the Cultural Dynamics of Sino-Western Educational Cooperation, *CQ* 104 (December 1985): 676-699.
7. Ch'en, *China and the West*, p. 270
8. Hu Sheng, *Imperialism and Chinese Politics*, pp. 96-103; Ch'en, *China and the West*, pp. 265-270.
9. Cited in FBIS (14 February 1986), pp. K20-24.
10. *Ibid.*
11. *Ibid.*
12. Cited in Ch'en, *China and the West*, p. 185.
13. Cited in Ch'en, *China and the West*, p. 189. See also Yang Liqiang and Shen Weibin, "Symposium on Modern China's Bourgeoisie," *SSC* V:2 (June 1984), pp. 9-27.
14. Nora Wang, "Deng Xiaoping: The Years in France," *CQ* 92 (December 1982): 698-706. See Also Rice, *Mao's Way*, pp. 19-20.
15. For one scholarly account of the Twenty-eight Bolsheviks see Gregor Benton, "The Second Wang Ming Line," *CQ* 61 (March 1975): 61-94.
16. Schram, "The Cultural Revolution in Historical Perspective," in Schram (ed.), *Authority, Participation and Cultural Change*, p. 14.
17. Ibid.
18. Cited in Boyd Compton, *Mao's China* (Seattle: University of Washington Press, 1952), pp. 62-63, as noted in Schram, "The Cultural Revolution in Historical Perspective," p. 19.

19. Mao Zedong, *Selected Works*, Vol. 4, pp. 422-423.
20. Schram, "The Cultural Revolution,", p. 7.
21. Hayhoe, "Sino-Western Educational Cooperation," p. 682; Gordon White, "The Post-Revolutionary Chinese State," in Nee and Mozingo (eds.), *State and Society*, pp. 29-32; Ying-Mao Kau, "Patterns of Recruitment and Mobility of Urban Cadres," in John W. Lewis (ed.), *The City in Communist China*, (Stanford: Stanford University Press, 1971), p. 113.
22. Cady (ed.), *Economic Reform in China*, pp. 6-33; Donnithorne, "China's Cellular Economy,", pp. 605-619.
23. The following is from Jonathan Pollack, *The Chinese Electronics Industry in Transition* (Santa Monica: Rand Corporation, 1985), pp. 5-12.
24. *Far Eastern Economic Review* (18 September 1986), p. 47.
25. Cited in FBIS (15 May 1986), pp. K10-K15.
26. See John Sheahan, *Alternative International Economic Strategies and Their Relevance for China*, Staff Working Paper #759 (Washington D.C.: World Bank, 1986), for a Western analysis of conflicts and options in China's departure from "double-layered insulation."
27. Cited in XINHUA in JPRS-CEA (19 September 1985), pp. 78-82. See also Ma Hong, *New Strategy for China's Economy* (Beijing: New World Press, 1983) especially pp. 33, 39, and 63-63.
28. Quoting: "The workingmen have got no country. We cannot take away from them what they have not got" in "Communist Manifesto," Elliott (ed.), *Marx and Engels*, p. 373.
29. "Grundrisse" in Elliott (ed.), *Marx and Engels*, pp. 112-114.
30. See "Wage Labor and Capital" in Elliott (ed.), *Marx and Engels*, pp. 275-276; M.C. Howard and J.E. King, *The Political Economy of Marx* (London: Longman, 1985), pp. 225-237; Ben Fine and Laurence Harris, *Rereading Capital* (New York: Columbia University Press. 1979), pp. 146-170.
31. See A.G. Frank, *Capitalism and Underdevelopment in Latin America* (New York: Monthly Review Press, 1969); A.G. Frank, *Lumpenbourgeoisie: Lumpendevelopment* (New York: Monthly Review Press, 1972).
32. "Capital" in Elliott (ed.), *Marx and Engels*, pp. 164-172.
33. See Laclau's criticism of Frank in "Feudalism and Capitalism in Latin America," *New Left Review* (1971), No. 67.
34. See Li Honglin, "Open Policy Essential to Socialism," in Zhou Guo (ed.), *China and the World*, p. 9, 24.
35. See "Theory Based on a Natural Economy or Theory of an Economy Based on Planned Products?" *Jingji Yanjiu* (20 August 1985), pp. 59-65 (in Chinese).
36. Sun Xiangjian, "The Question of the Profitability of Foreign Trade to the National Economy," *SSC* II:1, pp. 35-60; Yuan Wenqi and Wang Jianmin, "We Must Review and Reevaluate the Role of Foreign Trade in the Development of the National Economy," *Guoji Maoyi*, No. 1 (1982), pp. 22-28 (in Chinese).
37. Yuan and Wang, "Reevaluate the Role of Foreign Trade," pp. 22-28.
38. See Yuan Wenqi, Dai Cunshang, and Wang Linsheng, "International Division of Labor and China's Foreign Economic Relations," *SSC* I:1, pp. 22-48; and Sun Xiangjian, "Profitability of Foreign Trade," pp. 35-60.
39. See *Kaifang* in JPRS-CEA (1 November 1985), p. 20; FBIS (16 May 1986), pp. K5-9; FBIS (22 May 1986), pp. K10-13; FBIS (19 May 1986), pp. K13-18.

40. Teng Weizao, "Modernization and Foreign Trade," in Xu Dixin (ed.), *China's Search for Economic Growth* (Beijing: New World Press, 1982), pp. 172-192.
41. Cited in *Jingji Wenti Tansuo* in JPRS-CEA (19 September 1986=5), pp. 19-26.
42. Cited in FBIS (13 August 1986), p. K5.
43. See Liu Guoguang, "Certain Problems Regarding the Reform of the System of Ownership," *Jingji Ribao* (4 January 1986), p. 3 (in Chinese).
44. See CPC, *China's Economic Structure Reform* (Beijing: Foreign Languages Press, 1984), p. 7.
45. Cited in FBIS (18 July 1985), p. K9.
46. Cited in FBIS (23 June 1986), pp. K14-24.
47. "On the International Environment of China's Open Door Policy," *Shijie Jingji* (10 February 1985), pp. 25-29 (in Chinese).
48. Interview with the author, Beijing, 14 January 1987.
49. See *China Daily Business Weekly* (11 February 1987), p. 1; *Jingji Daobao* in JPRS-CEA (3 September 1985), pp. 85-88; and three articles by Chen Dongsheng, "China's Layout of Productive Forces," *Guangming Ribao* (20-22 February 1986). See also FBIS (4 April 1986), pp. K17-19; FBIS (26 June 1986), pp. K6-10; and JPRS-CEA (9 July 1985), pp. 11-12.
50. *Shijie Jingji* (10 February 1985), pp. 25-29 (in Chinese).
51. *Guoji Maoyi* in JPRS-CEA (23 September 1985), pp. 61-65.
52. *Xuexi Yu Yanjiu* in JPRS-CEA (13 August 1985), pp. 84-86, 112-115.
53. *ACFERT* (1986), p. 492.
54. Richard Baum, "Modernization and Legal Reform in Post-Mao China: The Rebirth of Socialist Legality," paper presented at the Regional Seminar in Chinese Studies, University of California, Berkeley (25 October 1986). Baum concludes: "New and increasingly articulate social forces are taking shape in China . . . and they are buttressed by a new system of institutionalized legal safeguards."
55. *Documents of the First Session of the Fifth National People's Congress*, p. 92; Deng Xiaoping, *Selected Works*, p. 136; Werner Pfennig, "Political Aspects of Modernization and Judicial Reform in the PRC," *JCS* I:3 (February 1984), pp. 79-103; Stanley Lubman, "Emerging Functions of Formal Legal Institutions in China's Modernization" in U.S. Congress, Joint Economic Committee, *China Under the Four Modernizations*, pp. 235-289.
56. Cited in FBIS (26 August 1986), pp. K27-28.
57. See *Documents of the CPC National Conference, September 1985* (Beijing: Foreign Languages Press, 1985), p. 82.
58. Ibid.
59. Cited in FBIS (10 March 1986), pp. K1-3.
60. See Lawrence Sullivan, "The Role of the Control Organs in the CCP, 1977-83," *AS* XXIV:6 (June 1984), pp. 597-617.
61. Pfennig, "Modernization and Judicial Reform," p. 94; Joseph Needham, *Science and Civilization in China II* (Cambridge: Cambridge University Press, 1969), p. 544.
62. Yu Haocheng, "The Double Hundred Policy and Its Guarantee by the Legal System," *Renmin Ribao* (30 May 1986), p. 5.
63. Brantly Womack, "Modernization and Democratic Reform in China," *JAS* XLIII:3 (May 1984), pp. 417-439.

64. FBIS (11 August 1986), p. K8; *BR* 40 (1983), pp. 19-21.
65. CPC, *Resolution on CPC History*, p. 79.
66. Cited in FBIS (4 August 1986), pp. R1-3.
67. Interview with the author, Beijing, Institute of Politics (CASS), December 1986.
68. Cited in FBIS (28 May 1986), pp. K11-22.
69. Interview with the author, Beijing, 14 January 1987.
70. Nina Halpern, "Learning from Abroad: Chinese Views of the Eastern European Experiments, January 1977 to June 1981," *MC* X:1 (January 1985), pp. 77-110.
71. *Guoji Maoyi Wenti* in JPRS-CEA (19 September 1985), pp. 86-89.
72. *Liaowang* in JPRS-CEA (9 October 1985), pp. 76-77; XINHUA in JPRS-CEA (29 August 1985), p. 48.
73. Li Honglin, "Open Policy Essential to Socialism," in Zhou Guo (ed.), *China and the World*, p. 29.
74. Nathan, *Chinese Democracy*, pp. 3-44.
75. Cited in FBIS (19 August 1986), pp. K22-33.
76. FBIS (28 May 1986), pp. K11-22; Peng Zhen, "Be Good at Wielding the Weapon of Marxist Philosophy," *Hongqi* (16 March 1986), pp. 3-6 (in Chinese).
77. "Political and Economic Reforms Complement Each Other," *Wenhui Bao* (8 August 1986), p. 4 (in Chinese).
78. *Renmin Ribao* in JPRS-CPS (28 April 1986), pp. 13-15.
79. FBIS (25 February 1986), pp. K2-5.
80. Lowell Dittmer, "Chinese Communist Revisionism in Comparative Perspective," *SICC* XIII:1 (Spring 1980), pp. 3-40.
81. FBIS (25 August 1986), pp. P1-2.
82. Li Fan, "Are Concepts and Mentality Changing? An Explanatory Discussion on the New Technological Revolution and the Modernization of Mentality," *Chinese Sociology and Anthropology* XVII:3 (1984) pp. 107-115.

Part II

Facts

4

The Opening to the Outside World

With the Opening to the Outside World, foreign trade has reached an unprecedented importance in China's economy. One Chinese analyst noted that in 1984 additional imports allowed production to rise approximately 3 percent, or more than 25 percent of the increase in gross industrial output value.[1] China's economy also grew substantially from 1978 to 1986, per capita Gross Social Product rising 11.8 percent annually—more than the Cultural Revolution rate of 5.1 percent and even the First Five-year Plan's (1952–1957) 6.0 percent. Together, rapid growth and a trade orientation appear to have enhanced China's place significantly in the international political economy.

DOMESTIC DEVELOPMENTS

Agriculture was the first area to be affected by the reformers. A dramatic jump in productivity resulted from the 1978 introduction of the responsibility system which provided that individual households could produce goods of their own choosing for the open market after having fulfilled state quotas. Rural per capita income tripled from 134 yuan (about $US 45) to 355 yuan (about $US 118) between 1978 and 1984.[2] Cooperatives reappeared in force, replacing the premature collectives.

In 1985, however, with more comparatively well-off households devoting production to more profitable "sideline industries" and away from staples, the grain harvest dropped ominously. Renmin Ribao published a less-than-enthusiastic investigative report on living conditions in Heilongjiang's countryside on August 17, 1985, concluding "some cadres have overestimated the degree of prosperity of the peasants . . . many cite the number of '10,000 yuan households' in existence, and the number of 'color television villages' . . . But is this really the case? No. Those peasants who have become better off are still a minority of the rural production . . . more than one-fifth of the rural population has not yet solved the problem of sufficient food and clothing." This in turn led some to question the advisability of too great decentralization in agriculture and a policy of encouraging grain production by both price incentives and administrative penalties. To quote Chen Yun at the September 1985 CPC National Conference: "We must continue to pay attention to grain production. . . . The trouble is that the slogan 'no prosperity without engaging in industry' is heard much louder than the slogan 'no economic stability without agricultural development.'" Devolution of production to the household also did not allow funds to accumulate for infrastructure development. Whereas under the bad old days of collective farming there may have been quite a lot of hunger in the poorer regions, there was evidence of substantial improvement in the general environment in which the rural people lived. Ironically, Deng's reform may have undermined the provision of these services.[3] Perhaps in recognition of this, the Seventh Five-year Plan and most of the major key projects since 1982 have focused on developing the infrastructure and maintaining the stable supply of key national commodities such as grain, oil and steel.[4] Spending on telecommunications, energy, and transport in particular has increased sharply as a percentage of the government budget since 1983.

The reforms of enterprise autonomy announced in the early 1980s also reversed the Maoists' emphasis on state intervention to ensure equality. Originally introduced in October 1978 in Sichuan, these industrial reforms were officially extended in 1984 to over 6,600 enterprises accounting for 60 percent of total output value. Three ministries—in particular, Machine-building, Foreign Trade, and Commerce—were also chosen to be "decentralized" [xiafang] and all enterprises directly supervised by them placed under local jurisdiction.[5] Generally, local administrative bureaus were to withdraw from enterprise supervision; enterprises were now directly responsible for their profits and losses; and the factory manager replaced the party secretary as the enterprise manager.[6] Efficiency was to be improved by the integration of industry and trade in both the countryside and the cities.[7] By giving factories the right to market their goods themselves and encouraging sideline production in the villages, the atrophied commercial and distribution sector would develop efficiently. While many of the elements of the reform are still subject to political argument, especially those pertaining to the party's involvement in production and the ultimate source of investment funds, some results of the policy have been dramatic. Market trade has more than quintupled between 1978 and 1985 to a total volume of 71 billion RMB, or about $20 billion.

One man's benefits, however, could be another's disadvantage. Some of the reformers saw that the role of the state was to ensure the socialist distribution of "common prosperity" by using more efficient market tools or economic levers such as taxation, credit and subsidies to manage the national economy in the state's interests. Quoting from the Seventh Five-year Plan: "We shall gradually shift the emphasis in our planning from direct control to indirect but more comprehensive control, chiefly using economic policies and measures to regulate the macroeconomy." Here, though, political conflicts (as with the factory responsibility system) have been apparent between those who hold economic levers have an "incentive" function as opposed to a "regulatory" function.[8] The former have emphasized that common affluence requires some to get rich faster than others, while the latter specify the state must ensure polarization cannot occur. To quote from one journal: "Those who get more income by having more means of production and those who do so by relying on competent operating skills, a high technical level, and high efficiency cannot be treated on the same footing... Those who derived higher income by possessing more means of production should be brought under proper control."[9] As Deng Xiaoping commented wryly to Dan Rather in 1986: "In China, it is very difficult to become a millionaire."

Regardless of these political differences, almost all reformers have agreed on the need for the creation of a modern tax and credit system and on the need for labor and financial reforms such as contracts and the diversification of the People's Bank, aimed at creating more liquid labor and capital markets, respectively.[10] Taxation reform was intended both to ensure more stable revenues for key national projects and to provide a means of economic management, a so-called leverage function.[11] Whereas in 1978 the state received more revenue from its factories than from taxes, by 1984 state revenues from taxation surpassed those from state-owned enterprises by more than 200 percent! Efficient producers should be encouraged as state subsidies lessened. Quoting senior economist Ma Hong: "Top priority must be given to the economic returns of investments. The various departments should fix a reasonable time limit for recovering investments as well as minimum standards for rational investments."[12] The tentative introduction of "socialist joint-stock" companies likewise would allow for more individual initiative under socialist ownership.[13]

Most importantly, price reform would be necessary to correct irrational market relationships embodied in a price structure set as far back as the 1960s. Pricing was particularly important to the foreign trade sector due to the deficits incurred by state-owned trade enterprises buying at high fixed prices and then exporting at fluctuating international prices. Xue Muqiao noted authoritatively: "At present, the major shortcoming in our price control work is that price varies from value ... major products urgently needed by the state are priced too low while secondary or overproduced goods are priced too high ....Rigid control over prices without any competition hinders the exchange of goods. It should be changed because it does not help consolidate socialism but hinders socialist economic development."[14]

While agriculture boomed, the reformers had mixed success in encouraging industrial reform, especially when confronting entrenched feudal-bureaucratic interests and the cellular economy. Evidently peasant farmers were more effective "agents of change" than the urban proletariat. Heavy industries kept their perks through the period of readjustment for the most part. For example, of the top nine industries allocated computers (mainframes and minicomputer only) representing 62 percent of China's installed base as of 1986, two of the top three noneducation ministries were in heavy industry—Metallurgy, Electronics, and Machine-Building. Not one of the top nine was light industry related.[15] Those in charge of reform in turn have realized that the only way to shake the heavy industrial grip on investment funds may be to channel more funds to the local level. To wit, sources of capital construction investment from outside the state budget grew from 5.7 billion RMB or 9.7 percent of the total in the first five-year plan period of 1953–1957, to 171 billion RMB or 50.2 percent of the total in the sixth five-year plan period 1981–1985, the vast majority of this change coming since 1978.[16]

CHINA AND ITS TRADING PARTNERS

From the foreign perspective, the Opening to the Outside World has been at least as important as these domestic developments. China had for centuries been a potential source of business, but never an urgent prospect for foreigners, especially Westerners. Missionaries, the major Western presence in earlier days were chiefly attracted by the obvious opportunities for conversion. As Robert Morrison, a Presbyterian sent by the London Missionary Society in 1807, defined his goal: "the light of science and revelation will ... peacefully and gradually shed their lustre on the Eastern limit of Asia and the islands of the rising sun."[17] Businessmen on the other hand, were frustrated by the elusivity of the fabled China market. At no time during the 19th or 20th centuries did China control either a strategically important commodity for the West (not even tea) or did total trade bulk large enough to become politically or economically significant.

In 1986, China remained a relatively small player in global trade. Of the world's major economic powers only Japan was marginally affected by its trade policy, China buying approximately 5 percent of Japan's exports in

1986. Within the decade of the Opening though, much had already changed. As Chinese policy-makers began to emphasize the importance of building global links, international law was once again studied and China appointed its first judge to the Hague Court in 1985. China signed multilateral accords including the Multi-fiber Agreement, joined major international financial institutions, and applied for membership in the General Agreement on Trade and Tariffs. As one of the leaders in the 1986 breakthroughs in superconductivity, Chinese physicist, Zhao Zhongxian, participated in a landmark meeting of international scientists. Chinese students studied abroad and Chinese official media began overseas circulation.

The change in attitude renewed the economic relationships between China and its erstwhile trading partners. It was the British who had decisively changed the balance of power between China and the outside world in initiating the Opium Wars in 1842. Prior to that Russian caravan trade and Portuguese, Dutch and Spanish traders had all visited, all more or less conforming to the tributary system of trade.[18] In 1793, though, Lord Macartney's embassy to Peking to seek more trading rights failed over the symbolic issue of the kowtow. A second mission by Lord Amherst, in 1816, failed completely—so much so that all foreign envoys were thence banned from Peking. Afraid of domestic unrest if the foreigners intruded, the Qing court put its head into the sand. Modern Chinese scholar Hu Sheng noted that the Qing government was prompted both by irritation at "marauding European merchants" and the desire to save its own regime because "danger from without" generally coincided with "trouble from within." Li Shiyao, Viceroy of Guangdong and Guangxi, said as early as 1759: "When uncultured barbarians, who live far beyond the borders of China, come to our country to trade, they should establish no contact with the populace except for business purposes."[19] As the opium trade grew in importance, however, and the East India Company's monopoly on the China trade was abolished in 1834, the demonstration of modern military prowess in the Opium Wars effectively secured British trading rights, giving them the lead in the China trade. In 1826, they accounted for 25 out of a total of 76 merchants in Canton, for 32 of 83 in 1831, and for 158 of 213 in 1837, the brink of the Opium War.[20]

The period from the conclusion of the Opium Wars in the 1860s through the establishment of the Nanjing government in 1927 was one of increasing instability as central authority dissolved in China and feudal warlords contended for power. Throughout, the developed economies maintained the major portion of the China trade. Japan replaced Russia as the dominant power in Northeast China following the Sino-Japanese War in 1894-95 and the Russo-Japanese War of 1905. By 1931, the United States also rose to challenge Japan for second place to the British empire in China's trade.[21] China effectively became a dependent nation as the great powers established spheres of influence and dominated trade within them.

With 1949, socialist countries took the lead in China's trade until the early 1960s. In 1957 centrally planned economies took up 67 percent of China's total trade; the Soviet Union alone accounted for more than 44 percent. The explanation for most of the early socialist preponderance lay in the Soviet Union's lending program. From 1950 onwards, the Soviets supplied the bulk of industrial inputs under medium term credits into the Chinese economy in a policy that came to be called "leaning to one side," namely, the Soviet Union and the People's Democracies.[22] In the heyday of the program from 1950 to 1956 or so, it rapidly introduced a measure of industrialization and bolstered China in the face of the Korean War. It has been described as perhaps the most massive instance of technology transfer ever. Disastrously though, with the split in 1959, the Soviets tore up their contracts and demanded early repayment. Some foreign observers persuasively described the Sino-Soviet conflict as the continuation of an age-old conflict between Empire and outside world, as manifested in the Chinese, specifically Mao's, unwillingness to accept bloc relationships as understood by the Soviets.[23] Regardless, in August of 1960, more than 1,000 Soviet advisors and technicians in China were withdrawn, taking their blueprints with them.[24] The sizable positive balance of Sino-Soviet trade from 1960 to 1966 reflected the accelerated repayment of credits. With the last repayment in 1966, trade between the two nations virtually dried up.

As early as 1960, market economies had surpassed the centrally planned ones in China's total trade. In fact, already in 1958 market economies assumed a greater share of China's imports, while market economies' share of China's exports took another 4 years to grow predominant by 1962. From 1963 to 1966, China signed contracts for more than 50 plants financed under medium-term credits mostly from the West. These imports were relatively small compared to the 1950s. Even in 1966 and the beginning of the Cultural Revolution, however, the direction of China's trade continued to be towards the West. Trade with the developed countries rose from 37 percent of total in 1965 to 54 percent in 1975, while the alliance with the Third World, declared in Mao's global three-zone analysis, seemed to be lacking in economic content.[25] Trade with the Less Developed Countries (LDCs) actually fell from 46 percent in 1965 to 39 percent in 1975. Aid drawn on China by the Third World between 1954 and 1974 amounted to less than a third of the Soviet Union's $5.7 billion.[26]

With the Opening, the foreign reaction to China was a tourist explosion. Annual visitors multiplied ninefold from 1.8 million in 1978 to 17.8 million in 1985. China's financiers hoped it would continue as tourism was a steady source of foreign exchange, bringing in $1.25 billion in 1985, alone. Moreover, many overseas Chinese visitors were motivated not only by a desire to see China but also to do something for their motherland. Several major Chinese business groups from various Southeast Asian nations invested in China, among them Thailand's Charoen Pokphand Group (Shanghai Ek-Chor Motorcycle), Indonesia's Liem Sioe Liong (a Fujian oil refinery) and Malaysia's Robert Kuok (Beijing Shangri-La Hotel). From the U.S., An Wang's Wang Computers established a computer assembly operation in his hometown Shanghai. These investments of course were not entirely altruistic. To quote one Thai-Chinese businesswoman: "Patriotism never means that we aren't going to make money."

Of foreign visitors in China, such overseas Chinese [*huaqiao*] were by far the largest group. Indeed, the Chinese government made a concerted effort to attract them, offering special discounts on meals and lodging, as well as airfare on CAAC and regular tour packages. From 1978 to 1985, they made over 90 percent of all visits to China, for a total of about 58 million visits received. After the *huaqiao*, the Japanese constituted the second largest group of foreigners in China with 470,000 visitors in 1985. In 1986, the U.S. lagged somewhat behind with approximately 290,000 visitors to China, and 50,000 Chinese visitors to the U.S. The U.S. to China traffic was distinctly less business-oriented (32 percent of the total) than U.S. to other Asian destinations (42 percent), reflecting the relatively nascent amount of foreign investment.[27] China's appeal as a tourist resort, however, did spark a boom among foreign hoteliers—in 1988 and 1989 alone, 5 Holiday Inns, 3 Meridiens, 2 Movenpick, 1 Sheraton, 1 Intercontinental and 1 Hyatt were scheduled to open.

Both Japan and the United States have also returned as major trading partners, coincident with the expansion in China's overall trade volume. Trade with Japan and the United States rose at annual rates of 19.6 percent and 57.7 percent, respectively, from 1976 to 1984, and Japan eclipsed Hong Kong as China's major trader. European trade increased as well and West Germany in fact surpassed the United States in the first half of 1985 as China's leading technology supplier with 69 contracts amounting to about DM 1.8 billion.[28] Overall in 1986, Japan accounted for 24 percent and the U.S. for 11 percent of China's total trade, with Hong Kong slipping to second place with 19.4 percent. Japan especially benefited in consumer electronics where both of its major rivals South Korea and Taiwan have been politically constrained. In 1984, Japanese firms captured up to 90 percent of the Chinese color TV market and China became Japan's second largest electrical goods market.[29]

Japan resumed diplomatic relations with China in 1972 and in 1973 first began to import oil. Since 1974, oil and chemical products consistently ranked first among the Chinese commodities exported to Japan. Between 1979 and 1984, the Japanese government also loaned 300 billion yen to China to build six construction projects. Among other projects, joint

China-Japan natural resource exploration has taken place at the Anqing copper mine, the Oujiang hydroelectric project, and both offshore and on-shore oil fields.[30] Japanese engineers have also taken the lead in technical exchanges with Chinese factories. In 1985, the State Economic Commission undertook an exchange whereby 651 Japanese managers came to China from the Ministry of International Trade and Industry to diagnose the problems of 131 Chinese enterprises and offer proposals to improve. Based on this, 60 Chinese enterprises signed contracts with their Japanese counterparts in technological transfer and equipment import, in the total amount of $100 million. Further, according to Vice Minister Zhu Rong Ji, some of these enterprises considered setting up joint ventures for export.[31]

Though Chinese trade officials did not seriously discourage the Japanese onslaught, neither did they appear entirely satisfied. Disputes focused around market barriers to Chinese products in Japan and the per-ceived unwillingness of Japanese companies to invest in China.[32]. More-over, the Chinese looked forward to returning the favor in the future. One article took to heart some lessons from Japanese sales techniques—first, concentrate on "small wins" or small projects able to rapidly produce ex-port earnings rather than large multi-year efforts; second, publicity and sales promotion needed to be strengthened as Japanese customers would not buy expensive Chinese jades without explanatory notes attached to the item; third, exporting needed to be better coordinated to avoid ram-pant price cutting. For example, in 1984, faced with a bumper harvest of chestnuts, the chestnut-producing regions refused to coordinate with one another and exported independently so that price cutting ensued as the Japanese market saturated at approximately 22,000 tons annually and volume rose above that level.[33]

While Hong Kong declined within China's trade, China on the other hand became a greater part of Hong Kong's revenues, as entrepot trade in-creased.[34] In 1985, China supplied 26 percent of Hong Kong's imports, up 6 percent on 1984, and received 12 percent of its exports, up 35 percent. Hong Kong transshipments were another significant measure of China's economic importance to the territory as 10 percent of China's total trade ($5.9 billion) passed through Hong Kong in 1985.[35] Overall Hong Kong's China trade boomed, growing at a 35 percent annual pace from 1976 to 1986.

Hong Kong naturally was also the overwhelming source of overseas Chinese visitors, even if slightly overcounted as a port of entry as well. Hong Kong residents had free access to China, especially the Special Economic Zones. With the prospect of reversion to Chinese control in 1997, major Hong Kong financiers invested considerable sums in "name" projects such as Y.K. Pao's university in Ningbo. As of 1986, Hong Kong investors accounted for the overwhelming majority of all foreign invest-ment in China, mostly in light industry and processing-and-assembly agreements. Non-Hong-Kong investors also increasingly viewed Hong Kong as a gateway to China. In one poll, American executives ranked Hong Kong's geographic location and its international communications facilities as the most important factor in their decision to establish a presence in Hong Kong. Chinese and Hong Kong executives responded similarly, adding the factor of connections to Chinese trading companies in Hong Kong. China itself invested in Hong Kong manufacturing and in 1987 was the third largest presence in the colony with over HK$ 2.9 billion or 18.4 percent of the total.[36]

In an even more significant development, Hong Kong served as the entrepot link between China and two now booming but politically difficult Asian economies—Taiwan (especially) and South Korea. Total Taiwan-mainland trade rose from HK$ 219 million in 1978 to almost HK$ 7.9 billion, or US$ 1 billion, in 1985. China sold mostly medicinal herbs, wool, and animal hair to Taiwan which in turn exported mainly textile yarn and consumer appliances. For the duration of the relationship, Taiwan has enjoyed solid surpluses—in 1985 amounting to at least HK$ 6 billion, or greater than a 4:1 advantage. While the Taiwan government has expressed repeated concerns about growing dependent on the mainland economy, the likelihood seems slight given the mainland's still insignificant share (2 percent) of Taiwan's exports. The mainland's intentions in sponsoring this trade have clearly been political, however, not economic in nature. Mainland authorities have regularly granted special deals to Taiwanese compatriots offering the same terms as foreigners while continuing to regularly advance proposals for reunification.[37]

Only slightly less sensitive has been China's growing trade with South Korea, legalized in 1988 after many "black" years. In the previous decade, Daewoo and several other Korean companies already established joint ventures in southern China through their Hong Kong branches. With legalization they will now be encouraged to compete with the Japanese in the northern ports of Shandong. In 1985, Hong Kong entrepot trade with South Korea amounted to over US$ 600 million.

China's impact on the developed market economies, both as exporter and importer remains to be seen. The Seventh Five-year Plan projects that China's exports will reach the sum of $100 billion in 1990, a not insubstantial amount but still a drop in the bucket of world trade.[38] In 1985, China ranked 16th among world exporters with 1.4 percent of the world total compared to Taiwan's rank of 11 and South Korea's rank of 13. This position is at odds with China's vastly larger population.[39]

On the other hand, the political significance of China's Opening is readily apparent. The more pragmatic trading approach has already sold Silkworms to Iran and missiles to Saudi Arabia; boosted Taiwan trade to $1 billion; and led to a partial normalization with South Korea. In a dramatic contrast to its recent dependent past, China now appears able to play one nation off against another for the most concessions it can get. For example, in the early 1900s, China negotiated a mutual protection treaty with the Russians against the Japanese at the price of concessions that virtually turned Manchuria into a Russian sphere of influence. In 1986, one of China's preconditions for better relations with the Soviet Union was larger markets for Chinese textiles.

TOWARDS INDUSTRIALIZATION

China's import profile has remained fairly constant over the 37 years from 1949 to 1986, consisting mostly of industrial inputs, with a gradual switch since 1978 away from importing complete plants to individual sets of equipment and semi-finished materials. In a prescient analysis, a British commercial attache noted in 1933: "It can at once be said that the future import market of China will consist far more of capital goods than consumable goods, at least for several years."[40] Of the notable items, in the years between 1950 and 1960, more than 90 percent of foreign exchange spending on technology was for complete sets of equipment of which the Soviet Union supplied 156 sets.[41] During this period of Soviet tutelage distinctly more heavy equipment was imported than in later decades; machinery made up 50 percent of all imports in 1960 as opposed to 10 percent in 1963. With the withdrawal of Soviet aid, however, the import substitution campaign initiated for consumer goods in the 1950s apparently broadened to include complete plants. Again complete plants showed a brief jump in 1974 but were quickly restored to their customary level of 10 to 20 percent of imports. In their stead, Chinese imports have emphasized semifinished goods and industrial materials, especially steel, nonferrous metals and cement. According to Zhou Chuanru, Director of the Import and Export Bureau of MOFERT, in 1985 China imported 19.63 million tons of steel products, 1.128 million tons of copper, aluminum, zinc, and lead, and 1.83 million tons of cement, making it one of the world's largest importers in each. Overall, import of means of production, raw materials and other materials vital to the national economy and people's livelihood accounted for over 92 percent of the total import paid for with the foreign exchange under the control of the central government in 1985.[42]

The other significant Chinese import has been wheat. Until 1960, as the result of a number of good harvests, China had not imported any sizable amounts of grain since 1949. However, the disruptions of the Great Leap Forward from 1958 to 1960 coupled with the famines and floods of 1959 to 1962, severely damaged agriculture. Between 1960 and 1961, wheat imports jumped from nothing to 3.9 million tons. Since then they have remained at or around this level, as China has actively exported rice to take advantage of the higher international price and maintain a balanced foreign exchange account. An abundant wheat supply is moreover a politically sensitive subject in China. Senior politicians have warned that rural industrial output will distract peasants from the essential task of grain production.[43] Historically grain shortages have often led to revolts by China's peasantry against the center. For example, in 1960, the People's Liberation Army (PLA) daily soldier ration was reduced to 1500 calories, whereupon widespread discontent grew and mutinies were reported in hard hit provinces.[44]

On the exports side, a substantial argument can be made that export growth and industrialization should be closely linked to domestic economic progress.[45] In the large majority of those countries that experienced rapid economic growth in the 1960s and 1970s exports also grew quickly, specifically manufactured goods exports. The Asian newly industrializing countries are the classic examples of this "export-led" growth. In 1985, trade represented 84.6 percent and 70.4 percent of Taiwan and South Korea's gross national product, respectively, although admittedly each had a much smaller economy in comparison to China. Manufactures, however, bear out the rapid progress as these goods accounted for 86 percent and 91 percent of each country's exports in 1984, with a steady trend towards higher value-added goods.[46] China has stagnated relatively: a quarter of the world's population produced only 1.26 percent of its exports in 1985 and of these only 46 percent were manufactured goods.[47] Of course, this far outstrips China in the 1930s when manufactured goods were a negligible portion of exports.

In fact, since 1949 to 1984 slow 10- to 20-year shifts are apparent in the composition of China's exports from basic agricultural products to textile goods to machinery. Extending the analysis back to the 1800s illustrates the stagnation in China's export production mix prior to 1949. In the 1850s, tea and silk accounted for almost 92 percent of total exports. Tea exports from China succumbed to Indian exports shortly thereafter. Silk maintained a 30 to 40 percent share as late as 1908.[48] By 1932, though, China's exports had fragmented into a variety of agricultural products or "muck and truck," the largest of which was beans and beancakes with a 16 percent share in 1932, not the hallmark of an industrializing country.[49]

Comparing China's overall export composition growth since 1949 to that of Taiwan, as in Chart 2, indicates that there seem to be common stages for the two developing economies. The steps in the ladder of industrialization are reflected in their export profiles, and in 1986 China appears to be about ten years behind Taiwan. Only in the mid-1980s is China beginning to develop a significant electronics export capacity whereas Taiwan's existed in the 1950s. While China has had the added advantage of substantial energy exports, which came on-line in the early 1970s and now account for between 20 percent and 25 percent of all export earnings, the depressed state of oil prices decreased foreign exchange in-

CHART 2
Composition of PRC and Taiwan Exports, 1953–1984
(100% = US$billions)

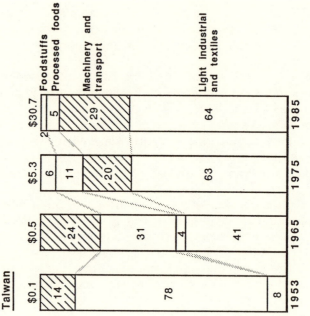

Taiwan

	1953	1965	1975	1985
	$0.1	$0.5	$5.3	$30.7

Foodstuffs
Processed foods
Machinery and transport
Light Industrial and textiles

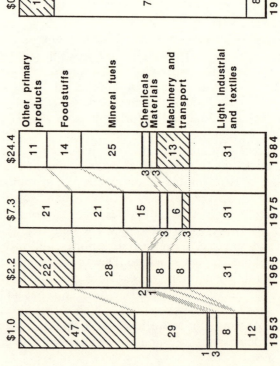

PRC

	1953	1965	1975	1984
	$1.0	$2.2	$7.3	$24.4

Other primary products
Foodstuffs
Mineral fuels
Chemicals
Materials
Machinery and transport
Light Industrial and textiles

Source: ACFERT (1986), pp. 956-957; Taiwan Statistical Databook (Taiwan: Council for Economic Planning and Development, 1986) pp. 205-206

come from oil by $2.3 billion in 1986,[50] with about the same export level as in 1985. This drop appears to force China both to boost its foodstuffs output in primary goods exports and to put more effort in to expanding machinery and other manufactured goods exports, if it is to continue its export-development program. Textile growth is basically limited under the conditions of the Multi-fiber Agreement, to which China is a signatory. A decade-long decline in the world commodity prices from peaks in the 1980s has further encouraged China to switch towards higher value-added goods with greater market potential. Promisingly, in 1986, China's export of mechanical and electrical products reached a new high of about $2 billion, although the automotive and shipbuilding industries suffered declines.[51]

Long-term, the consequences of China's lengthy isolation appear to be important obstacles that limit the ability of Chinese products, especially manufactured goods, to compete internationally. Western buyers often complain of the inconsistent quality, slow response time and generally poor performance of the Chinese. In a 1982 study of the competitiveness of products from the Asian NICs, China and Japan, Chinese economist Qian Zongqi reports that China placed first only in "cheap prices," and last in terms of "product quality," "new product development," "design and packaging."[52] These "unhealthy tendencies" appear to be China's long-term challenge in export growth and industrialization.

THE TERMS OF TRADE

In 1933, Beale noted: "The outstanding feature of China today is the desire—one might with truth call it the definite plan—to become self-supplying in the everyday needs."[53] Early Qing and Nationalist rulers sought to maintain a status quo between people, rulers, and foreigners, not to seek growth. Somewhat similarly, the Sixth Five-year Plan (1980-1985) declared: "The aim of expanding our foreign economic and technological exchanges is of course to raise our capacity for self- reliance." In the Seventh Five-year Plan (1986-1990) however, no such admonition was present. Rather, to quote Wang Junsheng, Vice Minister for Foreign Trade in 1978: "We have now entered into a new period of construction and we have a greater need to develop international trade." Conservative Premier Hua Guofeng had used Lenin and Stalin to justify the speed-up in trade— "[they] effectively made use of such exterior factors as accepting foreign loans, importing foreign machines and experts, accepting technical aid from the West, and organizing joint companies with foreign capitalists."[54] Deng Xiaoping has displayed even fewer "self-reliant" sentiments.

As if to test the reformers, developing foreign trade since 1949 has not been an easy task. China has had sizable deficits, some of which have been linked to fluctuating international prices for China's agricultural and oil exports and some to adjustments in the domestic pricing system of imports and exports.[55] Irresponsible leaps in imports by both provincial and central authorities have also played a major role. While previous government policy has reacted by conservatively curtailing imports in order to balance the account, the Opening to the Outside World has, however, encouraged export growth and the use of diversified capital, while tolerating the largest deficits in China's history. To quote economist Wang Jian: "Although measures adopted simply to reduce imports can achieve a foreign exchange balance, they can also ignite fluctuation in economic growth. . . . Under the present conditions where there is too little foreign exchange, we must encourage additional exports . . . exports represent increases in the domestic value of output; they can promote domestic economic growth."[56]

In the early 1950s China ran a deficit with the Soviet Union as it bought complete plants, capital goods, and technicians' services on medium-term credits extended by the Soviets. Then, with the Sino-Soviet schism, the Chinese embarked on an accelerated repayment drive combined with a sharp cut in imports and cleared up the balance-of-payments problem by 1962, albeit painfully. Robert Dernberger has calculated that the pro forma effects of the Soviet pullout were a 20 to 30 percent reduction in China's estimated rate of growth. Exports to the Soviet Union accounted for between 18 percent and 26 percent of all trade from 1959 to 1962, while China's total worldwide trade volume dropped 15 percent each year. Added to this, at the same time as the Sino-Soviet rift occurred, and the Great Leap Forward created domestic dislocations raising export prices, international prices of agricultural commodities—China's major exports—dropped 10 percent from 1958 to 1960.[57] For the next twelve years, China was to maintain a self-reliant, balanced foreign trade account, importing only what was absolutely necessary and exporting solely to balance accounts. In effect, the policy reduced the overall importance of foreign trade in the possibly simplistic belief that a larger volume of foreign trade would produce larger deficits. Economist Xiang Yin notes that this attitude persisted in 1984. According to him, the foreign trade *export* plan in 1984 was reduced 17 percent below that of the previous year in order to reduce the deficit.[58]

Deficits first occurred in 1974 and 1975 as the result of hasty expenditures made in the previous years. In 1972, China suddenly purchased a number of complete plants from Japan and Western Europe, the volume of which increased rapidly over the next two years. Contracts of $58 million were signed in 1972, rising to $1.2 billion in 1973, $850 million in 1974, falling off to $364 million in 1975 and to only $200 million in 1976.[59] Overall, imports rose 80 percent and 48 percent, respectively, in 1973 and 1974. Beginning in 1975 readjustment measures were taken—at least partially in light of the $670 million deficit of 1974—and the deficits dropped off along with imports as a whole. Via the centralized foreign trade apparatus, the domestic "allocation" charge paid to foreign trade departments by domestic purchasers was increased from 60 percent to 80 percent, thereby transferring import pricing differential profits from domestic to foreign trade departments and rectifying the foreign trade account balances.[60]

A similar set of events occurred in the late 1970s, during the early stages of the Opening to the Outside World when, in 1977, Hua Guofeng announced unrealistically large goals for the economy. As Hua declared at the 1977 National Conference for Learning from Daqing in Industry: "the question of the speed of construction is a political rather than a purely economic question."[61] To induce speed, Hua also favored large-scale imports, especially for heavy industry. But, as imports gained 51 percent in 1978, domestic production failed to keep pace and exports rose by only half of imports. Chen Yun among others frankly criticized Hua's goals in 1979, specifically the excessive speed and volume of investment in heavy industry capital construction to the detriment of agriculture.[62]

At the end of 1978, Hua found himself increasingly with his back to the wall both in foreign trade and domestic production. A December *Renmin Ribao* commentator wrote: "there is no other way but to squeeze ourselves a bit. Particularly in the cases of those commodities that are not essential to the people's livelihood, we must make a determined effort to cut domestic consumption and make them available for export."[63] As the Central Committee met in the waning days of the year to find ways and means to cope with economic difficulties engendered by Hua's plan (for example, the rising deficit of $2.02 billion in 1979), nervous factory managers saw their chance and in the space of 10 days, signed nearly $3 billion worth of import contracts. As the managers had surmised, the Central Committee meeting (the momentous 3rd Plenum of the 11th Congress wherein Deng Xiaoping's economic reforms were first put forward in comprehensive scope) resulted in shelving of Hua Guofeng's Ten-year Plan and instituting a short-term policy of "readjustment, reform, consolidation and improvement." Both imports and exports were curbed and deficits fell. On February 28, 1979, Beijing informed Japanese firms that it was suspending approximately 22 contracts, including that for Baoshan steel complex, worth in the aggregate some $2.6 billion. In so doing, however, it also committed itself in April to buying $8 billion worth of technology up to 1985.[64] By 1981 imports grew only 10 percent, and proceeded to fall 12 percent in 1982, rising only 11 percent in 1983.

In 1986 then, it seemed ominous that the largest deficits in China's history should be occurring under Deng Xiaoping's tenure. Imports rose 28 percent in 1984, 55 percent in 1985, and in the first six months of 1986, alone, the trade deficit reached $6.4 billion (three times that of 1978) mostly with Japan, first, and then the United States. As the key to reversing negative balances, however, a major change in policy appeared to favor export growth and the judicious use of international borrowing over clamping down on imports. To quote Vice-Premier Yao Yilin's speech to the 1985 National Planning Conference for Foreign Economic Relations and Trade: "Do we need to seek foreign loans? Yes, we do. However, we should seek foreign loans on the basis of the volume of our exports." Compare this to the more cautionary tone of a key *Hong Qi* document on foreign economic relations, published in 1982 which stated: "Discretion is needed in soliciting commercial loans. All loans have to be paid off, and complemented with domestic financing. Because of this, their use is bound to be limited."[65] Unlike previous government policy, the newly issued Seventh Five-year Plan (1986-1990) also appeared to encourage financing deficits through debt.

In another departure from the past, the 1984-86 deficits were largely caused by the reaction of provincial authorities to powers newly acquired under the economic reforms, hence less subject to central government control. Runaway imports were directly attributable to the partial removal of the institutional barriers of MOFERT through the introduction of the agency system and generally to the inconsistencies of the economic reforms—for example, geographic price differences, lack of expert personnel, foreign exchange black markets, and inadequate credit control. In line with the financial reforms, bank credit grew from RMB 343 billion in 1983 to RMB 591 billion in 1985 annually increasing 29 percent and 34 percent and much of it was used by enterprises to finance foreign-exchange purchases. Poor coordination between localities also resulted in overlapping imports.[66] Export freedoms led to drastic price-cutting among enterprises and reduced export income. Consequently, MOFERT recentralized export license control on most textile and agricultural exports to Hong Kong in February 1985. To curb these new deficits the old remedy of cutting off imports now only partially effective had to be supplemented with export-boosting measures. During the Sixth Five-year Plan (1980-1985) over 800 processing enterprises and 33 comprehensive production bases were set up and dedicated to export production exclusively. The Seventh Five-year Plan envisioned the creation of geographically specialized export bases capable of developing competitive scale production facilities. An Export Development Fund was established, and some export-oriented factories allowed wages and social welfare entitlements higher than domestic-oriented factories.[67] This new attitude was also reflected in the increased and diversified use of foreign capital.

FOREIGN CAPITAL

As China's trade was no longer rigidly balanced, it might be expected that the use of foreign capital would increase. The traumatic experience with Soviet credits, however, left a very conservative Chinese policy in the use of external funding. Following the last Soviet repayments in 1966, it was not until 1972 that China resumed using credits to buy equipment. As late as 1974, Li Qiang, Minister of Foreign Trade, stated: "[China] will never go in for joint management with foreign countries, much less grovel for foreign loans as that superpower [the Soviet Union] does." Li was actually being misleading, as during 1972 and 1973, credits advanced to China for complete plants and other equipment totaled approximately $1 billion. It was 4 years later when the same Li Qiang announced that China would accept loans and admitted that it had been doing so all along in the guise of deferred payments.[68] Later, in 1985, an article in *Shijie Jingji* complimented the Soviet Union on the same use of foreign capital, noting: "Technology import and resource development, in particular, have benefited tremendously from Western credits."[69] Still, the old suspicion remained—many Chinese leaders remembered the crippling weight of feudal China's debt. Before World War II, most foreign investments in China were not in manufacturing but in commerce, and it was through the banks that the West, especially the United States, attempted to manipulate the Chinese government. Both Chinese and Western observers have agreed that the financial consortiums, though of limited success, were a concerted effort by the West to check Japan and enhance their own interests at China's expense.[70]

Nonetheless, in 1979 significant lending to China shakily got under way. The World Bank, the International Monetary Fund, and Japan were the initial major lenders. Though they and others professed willingness, all were conscious of the sketchy legal environment and lack of familiarity with the area. For example, in 1986 the $475 million megaloan for the Pingshuo-Occidental Petroleum coal mine joint venture led by Bank of China and four other major banks, was subscribed to by only 34 banks—the large majority Japanese and only one North American bank. Said one Japanese banker: "I would use a Japanese saying, 'a snake in the forest,' to describe the loan. There are so many uncertainties that you may get bitten somewhere as you proceed."[71]

Between 1979 and 1982, of the initial $12.8 billion lent, 61 loans or about 50 percent of the total went to the Baoshan Steel Works and 21 other metallurgical and petroleum related key projects. Among the single largest loans approved by the World Bank in this period, one was $162.4 million for drilling rigs and other equipment at the Daqing oilfield and another was $124 million for port improvements in Shanghai, Huangpu and Tianjin, in line with national priorities. Technological modernization of existing facilities, in particular energy and transportation, remained the government's priority in soliciting funds.[72] Commercial bankers were, however, stymied as loans from governments and international financial institutions continued to account for 36 percent of the aggregate in 1986 (see Table 2). The inefficiency of Chinese enterprises appeared to be a major limit on the opportunities for Western commercial bankers. Some Chinese factories have reportedly defaulted on domestic loans at 6 to 8 percent interest, let alone standard 7 to 10 percent rates on the international commercial finance market of the 1980s.[73]

Volume of lending slowed dramatically in 1983 and 1984, rising again in 1985. This drop in lending coincided with reintroduction of decentralizing reforms in the domestic economy and therein lies a tale. Audrey Donnithorne reports that direct foreign trade by Sichuan provincial organs started as early as 1977. In 1980 decentralization accelerated and, in retrospect, its hasty implementation was apparently responsible for the $1.9 billion deficit that year—contributing to an inflation rate of 6 percent, and retail food prices rising 13.8 percent. After a period in 1981 of some retrenchment on decentralization reforms, their reintroduction in 1982 and 1983 coincided with specific policies regulating foreign capital use.[74] Some Chinese economists may also have taken note of the experiences of other socialist economies—especially Poland, which wandered into such a morass.[75] Nonetheless, the Seventh Five-year Plan (1986-1990) called for a further $40 billion in capital to be raised, most of which would come from the private sector.

While lending dropped in 1982, other means of raising capital were attempted. Fourteen times, from 1982 to the end of April 1986, China issued bonds in foreign currencies in West Germany, Japan, Hong Kong, and other areas, raising funds totaling $1.5 billion.[76] Led by Rong Yiren, Shanghai textile magnate and one of China's biggest prerevolutionary capitalists, the Bank of China (BoC) and the China International Trust and Investment Corporation (CITIC) have been the trailblazers, issuing bonds five and six times, respectively. As these institutions revisited old haunts, however, ghosts seemed to appear—the British Central Bank would not allow China's 1986 Eurodollar debut to take place in London because China had defaulted on bonds issued by the Qing dynasty early in the century![77]

Another major change was the encouragement of Direct Foreign Investment (DFI). In 1979, with the passage of the Joint Venture Law the first negotiations began. China's goals in attracting DFI were to promote exports, introduce technology and management skills, and renovate existing enterprises while retaining control of the domestic market.[78] The economic results, however, were less than impressive in the first seven years.

TABLE 2
China's Utilized Foreign Capital, 1979–1986
(US$ Billions)

	1979-86	1979-81	1982	1983	1984	1985	1986
EXTERNAL LOANS	$20.74	9.09	1.78	1.06	1.29	2.51	5.01
GOVERNMENTS	4.24	0.93	0.55	0.72	0.72	0.49	0.84
INTL FIN INSTS	3.14	0.93	0.00	0.07	0.18	0.60	1.34
BUYERS CREDIT	0.94	0.21	0.19	0.11	0.13	0.13	0.18
COMMERCIAL LOANS	9.71	6.70	0.86	0.00	0.13	0.53	1.49
OTHER	2.72	0.33	0.18	0.17	0.12	0.76	1.16
EXTERNAL LOANS BY ORIGINATOR							
Japan					0.85	1.28	2.90
World Bank					0.18	0.58	0.61
I.M.F.					0.00	0.00	0.71
Others					0.01	0.40	0.05
Britain					0.03	0.03	0.05
F.R.G.					0.02	0.13	0.37
U.S.A.					0.03	0.02	0.41
France					0.04	0.05	0.11
Kuwait					0.05	0.02	0.04
Balance of Buyers Credit					(0.04)	0.00	0.00

Source: ACFERT (1986), pp. 1212-1214; ACFERT (1984), p. 1092-1095; ACFERT (1987), p. 547

Only $20 billion was pledged and of that only $8.3 billion utilized as of the end of 1986. Moreover, the first nine months of 1986 showed a drop of 42 percent in new commitments over the same period in 1985. Investment approvals would, however, rise again in 1987, 30 percent over 1986. Comparing China to other, smaller nations actively seeking foreign investment showed how far behind it lagged. In 1984, DFI stock in Malaysia amounted to $7.4 billion or 25 percent of GNP, $15 billion in Mexico or 9 percent of GNP, and $25 billion or 11 percent of GNP in Brazil. In contrast, DFI stock totaled only 0.8 percent of China's GSP in 1984.

From a realistic perspective, foreign business came for a market that was not a billion people but more like 20 million high-income urban and 100 million high-income rural familes. These high-income households had average annual net income per person above $288 in urban areas and above $200 in rural areas.[79] Consumerism was still growing as peasant families and others acquired the disposable income to make material purchases. Refrigerators, television sets and other large appliances appeared to have considerable room for expansion. Other opportunities would lie in industrial markets as Chinese factories and farming automated. A NYNEX spokesman commented: "The tremendous potential market in China and India will dominate global telecommunications trade into the next century." Foreign manufacturers noted China held commanding positions in a number of products, leading to theoretically enormous economies of scale for the entity that controlled those resources. In 1986, China was the world's largest producer of washing machines, with 9 million, and of electric fans, with 33 million. China was also the world's number 3 producer of chemical fertilizer, number 4 in steel, number 5 in crude oil, number 6 in chemical fibers, and number 2 in television sets.[80] In global businesses such as electronics the possibility of a strategic alliance was an increasingly likely possibility given their ever-increasing use by such firms as Sony, Fujitsu, Olivetti, and Xerox.[81]

China, though, throughout the decade competed with the Newly Industrializing Countries and other large developing nations such as Brazil, Malaysia, and Indonesia, for the foreign investment dollar/yen. In all of these countries foreign companies played important roles in developing native industrial expertise. Even in relatively restrictive Japan, Fuji-Xerox, Chrysler's Mitsubishi investment, and Intel and Motorola's licensing agreements with Japanese semiconductor firms, were examples of successful foreign investment. In Brazil, Ford, Volkswagen, Fiat and General Motors helped create a native automotive industry. In Korea, Westinghouse and Framatome developed atomic power, and Western Electric and Siemens made commitments in telecommunications. Singapore founded its entire development strategy on the presence of multinationals.[82] Most of these investment havens competed favorably with China on the basis of industrial infrastructure, receptiveness to foreign investment, presence of other companies, and even political stability. Moreover, a number of them had industrialized more rapidly and were farther ahead of China on the export ladder.

Most foreign companies thus made only trial investments in China. A rough survey of those with representative offices would identify at most 20 percent of the Fortune 500. The average size of manufacturing investment in most cases is smaller than the balance-sheet rounding error. Beijing Jeep and Shanghai Volkswagen had two of the most significant manufacturing ventures in China yet paid-in capital from the Western partners represented only $16 and $90 million in each case. This is compared to $1,153 million in AMC's worldwide capital investments in 1985 alone.

What investment there has been is mostly in property and services (including even oil-related investment) with 63 percent of all investment coming from Hong Kong and Macao by 1986. The major developed countries of Europe, the United States and Japan, who together make up the overwhelming 80 percent of global investment, are underrepresented in China. Shenzhen, Hong Kong's border SEZ, accounted for 19 percent of all foreign investment utilized in China as of 1986. Next door Guangdong province utilized $2.7 billion worth of DFI between 1979 and 1985, or about half of China's total.[83] Shenzhen investment tended to be in either hotels or processing-and-assembly plants of mostly consumer electronics goods, *not* high-technology. Western observers commented unfavorably on Shenzhen's industrial base. For example, Shenzhen's one university graduated only 100 engineers in 1987. Said one bank manager: "Shenzhen is not yet ripe for absorbing high-technology industries. Lets call it an accumulation of isolated factories which do not have the support of related operations."[84] The SEZs, Shenzhen in particular, have also spurred concern of the top Chinese leadership over "unhealthy tendencies" like currency black markets, smuggling, and "spiritual pollution." From November to March of 1985, Shenzhen authorites checked more than 300 companies dealing in imports and exports and found that 66 had violated foreign exchange control regulations. In August of 1984, the Shenzhen City Communist Party Committee announced that cadres needed more guidance in the area of basic Marxist theory. Since then some 3,000 cadres are studying *Das Kapital,* and 50,000 other citizens are studying political economy.[85]

There many be another story, however, beyond what the numbers suggest. C.B. Sung, a significant China investor noted: "The amount of money China needs to reconstruct is far more than it can possibly get from foreign investors or than it can borrow. The real issue is whether foreign ventures can have multiplying and demonstration effects for Chinese enterprises surrounding it." Through "demonstration effects" foreign ventures may serve as models for Chinese factories.[86] For example, a number of Chinese enterprises have imported foreign managers to help improve management. One of them, Werner Gerich of the Wuhan Diesel

Engine Plant, was eulogized in 1986 for taking "an axe in his hand and chopping down many bureaucratic practices and lazy habits." Said journalist Su Zhong: "It is wrong to say that China does not have people as knowledgeable and capable as Gerich. The truth is that the Chinese 'Geriches' are tied up by old traditions, by the 'relations snare' they have formed over the years, and by the imperfect economic and political system of the country."[87]

Also available are case examples of issues such as pay for performance systems, the role of labor unions, the importance of developing component industries, and others that can be gleaned from the histories of ventures like Beijing Jeep (AMC), Fujian Hitachi, and Guangmei Foods (Beatrice). The well-publicized Beijing Jeep case revolved about foreign exchange—the number one problem in most Western investors' minds. Briefly, a temporary impasse was reached when Chinese authorities refused to release foreign exchange to buy kits for assembly in the Beijing factory—no foreign exchange, no kits, no jeeps! A similar set of events happened to Fujian Hitachi. Eventually, the Jeep case was resolved in May of 1986 through the reported personal intervention of Zhu Rongji, who arranged for foreign exchange flow and an accelerated schedule for localization of components. Zhu has since been appointed Mayor of Shanghai (in 1988).[88]

And in some localities, especially Tianjin, Chinese bureaucrats and managers have taken foreign investors' management concerns seriously. Li Lanqing, formerly vice-mayor of Tianjin was promoted to become a vice-chairman of MOFERT in late 1986, apparently as a reward for his activities in improving Tianjin's investment climate. Western joint ventures such as Tianjin Otis, Tianjin Liming (Wella), and Tianjin Otsuka have been very complimentary of local officials in interviews. Problems exist even in Tianjin, however, as for example, with the Japan China Oil Development Company. There the two sides cannot agree on new contract terms with the drop in oil prices and are so separated that the company has two planning departments, one Chinese and one Japanese.[89]

A final major change has been the expansion of China's overseas investment since 1978. From 1954 to 1976, total economic and military aid from China to the Less Developed Countries (LDCs) was $2.9 billion, averaging slightly more than $130 million each year. Since 1976 this has increased until, in 1984, aid grew to $2.1 billion in one year alone. The composition of this aid has also changed dramatically—in 1976, 75 percent of accumulated aid given to the LDCs was economic but for the year 1984, fully 90 percent was military in nature. Of the other $526 million in economic aid extended to LDCs, the direction remained oriented towards China's historical aid focus, Africa and the Middle East, 92 percent of the total. Likewise, 87 percent of the 3,765 military trainees from LDCs received by China between 1955 and 1984, came from Africa and the Middle East.

Apparently, China has also decided to embark on a more active Third World foreign policy via both military giving and inexpensive construction projects—a kind of Chinese Marshall Plan. As Premier Zhao Ziyang declared on a state visit to Brazil in 1985: "The Chinese people share weal and woe with the Latin American people and there are no fundamental conflicts of interest among us. Both sides require mutual political support and close economic cooperation." Iraq and North Yemen, unlikely bedfellows, accounted for 40 percent of China's foreign contracted projects and labor service cooperation agreements, or about $2 billion from 1976 to 1985. And in 1985, China signed loan agreements with Guinea, Papua New Guinea, Kenya and Nicaragua.[90] As of 1984, there were a total of 41,755 Chinese economic technicians in LDCs, of which 17,000 were in Iraq and 11,585 in other parts of the Middle East, principally Jordan and Kuwait. Since 1979, these technicians have also been contracted by host countries to participate in either contract labor or engineering service projects. From 1979 to the end of 1984, China signed a total of 1,950 international engineering and labor service contracts for $3.9 billion. In other words, China received almost as much foreign exchange from contract labor abroad as it did from all direct foreign investment in China in the five years from 1979 to 1984.

China has also turned enough from its socialist international duties in the Third World, however, to begin investing in more developed areas, specifically Hong Kong, the United States and Australia. CITIC's overseas branch has bought several timber mills in the United States and in 1986 concluded a mining joint venture in Australia. Over the four years from 1980 to 1984, China has invested a total of $150 million in 113 joint venture enterprises, progressively increasing the scale of its investments. Through these investments in developed economies China has appeared to be seeking access to more advanced technologies applicable to domestic conditions, especially in exploiting natural resources.

In Hong Kong, China's motives have been somewhat different, which is reflected in the nature and size of its investments. Beginning in 1984, Beijing began to take an active role in Hong Kong's finances in an effort to allay fears over the 1997 transition. These initial attempts for the most part have been ham-handed and occasionally even embarrassing. Wang Guangying, China's "red capitalist" and Liu Shaoqi's brother-in-law, had to be saved from losing his shirt in the Hong Kong property market by tycoon Li Kashing. In January 1984, Everbright concluded a $1 billion deal to purchase some residential properties in Hong Kong from Li Kashing. The move boosted confidence in the Hong Kong investment climate but, in June 1984, Everbright withdrew from what appeared to be a deal beyond its technical ability to execute. In doing so, it revealed a secret opt-out clause designed by a cautious Li Kashing that allowed Everbright to withdraw its deposit without loss. Li was subsequently investigated and found culpable of insider trading by a Hong Kong tribunal. Since then, Everbright has been less visible.[91] In mid-1984, China Resources, China's major trading company in Hong Kong, also injected $60 million in the failing Hong Kong electronics firm, Conic—18 months later, that investment remained unprofitable. It was estimated that the Bank of China and China Resources lost at least HK$ 100 million on the deal.[92] Other ventures included loans to several failing Hong Kong family groups including the Tung family, long known for their involvement with Nationalist China's Kuomintang.[93] The Bank of China has fast become known as Hong Kong's lender of last resort. Some Hong Kong economists did not see this, however, as a helpful development. According to one: "Such attempts [Conic, Everbright] are harmful to Hong Kong in the long run because Hong Kong entrepreneurs will be induced to invest their time and resources to seek Chinese hand-outs instead of improving efficiency and competitiveness."[94]

Cumulatively, China's dramatically increased participation in the world economy via increased foreign capital, direct investment, export-boosting measures, and overseas investments, constituted a remarkable change in attitude on the part of China's leadership. It appeared to reflect a growing recognition of the political and economic benefits that foreign economic relations could bring if properly directed. The problems of mismanagement, however, became equally apparent at this time. In particular, foreign business encountered major obstacles when investing in China, obstacles directly linked to China's "feudal" heritage.

NOTES

1. *Guoji Shangbao* in JPRS-CEA, (15 October 1985), p. 70.
2. *SYC* (1985) p. 185, 235.
3. Anthony Tang, "Economic Development of the Chinese Mainland Under the PRC with Reference to Agriculture," paper presented at the Symposium on Economic Development in Chinese Societies, Hong Kong Economic Association (18–20 December 1986), pp. 42-49; *Documents of the CPC National Conference—September 1985,* pp. 91-92.
4. David Denny, "China's Seventh Five Year Plan, " *CBR* XIII:4 (July/August 1986), pp. 12-16.
5. Kjeld Brodsgaard, "Paradigmatic Change: Readjustment and Reform in the Chinese Economy, 1953- 1981," [Part 2], *MC* IX:2 (April 1983), pp. 264-265.
6. See Ma Hong, *New Strategy for China's Economy,* pp. 83-115.
7. *Guoji Maoyi* in JPRS-CEA (9 July 1985), pp. 78-82.
8. FBIS (7 February 1986), pp. K21-23.

9. *Liaowang* (24 March 1986), p. 4 (in Chinese).

10. FBIS (12 December 1985), pp. 31-37; FBIS (8 April 1986), pp. K1-6.

11. *Caimao Jingji* in JPRS-CEA (9 July 1985); Wang Chuanlun, "Some Notes on Tax Reform," *CQ* (1984), pp. 53-67. Wang concludes: "It is obvious now that the leverage function of taxation will certainly increase in the future."

12. Ma Hong, *New Strategy for China's Economy,* p. 63.

13. *Jingji Yanjiu* in JPRS-CEA (February 1986), pp. 7-16.

14. See Xue Muqiao, *China's Socialist Economy,* pp. 122-145.

15. *SCMP* (25 November 1986), p. B1; Solinger, "Economic Readjustment," pp. 24-26.

16. State Statistical Bureau, *China: A Statistical Survey in 1986* (Hong Kong: Economic Information & Agency, 1986), p. 73.

17. Cited in Ch'en, *China and The West,* pp. 94-95.

18. See Mancall, *China at the Center,* pp. 60-64, 70-80, 93-104; Ch'en, *China and the West,* pp. 59-61, 332-334; Hao, *The Commercial Revolution,* pp. 32-34.

19. Cited in Hu Sheng, *Imperialism and Chinese Politics,* pp. 3- 4.

20. Hao, *The Commercial Revolution,* p. 33.

21. Beale, Pelham and Hutchinson, *Trade and Economic Conditions,* p. 37.

22. Mao Zedong, *Selected Works,* Vol IV, p. 415.

23. Mancall, *China at the Center,* pp. 400- 418.

24. Rice, *Mao's Way,* p. 179.

25. James David Armstrong, *Revolutionary Diplomacy: Chinese Foreign Policy and the United Front Doctrine* (Berkeley: University of California, 1977); and Alvin Rubinstein, *Soviet and Chinese Influence in the Third World* (New York: Praeger, 1975).

26. CIA, *Handbook of Economic Statistics* (Washington D.C.: Central Intelligence Agency, 1985), p. 109.

27. United States Travel and Tourism Administration, *Inflight Survey: October-December 1986,* Washington, D.C.

28. *Intertrade* in JPRS-CEA (1 November 1985), pp. 100-101.

29. *China Trade Report* (June 1985) pp. 12-14.

30. FBIS (20 April 1984), pp. D6-9.

31. Zhu Rongji, "To Expand Economic and Technical Cooperation Between China and the U.S.," unpublished speech delivered at Conference on Foreign Investment in China, Beijing (23-24 October 1986), p. 7.

32. *Guoji Maoyi* in JPRS-CEA (24 October 1985), pp. 46-49; *Guoji Maoyi* in JPRS-CEA (20 October 1985), pp. 89-92.

33. *Guoji Maoyi* in JPRS-CEA (20 October 1985), pp. 82-88.

34. A.J. Youngson (ed.), *China and Hong Kong: The Economic Nexus* (Hong Kong: Oxford University Press, 1983).

35. *ACFERT* (1986), pp. 742-743.

36. *SCMP* (7 February 1987), p. B1.

37. *China Trade Report* (February 1986), p. 1,4-5.

38. *ACFERT* (1986), p. 459.

39. *ACFERT* (1987), p. 773.

40. Beale, Pelham and Hutchison, *Trade and Economic Conditions,* p. 9.

41. *Intertrade* (February 1986), pp. 26-29.

42. *ACFERT* (1986), pp. 475-476.

43. CPC, *Uphold Reform*, pp. 91-92; Bachman, *Chen Yun*, pp. 153-155.
44. Thomas Bernstein, "Stalinism, Famine and Chinese Peasants," *Theory and Society* XIII:3 (1984), pp. 339-374.
45. Sheahan, *Alternative International Economic Strategies*, pp. 3-15.
46. *White Paper on Overseas Investment* (Tokyo: Ministry of International Trade and Industry, 1986); Edward Chen, "Export-Led Economic Development in Chinese Societies: The Existence and Transferability of the NIC Model," paper presented at Symposium on Economic Development in Chinese Societies (18-20 December 1986), pp. 3-6.
47. *ACFERT* (1986), p. 952, 957.
48. Hou, *Foreign Investment*, p. 190.
49. Beale, Pelham and Hutchison, *Trade and Economic Conditions*, p. 151.
50. *Asian Perspectives* (May 1986), p. 17.
51. *Intertrade* (January 1986), pp. 17-18; *China Daily* (14 November 1986), p. 1.
52. *Fujian Luntan* in JPRS-CEA (18 July 1985), pp. 17-20.
53. Beale, Pelham and Hutchison, *Trade and Economic Conditions*, p. 9.
54. U.S. Congress, Joint Economic Committee, *China Under the Four Modernizations*, p. 25; FBIS (24 August 1978), pp. E1-2.
55. *Guoji Maoyi Wenti* in JPRS-CEA (14 October 1985), pp. 76-83; *Intertrade* (March 1986), pp. 19-21; *Asian Perspectives* (May 1986), pp. 7-15.
56. *Guoji Shangbao* in JPRS-CEA (15 October 1986), p. 71.
57. Robert Dernberger, "Economic Development and Modernization in Contemporary China," in *Technology and Communist Culture: The Socio-Cultural Impact of Technology Under Socialism* (New York: Praeger, 1977), pp. 261-262; Victor Lippit, "The Great Leap Forward Reconsidered," *MC* I:1 (1972) pp. 92-115; Rice, *Mao's Way*, pp. 159-182; William Griffith, *The Sino-Soviet Rift* (Cambridge: M.I.T. Press, 1964).
58. *Guoji Maoyi Wenti* in JPRS-CEA (14 October 1985) p. 76.
59. Whiting, *Domestic Politics*, pp. 59-60.
60. *Guoji Maoyi Wenti* in JPRS-CEA (14 October 1985), pp. 80-81.
61. *On Learning from Daqing in Industry* (Beijing: Foreign Languages Press, 1978), p. 15.
62. Bachman, *Chen Yun*, pp. 153-154.
63. FBIS (6 December 1978), p. E5.
64. Macdougall in Gray and White (eds.), *China's New Development Strategy*, p. 164.
65. *ACFERT* (1986), pp. 381, 445-447, 448, 457.
66. FBIS (15 August 1986), pp. K7-11; *Asian Perspectives* (May 1986), pp. 11-15; *Jingji Lilun Yu Jingji Guanli* in JPRS-CEA (18 July 1985), pp. 36-41.
67. *ACFERT* (1986) pp. 497-499; *Fujian Luntan* in JPRS-CEA (18 July 1985), pp. 111-116.
68. FBIS (21 March 1979), pp. L17- L18.
69. *China's Foreign Trade* I:1 (1974), p. 43; *Shijie Jingji* in JPRS-CEA (23 September 1985), p. 101.
70. Zhou Xiuluan, "Development of China's Native Industries During World War One," *Chinese Sociology and Anthropology*, XVII:1 (Fall 1984); Frederick Field, *American Participation in the China Consortiums* (New York: Macmillan, 1931); Warren Cohen, "America's New Order for East Asia: The Four Power

Financial Consortium and China, 1919-1946," *Essays in the History of China and Chinese-American Relations,* Occasional Paper No. 7 (Michigan: University of Michigan, 1982), pp. 41-74; Hou, *Foreign Investments,* pp. 15-22, 52-59.

71. *Asian Wall Street Journal Weekly* (3 November 1986), p. 12.
72. *ACFERT* (1984), p. 390; *China Trade Report* (April 1984), p. 12; *CBR* (January-February 1984), p. 88.
73. FBIS (24 April 1986), p. K26.
74. *ACFERT* (1984), p. 390; Donnithorne, *Centre-Provincial Economic Relations,* pp. 23-31; *BR* 11 (1981), pp. 5-8.
75. *Xuexi Yu Yanjiu* in JPRS-CEA (13 August 1985), pp. 129-134; *Shijie Jingji* in JPRS-CEA (9 October 1985), pp. 91-98.
76. FBIS (12 June 1986), p. K21.
77. *Asian Wall Street Journal Weekly* (9 June 1986), p. 26.
78. Zhang Peiji, "Growth of Private Direct Investment in the World and Foreign Investment in China," unpublished speech delivered at Conference on Foreign Investment in China, Beijing (23-24 October 1986), pp. 2-4.
79. See "How Demand for Consumer Electronic Products Can Grow in China," Nomura Securities Memorandum (7 March 1985).
80. *SYC* (1986), p. 720.
81. See generally Kenichi Ohmae, *Triad Power* (New York: Free Press, 1985).
82. Sheahan, *International Economic Strategies,* pp. 3-15.
83. FBIS (4 August 1986), pp. P1-2.
84. *Jingji Wenti Tansuo* (20 April 1985), pp. 1-6 (in Chinese); cited in *SCMP* (9 October 1985), p. 1,3.
85. *BR* (30 September 1985), pp. 4-5; FBIS (16 April 1986), pp. P2-3.
86. *Guoji Maoyi* (27 June 1985), pp. 50-52 (in Chinese); *Fujian Luntan* in JPRS-CEA (15 May 1986), pp. 110-111; Ji Chongwei, "Foreign Investment in China and Sino-foreign Joint Ventures: Its Present Situation and Prospects," unpublished speech delivered at Conference on Foreign Investment in China, Beijing (23-24 October 1986), pp. 8-10, 15-16.
87. *China Daily* (4 December 1986), p. 4.
88. *SCMP* (24 May 1986), p. B1.
89. *AWSJW* (16 June 1986), p. 1, 19.
90. *ACFERT* (1986), p. 454.
91. *SCMP* (22 October 1986), p. 1.
92. *Jiushi Niendai* (July 1985), pp. 42-43 (in Chinese).
93. *AWSJW* (24 March 1986), p. 10.
94. Y.W. Sung, "The Hong Kong Development Model and Its Future Evolution: Neoclassical Economics in a Chinese Society," paper presented at Symposium on Economic Development in Chinese Societies, Hong Kong, (18-20 December 1986), p. 32.

5

Ventures in China

In 1982, China successfully negotiated the reunification of Hong Kong with the mainland under the banner of "one country two systems." Under the terms of the agreement Hong Kong would retain its capitalist ways for fifty years. With the introduction of the Joint Venture Law in 1979, foreign enterprises were likewise "reunified" with China. "One country two systems" in fact was already in place, albeit within a very circumscribed sector of the political economy.

Since 1978, joint ventures have faced formidable capital, market and sourcing constraints. Cultural and objective conflicts have further limited their viability. There have been many more attractive places for an investor to put his or her money than China. Yet for those who became "insiders" and laid out their objectives clearly, the long-term prospects have steadily improved.

THE CONSTRAINTS ON VENTURES

Foreign Exchange

The following material is primarily based on interviews conducted in Beijing, Shanghai, Guangdong province and other regions of China from 1984 to 1986 with both Chinese and Western businesspeople, officials, journalists, students and others. Some identities have been disguised at the request of the interviewees.

As with all developing countries China did not have enough foreign exchange in 1978 to meet all the pressing needs of its economy. Even Taiwan originally had a fixed multiple exchange rate from 1949 to 1958 to control imports.[1] In the eyes of mainland Chinese policy-makers, the unconvertible Renminbi (RMB) currency allowed them to shelter their underdeveloped economy from external forces and choose their own priorities. Hence, most individual ventures had to balance their own uses and sources of foreign exchange independently. This policy, though originally perhaps intended to restrict large-scale consumer goods imports, discouraged capital-intensive and high technology investments. These ventures complained that foreign exchange was needed not for dividend repatriation but more urgently for the import of necessary materials and components that could not be sourced in China.

After the initial capital infusion from the foreign parent for plant and equipment, most ventures found it difficult to impossible to find domestic sources. Even if a venture were permitted to repatriate foreign exchange, some complained that the rules were too restrictive.[2] The Ministry of Foreign Economic Relations and Trade moreover supplemented foreign exchange controls by requiring import and export licenses on 152 export commodities and 45 import commodities. Licenses were needed for, among other items, motor vehicles, computers, television sets, watches, steel, timber, tobacco, synthetic fibers, and washing machine assembly lines.[3] Joint ventures, especially those run by Westerners, ironically were particularly affected by these restrictions because of their high visibility and few numbers. Under the original Beijing Jeep venture agreement, the joint venture was profitably run (over 25 percent ROI) as a sideline of the extant factory operations. However, when the Jeep board decided to import $20 million of Jeep kits to be assembled, the venture was unable to come up with that amount of foreign exchange. According to a negotiator, an agreement was eventually reached whereby foreign exchange for the venture would be provided over a four-year period to coincide with a speedup in the localization of Jeep parts. Local enterprises on the other hand could sometimes avoid Beijing's scrutiny and coerce local authorities to look the other way. As one member of a large British firm commented: "The only people making money selling to China are the small-time Hong Kong traders who can play the black market foreign exchange game in Shenzhen."

In addressing the foreign exchange issue, foreign investors were first advised by the Chinese to export their products, thereby generating foreign exchange. There were, however, unavoidable problems in Chinese exports. Quality was generally not up to par and the venture's product was often too high cost to be internationally competitive. China's image as a low-quality producer also inhibited exports. Usually, the more complex the venture product, the greater the problem—Wella shampoo and Pepsi-Cola perhaps but not Wang microcomputers or Volkswagen Santanas.

High tech ventures instead usually resorted to selling parts and components as available.

Another way to obtain foreign exchange was import substitution, or selling domestically. Here the opportunities were usually limited to a relatively small portion of the venture's sales, and that only for a "technologically advanced" enterprise. Shanghai Ek-Chor Motorcycle, for example, was able to sell only between 5 percent and 10 percent of its output to Friendship Stores and other sources of foreign exchange.[4] Bureaucratic obstacles and sometimes Chinese customer preference for imported products further diminished the opportunity. In one extreme case, a major customer of a machinery venture discriminated against the plant by giving no credit for its RMB content, and ignoring import duty, service fees and lifetime service in its evaluation of the competing imported product. Many executives claimed Chinese customers really wanted not the product but an overseas trip. At any rate, State Planning Commission officials have many times stated that import substitution is a strictly short-term recourse. For example, in 1988, a major Shanghai venture received tariff protection but with a quid pro quo of 80 percent localization in two years.

If one could not export one's own product, one could always attempt to purchase another domestic product for export. Again bureaucratic obstacles and the lack of horizontal coordination between ministries made such deals difficult. Some Chinese trading companies were jealous to protect their own distributing arrangements and charged premium prices to foreign companies attempting to break into the trade. At least 3M's wholly owned tape and resin manufacturing venture in Shanghai, appeared to be able in cooperation with Shamash, a long-time China silk trader, to trade Chinese glassware, nails, and silk. A fourth approach, rare in the early 1980s, was to try to swap foreign exchange with another foreign exchange-rich business. This was also difficult, in the absence of established markets and the presence of unrealistically low official foreign exchange rates. Along the same lines, some ventures considered investing in foreign exchange-rich companies such as hotels but again only with limited success. One manufacturing venture investigated the opportunity to invest in a hotel, only to find that the investment proposal they were offered had a 19-year payback.

By the mid 1980s, however, the foreign perception of the foreign exchange shortage as an obstacle to investment began to be shared by the Chinese. Two ways to resolve the foreign exchange crunch existed: generate more or distribute what existed more effectively. On the generation side, China already planned to increase its use of loans to some $25-30 billion within the Seventh Five-year Plan. However, as one China International Trust and Investment Corporation official remarked: "China has no trouble getting money. We just don't know where to invest it in

China." Officials of the International Monetary Fund also noted, China's "external debts are no longer light, its debt structure is irrational and that its debt management is not well coordinated."[5]

Regarding redistribution, in 1986 the 22 Articles on Promoting Foreign Investment allowed for the first time a foreign exchange market to be formed between ventures. At the meeting where the 22 Articles were announced, one of the speakers delicately acknowledged: "While we have admitted that the principal aspect is good, we have noticed that there are some complaints from those foreign investors....The investigation done by us showed that much of their complaint is true, and some certainly being exaggerated." The speaker, adviser Ji Chongwei went on to elaborate the provisions of the 22 Articles, specifically the policy of granting foreign exchange loans to certain export-oriented and technologically advanced enterprises such as Beijing Jeep and Fujian Hitachi. Moreover "under the supervision of the Foreign Exchange Administration, the foreign investment enterprises could among themselves each make up the other's deficiency of foreign exchange from its own surplus." By 1988, this foreign exchange market (based partly on earlier experiments in Shanghai and Shenzhen) was functioning in over 30 centers in all the provincial capitals plus Hainan, Dalian and Ningbo. In 1987 $4.2 billion was exchanged at a rate which varied between 6.1 and 6.4 yuan to 1 US dollar. This represented a premium of 60 to 70 percent over the official rate of 3.72 and was within 1 yuan of the black market rate.[6]

Officials at the Foreign Exchange Administration attributed the higher rate to "a distorted demand for foreign goods." However, the government had intervened to keep the exchange rate constant so as to help manufacturers with the cost of imported components. Access to the market was restricted to enterprises who wished to buy imported components and products, to repay loans, and to repatriate profits. Domestic enterprises were allowed to participate to the extent they were able to retain foreign exchange. Generally, most enterprises could retain 12.5 percent of the foreign exchange they generated. This rate could rise to 30 to 40 percent in the case of textiles, hotels and other companies who had need of foreign exchange liquidity. Domestic textile and other light industry manufacturers made up the bulk of the market from 1986 to 1988, constituting over 80 percent of foreign exchange trading volume. The domestic banking system, however, was not allowed to participate as it was feared they would engage in wholesale speculation and dry up all the foreign exchange in the market.

In the longer-term, Chinese officials are committed to the convertibility of the RMB but this remains problematic. The issue of Foreign Exchange Certificates is one example of how complicated the problem is. An intermediate currency used by foreigners, they were to be phased out in 1987 as part of the ongoing program but this was postponed primarily due to administrative confusions and complaints by expatriates living in China. In time, the government would also like to see the network of foreign exchange centers expand into a national center and a series of local brokerages. The Hong Kong Shanghai Bank already operates as a local broker in Shanghai. For now, however, ventures still have to seek out pools of foreign exchange and rely on the local center officials to implement the Beijing decrees.

Operating Costs

Another major constraint on the economic viability of many ventures has been the excessive cost of operating in China. China has imposed artificially high living costs and overhead on foreign companies. Many basic services are arbitrarily priced and controlled by state and local monopolies, while poor infrastructure has further inflated costs. New import duties pushed the cost of a medium-sized Japanese car to close to $40,000 at one time. Beijing hotel rates were comparable to the finest in the West. Authorities such as FESCO, the People's Insurance Company, China Overseas Shipping Company, and Civil Aviation Authority of China exerted monopolistic pressures. Griped one Western executive: "Beijing is a captive market and the Chinese exploit it fully." Universities routinely, though illegally, charged $7,000 "finder's fees" to joint ventures seeking to recruit on campus. A particularly notorious case occurred when TOTAL, a French oil company, hired a Chinese expert through FESCO. Officially the expert was paid $9,000, but he actually received $54 as his take-home pay. This was still a bargain, though, compared to the average China expatriate cost of between $100,000 and $250,000 in 1988, depending on age, nationality, and experience.

Economic efficiency also varied widely by city, with industrial concentrations only in Shanghai and the Northeast. Many companies have had transportation bottlenecks tie up shipments at Tianjin and Shanghai docks for weeks, while a freight train may take 16 days from Shenzhen to Harbin at a minimum. In fact, IBM once resorted to the costly expedient of chartering aircraft to carry its computers in. Low technological standards of local industries have made local procurement difficult and local authorities take opportunities to levy new charges at will. For example, when Fujian Hitachi, a joint venture producing color televisions, bought parts from domestic nongovernment suppliers, it had to come across with a previously unannounced 13 percent "commercial tax." In Guangdong, one foreign investor found out only after the contract was signed that the local authorities planned to charge an additional 3 million RMB for the right to access municipal water and power lines. In many cases, these economics made investments prohibitively expensive.

From the Chinese perspective, the foreign parents may have seemed untrustworthy. At one failed venture, the Chinese press speculated that the Hong Kong partner was just seeking to dump raw materials and equipment.[7] A Chinese manager at another venture believed the foreign partner was making "big profits" on the parts it supplied. According to this manager, the solution to all cost problems was component localization. This he realized though would be difficult to achieve in the short-term, given China's acute lack of basic electronics capacity, e.g., for integrated circuits and PCBs. Lacking knowledge about external market conditions, the Chinese partner also sometimes suspected his partner of cheating him in the marketplace. China National Electronics Import-Export Corporation (CEIEC) officials in Guangzhou believed their Hong Kong floppy disk joint venture partner was engaging in price-cutting in the Hong Kong market, driving down Chinese margins while overcharging for components from Hong Kong. In the words of one: "Hong Kong investors are bloodthirsty for Chinese foreign exchange." Foreign ventures were also seen as privileged enterprises awash in cash, natural targets for hungry local authorities. Prices on these authorities' state-controlled products were being kept stable, while market reforms generally led to spiraling cost-of-living increases. Given this pressure, it was not surprising for a joint venture to be constantly pressed to do "small favors" from sending an influential person's child for overseas training to the constant rounds of banqueting.

Chinese factories were also generally fairly far down on the technology curve, making it difficult for them to supply high-quality components needed by many ventures to be economically viable. Automation was very low and what computerization there was tended to be misused. A Computerland executive noted in 1986: "About 50 percent of the computers in China are dark—either because they are broken or because people don't know how to use them.... The effort to bring machines in was a very smart move. What didn't work was the way foreign exchange allocations were misused."[8] This was partly due to the long neglect of management and systems skills in the job description of factory managers. Economics and finance graduates were in short supply throughout the Cultural Revolution, leaving a generation of untrained cadres unable in some instances to keep up with the pace of reform. Hence, some venture products had spotty quality and management could be lackadaisical. One of Nike's factories in Tianjin was consistently unable to turn out white shoes. Desperate, the Chinese manager suggested: "Why don't we just make grey shoes?" Nike moved to another plant.

China's low-cost labor was also frustratingly elusive. Low labor productivity more than offset low man-hour costs. One electronic joint venture said its productivity was one-twentieth that of its 1960s era U.S. plant. Some ventures were more successful than others, however, in realizing lower costs. The key appears to have been to demand more freedom for managers rather than bureaucrats to make decisions, hence the superior showing of small contractual ventures (usually in village industries), unencumbered with the established bureaucracy of a large Chinese enterprise. One Tianjin venture reportedly built its own plant and fought to set its own staffing levels. While it could not differentiate wages, it used a harsh system of monetary discipline. Hence, its productivity was equivalent to its non-Chinese operations and many times higher than similar Chinese enterprises. Likewise a Tianjin Japanese venture hired its own employees, mostly recent high school graduates, on a "green field" site with a new organization and had good productivity. Other enterprises who started with an existing Chinese factory found themselves saddled with both overstaffing and inefficient management.

High costs, however, were a long-term, strategic issue that would not go away. Only those enterprises able to work either within the Chinese system or devise efficient ways to "short circuit" it did have advantages in lowering costs. The more "in-plan" materials at low state prices the venture received, the better off its economics. Hence, some medium tech ventures with great effort appear to have been profitable selling 90 percent local content products at "imported quality" prices—e.g., elevators. The dual pricing system still generated some curious situations though. For example, one food processing venture paid more for rice in China than in California. They found that because farmers held back their best rice for private sales, state quota rice was in fact too low quality to use and they were instead forced to pay higher prices on the market.

Market Access

Most companies also perceived China to be a very tough market. The monopolistic nature of the Chinese bureaucracy left the seller very little leverage over his price. To quote one West German executive: "Here, you see every evil of textbook monopoly. Dealing with a state enterprise is like bargaining with a pistol at your head." Even Japanese companies were forced to accept prices 20 to 30 percent lower than those in the United States. In 1984, Japanese companies' average return on trucks sold to China was 3 percent as opposed to 10 percent worldwide; in steel the average price per ton was $307 versus $491; and in construction works completed profit rates ran 5 percent versus 11 percent.[9] Culturally, most foreigners were unprepared for the grueling style of negotiations. Chinese teams were large, members were interchangeable, sessions were long, and banquets frequent. To quote the account of one unsuccessful China trader: "After the initial round of welcoming banquets, I felt as if I had been put through a meat grinder; I had to repeat endlessly the same things to negotiators who would suddenly, inexplicably, disappear for a few weeks—replaced temporarily by another team—then just as suddenly reappear."[10] To Westerners the pace was generally excruciatingly and apparently inexplicably slow. A Swedish executive noted: "You cannot normally go straight from A to B because they will resist you; but if you make a detour, reaching B from the side as if you were sneaking up on it, they might well accept the same offer."

Of those companies who have made investments regardless, most have gone wrong initially by not realizing which segment of the Chinese market they participated in and what the key constraints were to be met in each. As an import substitute product, the key issue was foreign exchange. Tariffs against imports also helped as the venture's cost and quality had to be competitive. There was in addition usually a bias against "made in China" products among Chinese factories who wanted to get a "real" product. In this climate, import substitute ventures who did not gain the trust of the Chinese bureaucracy to impose tariffs on imports and encourage local factories to buy from the venture, were not economically viable. If the venture chose to sell domestically in RMB, ventures had to be careful not to build a too technologically complex product, pricing themselves out of the market entirely. The Chinese may also contribute to the problem by pushing for "state of the art" in the venture.[11]

Again, those ventures who did not do a good job of market research *prior* to entry faced serious economic issues. A baby-food venture in Guangdong is one notable example in which careful research was performed before entry, but this was surprisingly enough the exception, not the rule. Many ventures allowed the Chinese partner, who sometimes had different objectives and skill levels, to handle domestic sales and marketing. Regional jealousies prevented access to some markets. "Made in Shanghai" generally did not go well in Beijing. Finally, some ventures that were successful in cost-competitive manufacturing for the domestic market found themselves confined by a percentage ratio of export to domestic sales in their contracts.

In reply to these complaints, Chinese officials linked the market access issue to the undeveloped state of the Chinese economy. The potential of the China market was held as a carrot for foreign investors, and China's present poverty was the stick. Given GNP per capita figures, China's 1 billion people had the purchasing power of only 25 million U.S. citizens. How then could China afford the drain on foreign exchange that unrestricted currency control would lead to? Technology transfer and exports were the keys to success in the official mind. To quote a Shanghai official on one of the largest local joint ventures: "We will raise duties on products competing with the venture's as soon as the 'product maturity' issue is resolved. If only [the parent company] would be more open about the technology and quickly transfer it, we could jointly solve the problem."[12]

In this venture's particular case, it was indeed true that the foreign company had decided to make its money selling parts to the venture and as a result was less than enthusiastic about localization.

Bureaucratic Interference

Ventures also had to cope with bureaucratic interference. Not only a local Department-in-Charge, usually a bureau of the industrial ministry of the venture's partner, but also a variety of functional bureaus such as Finance and Labor supervised their functions. In one case in Shanghai a venture had to get approval from 33 different departments before starting business. In the usual Chinese enterprise before enterprise reform, these departments had direct access to the factory floor without going through the manager.[13] Most foreign companies were, however, used to making such resource allocation decisions on personnel and finance by a manager under the direction of a board. Joint ventures faced a real challenge in getting local functional bureaus to sever their links with venture departments and instead go through the general manager. One foreign general manager in Tianjin had to personally place an ad for personnel in the *China Daily* before his own Chinese advertising manager would consent to bypass the Labor Bureau.

Ventures, in addition, contended with the shadow structure of the Communist Party. While in theory the party and government had separate spheres of ideology and administration, in practice the party dominated government work. In joint ventures, party secretaries could be either progressive or retarding forces, but they were always factors. Reforms placed much emphasis on the separation of party and state but factory managers' power bases remained tenuous, especially in issues of labor relations. In joint ventures, as head of the trade union, party secretaries were legally empowered to a seat on the board of directors, to participate in deliberations on major questions, to negotiate collective labor contracts, and to supervise all decisions of the joint venture that have an impact on the personal interests of staff and workers. They were also responsible for organizing study sessions among the workers and staff, and encouraging observation of internal labor discipline.[14] With authorities thus unclearly defined, it was small wonder than one 1988 survey revealed over 38 percent of party secretaries and factory directors "do not coordinate their management efforts" and "come into conflict too frequently."[15]

The other form of bureaucratic interference many joint ventures faced was the parochialism that 2,000 years of a "feudal" economy engendered. Local rivalry and the lack of exchange produced some of the most thorough-going refutation of economic principles of specialization and scale economies ever seen. In 1985, for example, China produced approximately 400,000 motor vehicles from 1,300 factories, or an average of about 3,000 vehicles per factory. Although more properly perhaps called not bureaucratic interference but an excess of local economic democracy, these conditions, along with the small size of the ventures themselves, hindered ventures from achieving sourcing and sales targets. By 1986, one major automotive producer was able to localize only tires, radio and antennae. The only Chinese material in Wella shampoo was water. Shanghai Bell would be importing expensive integrated circuits for the foreseeable future.

The major upshot of both types of interference was the joint ventures' perceived lack of authority. Reforms perversely complicated this, as one Western businesswoman noted: "Decentralization means chaos in China." Many foreign companies entered China and became affiliated with the wrong ministry simply out of ignorance. A major semiconductor firm, for example, entered with a tie up with the Ministry of Aeronautics instead of the Ministry of Electronics. Once affiliated it was difficult to see the forest for the trees as horizontal coordination was far more difficult than the traditional vertical arrangements.[16] Where a strong partner could work wonders in clearing red tape, a weak one could prevent any venture from achieving its objectives.

To overcome bureaucratic interference, successful ventures first tended to be proactive in choosing their national partners. They took the time to understand their options and then sought not to hitch too closely to any one star but to spread their company name throughout the bureaucracy and out into the provinces. They realized no one partner could possibly help them manufacture, sell and distribute to the complex and divided China market. One supplier originally chose the old Ministry of Machine-building as its Beijing office sponsor only because it "was the best ministry to spread our way of thinking." This Beijing office, however, also maintained a directory of factory managers throughout China, conducted technical seminars in the provinces, and established independent links with factories throughout China. Likewise, An Wang chose the foreign trade corporation of the Ministry of Electronics to venture with because of old family ties but set up multiple operations in Beijing, Shanghai and Xiamen. Volkswagen's 1988 agreement with the Changchun Automotive Works appeared to have been totally separate from its existing Shanghai plant.

Once established, enterprises and specifically both Chinese and Western members of the board of directors also had to exert their authority to ensure the venture's interests were safeguarded. Both Shanghai Volkswagen's general managers and the board of directors appeared to share a common vision—to produce cars in Shanghai. At Otis, likewise, four of five Chinese board members were from the joint venture. On the other hand, another auto venture had a more fractious board where one manager complained: "Board members from other factories really don't understand [the venture's] problems. They don't have any authority either." Hence, foreigners grumbled that the local bureaucracy bypassed managers, and that the board did not resolve conflicts.

OBJECTIVE AND CULTURAL CONFLICTS

In addition to constraints, while the interests of foreign companies and the Chinese could theoretically complement each other, they could also conflict and perpetuate a communications gap. Cultural and value conflicts between socialist Confucian Chinese bureaucrats and individualist humanist foreign businesspeople were real obstacles. Companies generally saw China as a potentially huge market and possibly a low-cost sourcing alternative. The Chinese sought the kinds of foreign investment that would develop export-oriented industries and enable them to build the favorable foreign exchange balances needed for growth. To quote a State Council spokesman: "The state demands that these enterprises make profits and achieve better microeconomic results, but also that they contribute to rationalization of our production structure, our technological transformation."[17]

Objective Conflicts

Objective conflicts have translated into conflicts within the enterprise over strategy and operations. While the Chinese have wanted enterprises to develop immediately both design and process capabilities, foreign participants continued to do their research and development at home and only manufacture in China. Even China Hewlett-Packard, a relatively successful venture, foresaw R&D localization only sometime in the mid 1990s. The Chinese, moreover, have wanted to make immediately whole products where the foreign participant would often make components first. Thus, one of the largest U.S. manufacturers refused to enter into a venture with China because as one of its officials said: "The Chinese can't commercially build anything bigger than a microcomputer." Chinese managers also often wanted to keep control and minimize foreigners' influence in the workplace, which ran directly counter to foreign interests of increasing productivity and creating a dedicated workforce. At one Shanghai venture the foreign parent completely abdicated its management role. According to factory officials the board was very weak, outside bureaus continuously circumvented the general manager, and foreign managers were ignored. In a classic quote from one: "It's their project, they have bought your technology and are, frankly, embarrassed by the imposition of this JV fiction."

While the Chinese have sought to import the "highest" technology, Western companies would rather have used economically sound technology. According to a Western technical expert at a Shanghai venture, because the Chinese objective was to master manufacturing capability they chose the most advanced product 10 years before China would be ready for it. Worse, because profit assumptions were not adequately spelled out, the price set for domestic sale was far out of line with that of competing imports. Tianjin Otis and Shanghai Foxboro on the other hand, were able to persuade their Chinese partners to manufacture older rather than "state of the art" products as being more appropriate to Chinese conditions. Some Western companies such as Swarovski Crystal further feared creating new international competitors and were thus reluctant to transfer technology.

The above Shanghai venture illustrated how high-technology ventures in China usually lacked the necessary industrial infrastructure and market demand for beneficial economics and as a result found themselves in need of subsidies for long periods. The company originally assumed quicker localization than actually occurred. The foreign exchange deficit had been forecasted to end by 1987 but has continued beyond. Quoting a factory official: "[Our foreign exchange strategy is] . . . go to the wall. The PRC will bail us out." The products also cost twice as much as Japanese competing imports, sometimes backed by soft loans.[18] Likewise at Beijing Jeep, a venture that has received state support, at one time a jeep cost $18,000 as compared to $12,000 in the U.S. market.

Chinese officials desired to maximize the amount invested by foreign partners in the venture. Foreigners on the other hand preferred to minimize their capital risk. Hence many foreign partners argued about the value of technology as part of the venture contract and used financial leverage in lieu of cash. Beijing Jeep had 50 percent of its $16 million investment in cash, the rest being technology. Likewise 50 percent of Wella's $3 million venture was in the form of debt, as was 60 percent of the Shanghai Pilkington joint venture. Of Nabisco's $4.5 million total investment, $1 million was technology and training assistance. To counter the trend, especially among smaller Hong Kong companies, MOFERT in fact passed legislation in 1986 setting specific debt-equity levels for joint ventures.

The Chinese preference for ventures to have an export-orientation also conflicted with a Western company's mandate not to compete with itself in existing markets. Many ventures had existing overcapacity to meet their foreign market demands and hence exported from the venture reluctantly or not at all. The export-orientation issue also hindered foreign access to the Chinese domestic market. Wella for example was at one time reportedly constrained by a contract which mandated 50 percent of its products be sold overseas. Another problem occurred when the foreign partner focused exclusively on technology or production while the Chinese handled marketing. This was in most cases an inherently inefficient way of doing things as the Chinese factory often had no skills or experience in marketing and distribution while the foreign partner had never worked in a Chinese factory before.[19] A profitable enterprise like Hewlett-Packard China on the other hand began with a marketing and distribution agreement and only four years later added a small (10 percent of employees) manufacturing component.

In addition to Chinese-foreign objective conflicts, Chinese objectives have themselves been internally inconsistent. Almost no venture could simultaneously generate export earnings and transfer advanced technology.[20] Desired foreign capital would not be attracted to China without market access or control of the enterprise. Moreover, technology transfer ventures in particular, were only tenuously viable enterprises, their high costs and high tech not being economically viable in China's limited domestic market.

Given these conflicts it is no surprise that many ventures were frustrated. Fuzhou Hitachi and Beijing Jeep both shut down for a time because of foreign exchange problems. Foxboro faced disappointing sales from its 100 percent Chinese sales arm for a number of years. Hua Yuan, the Hong Kong floppy disk venture with CEIEC, faced serious distrust between partners and poor returns. Not only foreign but also Chinese managers were frustrated at this turn of events, blaming both bureaucratic interference and partners' incompetence.[21] This negative mood, of course, also resulted in a general "dump on China" mood in the press. Headlines such as "Joint Ventures: The Honeymoon is Over" and "Why Investors Are Sour on China" appeared, not doing much for the investment climate generally.

Only a few ventures were able to resolve objective conflicts successfully. Most did so by working out a compromise, keeping economic viability for both partners as the paramount criterion and meeting only those other objectives that did not conflict. Gould ensured the economic viability of its China office by risking only a limited capital exposure in China. Through a combination of foreign exchange sales and small technology transfer projects, they satisfied at least partially the Chinese objective of technology transfer as well as building the Chinese industrial infrastructure. After trailing rival Boeing for years, McDonnell Douglas entered the China market by agreeing to produce MD-82 planes in Shanghai only if the Chinese agreed to buy $1 billion worth of planes. Before closing the deal, McDonnell Douglas sourced aircraft doors in China for several years, trained Chinese engineers for the project, and persuaded the Chinese to drop the rival Yun-10 model as incapable of meeting international aviation standards. On July 31, 1987, the first Chinese-built MD-82 jet was delivered on time.[22] To quote Gareth Chang, McDonnell Douglas' chief negotiatior: "For a year we avoided conflicts, which is why we could not work together." For at least some successful ventures, if both sides decided to meet the other's interests within the single constraint of economic viability, success seemed to be much more possible.

Cultural Differences

Apart from the objective conflicts, cultural differences often accounted for venture problems. Personal relationships [guanxi] are the preferred way of doing business in China. The personal touch is much more important than in the West where relationships can often be impersonal. Rituals and prolonged contact are part of the relationship in China while for Westerners, such things are generally not part of the deal. Most importantly, in the West, personal relationships are subordinate to the terms of contract. In China, the rule of law is still subordinate to the rule of man. One Western electronics executive in Beijing noted that it is a general rule of thumb in a technology transfer contract that the more letters of credit there are in any deal, the more likely it is that the last one or two will not be opened. Instead, "the money will have been taken away by a higher Chinese authority for use elsewhere. In any other country that would be accounted breach of contract, but in China buyers generally do not accept the risk."[23] Guanxi, based on political power, supersede the contract. Efforts are being made to change this, but only in early 1987 was the first case (later settled out of court) brought to trial against a Chinese company by two foreign banks for breach of contract. One Chinese economist spelled out four points he felt could be immediately improved in 1985. He noted foreign businesspeople do not want to negotiate with people who need to ask for instructions in everything. Answers should be given regardless of embarrassment or fear of their discontent. Business secrets should not be divulged to rivals of foreign companies. Data prepared by foreign companies in negotiation should be given due weight. By implication, all these things are the case at present.[24]

Western companies, accustomed to explicit and binding contracts have had problems in this environment, especially when gaps in the legal structure are encountered. China had been rebuilding the structure only since 1978 and often rules were applied with partiality or not at all. For example, when United bought Pan Am's trans-Pacific routes in 1986, Chinese authorities insisted on renegotiating the entire contract rather than simply acknowledging the change of ownership. In the ensuing argument, United was prevented from picking up passengers in Beijing and had to fly empty planes out. Minimum requirements had to be spelled out in all contracts.

Often a Western company would assume that the Chinese understood they needed to make a profit. Often the assumption could be wrong and the Westerner could end up with a large amount of unconvertible currency and with no legal recourse.[25]

Whereas a Western company might have assumed that with the passage of regulations most problems could be avoided, everything in China had to be addressed both through contracts and personal *guanxi.* The lack of infrastructure was one area where foreigners not only had to have contracts with the local transport, power, and communications authorities, but also needed priority as granted by top leadership to be assured supply. In Guangdong province, for example, factories ran on less than a five-day schedule because of power outages. Often, unless the company was able to communicate with the top Chinese leadership and financial entities, delays and denials could continue. The Guilin Ramada, for example, found its water cut off after firing the son of the responsible local cadre.

While national labor guidelines have been published in Beijing, unless the venture had good relations with the local labor bureau and a powerful Chinese partner, it could also face unnecessary problems there. Shanghai Squibb illustrated the value of a good partnership. At one time, of a total of 172 employees, 108 came directly from the Shanghai Pharmaceutical Industrial Corporation (SPIC). Originally SPIC had nominated 400, of which Squibb tested and picked the 108 and then negotiated with their units. To quote one manager: "We're pretty lucky to have the support of the SPIC in getting experienced workers." The SPIC also retained Shanghai's Huang Pu District Labor Bureau to train local high school graduates. These graduates were selected by a test emphasizing math, chemistry and Chinese conducted by a local high school with the local District Labor Bureau. At universities Squibb could also pay the authorities to find a student to train for employment at a bargain cost of 1000 yuan.

Conflicts between foreign and Chinese management styles also proved difficult to resolve. Foreign managers complained that China could grind down an enterprise in red tape. Basic factory management techniques differed.[26] Experienced workers were usually not available and some ventures, reportedly Gillette's in Shenyang, had the experience of training workers and then seeing them commandeered by the labor bureau for other Chinese enterprises. In the enterprise, low utilization was frequently due to training costs, and featherbedding was usual in technical areas. At the Japanese joint venture Bohai Oil Company, Japanese technicians complained that it took three people to do a job that one could do alone— one Japanese technician, a Chinese trainee, and an interpreter. Sanyo Huaqiang, the largest Japanese presence in China, ran at 65 percent capacity in 1985 due to training costs.[27] One carburetor factory in Beijing produced 10,000 carburetors per year with 4,000 employees.

A further very common mistake made by foreign companies was to send engineers, whom the Chinese may have requested, instead of general managers, to run the joint venture. The engineers often found themselves consumed by unfamiliar day-to-day administrative and bureaucratic hassles, or creating adversarial relationships with technical departments within the venture. The role of "foreign experts" was undefined in these cases, unlike a venture where the foreign general manager was actually a professionally trained manager, capable of defining roles and carefully delegating authority. A more successful venture such as Shanghai Foxboro sent all of its Chinese staff for several months training in the U.S. with their counterparts. The expatriate general manager was full-time and lived in Shanghai. Shanghai Squibb likewise had a "China hand" who handled administration and relations with the bureaucracy, leaving the expatriate factory manager to run the plant effectively.

The management problem was just as bad from the Chinese perspective. Factory chiefs were not trained to act as general managers. They had difficulty in making and implementing resource allocation decisions between manufacturing, and finance and marketing departments because they never had before. Quoting one Chinese manager at a leading industrial joint venture: "It has taken three times longer to make decisions and get them approved than it did before we started the joint venture. The pressure has been terrible. I got all this grey hair in the last three years." Cultural misunderstandings further aggravated the problem—language being only the tip of the iceberg. For example, Nike at one factory tried to introduced a bonus system based on a worker's ability to reduce the number of blemished shoes. The scheme seemed initially to work well but to quote one official: "The Chinese really didn't get it. By the second year they thought it was automatic. They just came out with their hands open." For their part, lower level Chinese officials complained that the top officials did not give them enough guidance to deal effectively with foreign companies.

Foreign business tried to overcome these barriers by hiring the best overseas Chinese staff or the best Western talent fresh out of the Foreign Languages Institute in Beijing with fluent Mandarin skills. There was indeed a markedly younger tinge to the Beijing business corps, both men and women. Competent Chinese personnel were even scarcer commodities but extensive and prolonged training was required. For example, China Hewlett-Packard (CHP) trained all its university-recruited workers one-on-one with Westerners in sales techniques.[28] Its long-term objective was to have all posts manned by Chinese in 10 to 15 years—its Japanese operation was 100 percent Japanese. There were two types of training used—general employee orientation, usually in Beijing, and field training to get familiar with CHP products. For this, CHP employees could be sent almost anywhere. Product training was continuous and sales training was

conducted with individual managers under the responsibility of department heads. CHP's Western staff was made up almost entirely of overseas
Chinese, mostly from the United States or Singapore. President Liu Jin-
ming was a 17-year Hewlett Packard veteran. For those with fewer connections than CHP, quality often made up for quantity. One capable Chinese
general manager could often make the difference between success and
failure. To quote the head of the China Enterprise Management Association: "Problems in joint ventures come from two sources: unqualified
Chinese personnel and foreigners who do not understand China and the
Chinese. Western managers should train Chinese in real-life, hands-on
situations. Westerners also need to understand Chinese characteristics
such as deeply-engrained habits of small-scale production, the issue of
'face,' and vertical coordination's preeminence over horizontal. The success of a joint venture often depends on the compatibility of the
partners."[29]

Another type of cultural difference related to values—the ideological
and political differences between capitalist and socialist enterprise
decision-making. In Chinese factories, incentive systems, the right to hire
and fire, and other labor management tools were generally unavailable to
foreign investors. One Chinese manager at Bohai Oil exclaimed: "You
can't ask us to lay off our people. Where shall they go? This is still a
socialist country." Managers at the Shanghai No. 2 Radio Factory have
not hired directly through advertisements. Instead, the city government
had to approve all transfers from other units as well as any employees sent
abroad for training or sales. In 1986, personnel still could not be dismissed, but managers anticipated that with reform implementation the
general manager would be able to dismiss workers for discipline, wastage,
and refusal to accept assignment, and for redundancy in consultation
with the local labor bureau.[30] Of those few joint ventures able to work
around these obstacles, most found a way to introduce financially oriented worker motivation schemes. One Tianjin venture's managers were
actually quite enthusiastic about labor conditions in China, noting that
they have been able to institute productivity systems not usually available
in Hong Kong or other Asian countries. Apparently for foreign business to
take advantage of China's major competitive advantage, its low-cost labor,
a great deal of flexibility is required from the ideologues.

THE BENEFITS OF INSIDER STATUS

The major lesson from "one country, two systems" ventures appears to
have been that "insiders" in China have had successful experiences. The
insider's investment was based on a balanced agreement that began with
explicit recognition by each side of the other's interest, constraints and

risks. This agreement had to align the interests of the Chinese and foreign company to provide acceptable benefits and minimize risk for both. This did not entail sacrificing Western goals for Chinese or "going native." Rather, successful ventures developed a broad vision of phased development that subsumed both sets of interests under the primacy of economic viability.

To be successful, theoretically, Western companies could sell only technological products, invest in the economy, and generate exports, while the Chinese would open up the domestic market, reduce overheads and improve facilities, and Westernize their business practices. Such, however, was extremely unlikely to occur given all the conflicts and constraints present. Lack of foreign exchange led to risks of profit repatriation. A no-technology company faced inherent obstacles in developing *guanxi* and finding a buyer, while a too-high technology vendor found Chinese quality spotty and often a missing market.

Instead, Hewlett-Packard is an example of another kind of China success story. Rumor has it that the Chinese were first attracted to Hewlett-Packard (H-P) when aides in Nixon's 1972 delegation were spotted using H-P calculators. Regardless, in 1980 Bill Packard sent a letter of intent to Deng Xiaoping and later that year, a joint venture agreement was signed with the China National Electronics Import-Export Corporation (CEIEC). H-P's joint venture was unique, however, in that it involved not manufacturing but marketing and distribution. H-P China jointly sold H-P products throughout China using staff recruited by the venture directly from universities and ministries. In 1985, in response to Chinese requests, H-P added a small manufacturing component, occupying 20 of the total 200 employees. Sales in 1986 were over $30 million and H-P officials expect to sextuple them by 1990.

The reasons for H-P's success lay in the balanced agreement it made with its Chinese partner, CEIEC. Hewlett-Packard sold instruments, a needed high technology product meeting a market demand. By making an equity deal it supplied the Chinese interest in investment. By pledging to localize operations and operating with a minimum of expatriate staff, it cut its own costs and helped its access to the China market. By giving top management attention to the venture it developed high-level *guanxi* in the bureaucracy. For their part, the Chinese established a joint marketing office allowing H-P market access and the volume it needed to develop scale for economical viability. By allowing employees to be directly trained by H-P in sales and marketing techniques they increased the venture's efficiency. By relaxing restrictions on hiring and incentives, the Chinese gave the venture essential management rights. The long and short of it is that the venture was economically viable.

Other foreign companies were not so successful. The first Western investors into China were the oil companies in 1978. The South China Sea was suspected of being the next Prudhoe Bay. The Chinese distinguished themselves in the negotiations as being tough if unsophisticated bargainers. Western companies willingly accepted stringent terms, even as, in a foreshadowing of the problems to come, some found Chinese objectives unrealistic and contradictory.[31] Even Bohai Oil's venture with the Japan China Oil Development Company, on the face of it a culturally compatible match, encountered both an unpredictable operating environment and a lack of foreign exchange. Further, the Japanese were perceived as unwilling to transfer technology. In the aerospace industry, Boeing had no investment content in its bid and lost out to McDonnell Douglas in a $1 billion contract. Xerox with few technology transfer contracts fell behind its Japanese competitors in sales. AMC did not recognize a foreign exchange constraint in its contract and developed contractual problems, ironed out only at the highest level. In all these cases, failure to develop a balanced agreement contributed to the difficulties.

The implications for strategy and implementation in addressing these risks affect both the Western parent and its Chinese subsidiary. China is essentially a village economy and ventures have to play local politics, hence the importance of a local office. An effective China office like that of Gould demonstrated commitment to end-users, built local relationships, and asked the right questions before making an investment. While ITT Belgium Bell chose to plunge directly into China with a Shanghai manufacturing venture hoping to supply to all of China potentially thousands of System 12 switches, Gould's low-key multiple partnership strategy took much less risk. Likewise, Mitsui had a three-stage China strategy going from compensation trade to technology transfer projects to eventually a joint venture, specifically linking risk to economic scale. In 1981, Mitsui began with an agreement installing Mitsui equipment in a textile mill. In 1985, Mitsui established a joint leasing venture with the Shanghai China National Technological Import Corporation. Both Mitsui and Gould are profitable while Shanghai Bell was still unable to balance its foreign exchange in 1987.

The head office has an equally important, if not more so, role in devising and implementing a balanced agreement. Top management has to be able to give China appropriate attention while allowing the local office the independence to make the right decisions for the company. For example, McDonnell Douglas used a "China hand" like Gareth Chang to negotiate and manage—his father used to lunch with Deng Xiaoping during the negotiations between Nationalists and Communists. The project is now officially part of the Seventh Five-year Plan. Helmut Kohl cut the ribbon at the opening of Shanghai Volkswagen. United Technologies regularly sent former Secretary of State Al Haig, Company Chairman Harry Gray and several other high ranking company officials and directors on "dog and pony" tours to China.

The cooperative agreement must also employ a phased strategy for entry and growth. The venture must develop a more substantial, independent role as more specialized management insights and capabilities are developed to deal with more difficult risks. Initially foreign investment consists of nothing more than an export sales office. The foreign company is mostly intent on developing *guanxi*, finding the market, and gaining access to it, while the Chinese seek technology. With the development of a limited sales and marketing operation, however, the enterprise must also begin to be concerned about the Chinese demand for investment, significant operating costs, and the issues of management rights and profit repatriation. Finally, the developed China business unit must deal fully with the issues of becoming a significant sourcing operation such as quality of work, overheads, and manufacturing excellence.

At the export sales stage, three different investment vehicles offer the investor differing capabilities to minimize risk. Operating through an outside-of-China subsidiary makes it difficult to develop *guanxi*, identify markets or gain access. Moreover, only companies selling specialized services are likely to make contact with the right Chinese buyer this way. A number of small oil service and petroleum related companies have found themselves sought out by Chinese organizations and invited to China. On the other hand, Domes, Inc., a manufacturer of modular structures, spent four years and almost went bankrupt trying to sell an unfamiliar product with few immediately apparent uses to China. Video Technology and numerous other small Hong Kong electronics makers went under in 1986 following Chinese foreign exchange cutbacks. Trading companies similarly offer mixed prospects of developing relationships and products must compete generally on price basis.[32] Trading companies do have the flexibility to arrange for significant countertrade deals, however, and offer the foreigner unable to deliver management attention a reasonable ability to locate buyers. Kanematsu-Gosho and Citicorp have reportedly been successful in arranging flexible countertrade and barter arrangements. To represent it, Apple Computer has hired ACI Kaihin, a trading company joint venture between Singapore investors and the Chinese government.

The registered representative office has been the vehicle of choice for most investors. The office develops *guanxi*, can generate market demand, and can use geographic scope to penetrate. IBM trained Chinese engineers from its Beijing office and worked within the Chinese educational system to generate end-user demand. A large resident sales force, such as most Japanese companies have, enabled them to share leads and contact many different ministries. The representative office has the added benefit of being a formally recognized part of the Chinese foreign economic relations infrastructure with a legal framework.

With more significant investment, options grow correspondingly more complex. Processing-and-assembly, compensatory trade, contractual joint venture, equity joint venture, or a wholly-owned Chinese subsidiary are all choices. The decision rests on the foreign company's objectives and desire for exposure. For example, the Swire Group is one company with a longer history of China trade than most. Founded by Scottish opium smugglers in the mid-1800s, in 1986 Swire already had a number of compensation trade agreements with China. The company believed that equity ventures were more trouble than they were worth for small, nontechnological ventures. Hence, it concentrated on contractual ventures and compensatory trade agreements where Swire did not have to negotiate for land and labor and hence was not subject to artificially high costs. Terms were limited to 3 to 7 year contracts to minimize exposure and products made in compensatory trade agreements were exclusively for export, thereby minimizing foreign exchange constraints. Others such as Mikuni, a Japanese auto parts maker, and Mitsui agreed, and further saw such arrangements as the "springboard for expanding" into China. Licensing agreements usually subsumed under the contractual venture heading, were also popular for those seeking small exposure and low technology risk. For example, Hitachi and Victor Company of Japan (JVC) used technology transfer agreements to build cheap supply bases while becoming insiders.[33]

In this brief look at some of the constraints and conflicts of joint ventures in China, the contrast between strategy and implementation is stark. The strategists have been less than successful in getting foreigners to invest largely because the success of the investment has been conditioned by reactions at the local level. Those who have become successful "insiders" by working at least partially with, not against, the interest groups, have succeeded in overcoming constraints and managing conflicts. The decision to reinvest and ultimately the success of the Opening in attracting foreign business appears to be driven at least equally from the top and the bottom of the Chinese economy.

NOTES

1. World Bank, *China: Economic Structure in International Perspective* (Washington D.C.: World Bank, 1985), p. 15; and Lawrence Lau (ed.), *Models of Development* (San Francisco: Institute of Contemporary Studies, 1986), pp. 45-46, 90-96
2. Quoting a Xerox manager in Beijing: "The biggest problem in China today is the lack of foreign exchange. Not only that, but foreign exchange controls are too restrictive. Even if the money is there, if it is not spent in such-and-such a way, and within such-and-such a time, it can't be paid out."
3. *China's Foreign Trade* (June 1986), p. 27.
4. Interview at Shanghai Ek-Chor, Shanghai, 12 July 1986.
5. Cited in *FEER* (26 March 1987), p. 53.

6. Ji Chongwei, "Foreign Investment in China," unpublished speech at Conference on Foreign Investment in China, Beijing (23-24 October 1986), pp. 13-15; interview with officials from the State Administration of Exchange Control, Beijing (28 June 1988).

7. *BR* (29 February 1987), p. 21.

8. *Communications Week* (30 September 1986), p. 53.

9. *Nihon Keizai Shimbun* (30 April 1985), p. 13.

10. See, in general, Lucian Pye, *Chinese Commercial Negotiating Behaviour* (Cambridge: Gunn, Oelgeschlager & Hain, 1983).

11. A Western computer executive comments: "Introducing technology to China is a tricky thing. By making an investment, the Chinese imply they will grant most favored vendor status. However, because Chinese expectations are generally unrealistic and they lack experience, rushing into a "state of the art" technology transfer agreement can do more harm than good. That's why we haven't concluded an agreement yet despite Chinese pressure."

12. Interview with the author, Shanghai, July 1986.

13. In one well-known example, the local Labor bureau dismissed the Chinese manager of a joint venture out of hand. The Western side protested and was effectively ignored until, after much outcry, the Chinese press picked up the issue, articles were published in *Renmin Ribao* and the manager was eventually returned.

14. *Zhongguo Faxue Bao* in JPRS-CEA (20 November 1985), pp. 70-77.

15. *BR* (25-31 January 1988), p. 8

16. The Beijing head of IBM commented on this: "A big difference between doing business in China and the West, is that usually somehow the various governmental ministries share similar policies and coordinate in the West. In China they do not."

17. Cited in FBIS (25 April 1986), pp. W6-10; FBIS (28 April 1986), pp. W2-5.

18. Interviews with the author, Shanghai, 13 July 1986.

19. *Joint Ventures in the People's Republic of China* (Hong Kong: Business International Asia/Pacific, 1985), pp. 203-204.

20. For example, at one time it reportedly cost Schindler as much to make mechanical elevators in China as in Switzerland.

21. One Chinese manager complained: "Company X is very disorganized. It has not been able to coordinate different components from subsidiaries all over the world for technology transfer. The bureau in charge should help solve problems instead of interfering with the joint venture's management issues. The Board of Directors has no authority over personnel and operational issues."

22. Only time will tell if McDonnell Douglas' production decision was still premature. Before the planes fly they must all pass FAA-certification tests.

23. Interview with the author, Beijing, 3 August 1985.

24. *China Daily* in JPRS-CEA (19 August 1985), pp. 81-82.

25. See Michael Moser, "Foreign Investment in China: The Legal Framework," in Michael Moser (ed.), *Foreign Trade, Investment and the Law* (London: Oxford University Press, 1984), p. 136.

26. In 1986, Richard Goswell, plant manager of Cable and Wireless' Shenda Telephone Company, believed in establishing a management system operat-

ing on the assumption that the Chinese would be Chinese regardless of an initial Western management presence in the venture. For example, Shenda put across the importance of maintenance by physically combining the installation and maintenance crews instead of continuing the traditional separation and resulting minimal maintenance.

27. Interview with the author, Shenzhen, 5 July 1986.
28. Interview with the author, Beijing, 25 July 1986.
29. Interview with the author, Beijing, 12 January 1986.
30. Interview with the author, Shanghai, 14 July 1986.
31. Technology transfer, for example, was a key part of many contracts. British Petroleum (BP) once contracted to use a DEC VAX computer to train the Chinese in its use as well as to coordinate operations from Guangzhou. Authority to import the computer was held up, however, by officals concerned by foreign exchange expenditures. As a result BP dropped its effort and ran computer support from Hong Kong, thereby losing the convenience benefit to itself as well as the technology transfer element so desired by China.
32. After Zhao Ziyang visited Siemens' headquarters in Germany, the company discontinued its long-time Hong Kong trading representation, claiming according to one manager: "The Chinese dislike intermediaries."
33. JVC has signed technological cooperation agreements with 17 color television factories—about half of China's color television plants. Its exports, mostly kits, tripled from 1984 to 1985. Hitachi has technological assistance contracts that return royalties on every home electric appliance the Chinese manufacture through the use of its technology.

Part III

Interpretation

6

Interest Groups and the Opening

As the experience of joint ventures has indicated, interest groups do exist in socialist China and they have significantly affected reform policies. The leadership has however, generally proved more powerful in the decade of the Opening since 1978. Its policies have disrupted the old industrial and geographic coalitions and encouraged the rise of a managerial presence in the workplace. The displaced elements in turn have had to evolve more effective organizations to deal with the continuing pressures of scarce resources and growing grassroots demand.

DEFINING THE INTEREST GROUPS

Interest groups in China differ considerably from those in the West. They operate through *guanxi*-based informal networks, small-scale, and largely without a legal system or even an ideological affiliation. The Opening to the Outside World has affected them differently as the various groups have dissimilar goals. According to one 1987 survey, while local cadres made the least demands on reforms and were primarily interested in social status, farmers were most willing to take risks for more money and students demanded the most in the way of political reform.[1] The following chapter seeks to sketch those groups that have interests expressly related to the Opening, thereby interpreting its politics.

The Bureaucrats

Historically, the key to increasing trade in China has been to cut back the bureaucratic monopolies. The *likin* tariff on interprovince commerce and the restrictive treaty-port system were two of the first items attacked by foreign traders after the Opium Wars. Over a century later, the foreign trade monopoly enjoyed by MOFERT, and its constituent bodies since the 1950s, was also recognized as a major constraint on trade. To quote Li Lanqing, vice minister of MOFERT in 1988: "The main problem lies, as in the other sectors of the economy, in the system of state monopoly in income and expenses."[2] MOFERT and its subsidiary foreign trade corporations were functional ministries reporting to the SPC, the highest authority for all trade plans. The SPC set overall targets by consultation with the various foreign trade corporations. These plans were vague except for a few national commodities such as oil, and were originally refined and carried out only by the FTCs of MOFERT. The FTCs were themselves huge bureaucracies, divorced from factory production. The largest CNMMIEC and SINOCHEM, imported $6.5 billion and $3.6 billion worth of goods in 1985, respectively.

To supplement the FTCs, in the early 1980s import export companies directly attached to the various Ministries were also created, such as the CEIEC attached to the Ministry of Electronics. Some of these corporations had already been in de facto existence previously, for example, China North Industries which primarily sold armaments. By allowing industrial ministries and provincial authorities to set up their own foreign trade corporations, as well as giving independent foreign exchange privileges to export-oriented factories, the reformers believed they would spur competition, raise productivity and achieve greater gains in trade. Administrative and management power would be decentralized to local economic and trade departments. Foreign trade enterprises would have greater autonomy in making decisions for daily operations, in setting up new units, and in the assignment of cadres.

MOFERT on the other hand had a very proprietary notion of what constituted a bonified foreign trade enterprise. To quote from one of its mid-1980s directives: "The separation of the functions of the government from those of enterprises does not mean that the administrative departments will not administer the enterprises. On the contrary, the administrative departments should strengthen their leadership and administration." MOFERT's supervision specifically targeted Guangdong and Fujian province FTCs, as well as those in the SEZs. Moreover, newly established FTCs were now required to export $5 million after three years of trading in an attempt to eliminate so-called "briefcase" trading companies operating with little more capital than a telephone and *guanxi*. Despite MOFERT's efforts, though, miscellaneous foreign trade enterprises continued to thrive in the provinces.[3] The reformers pointed to the slow growth of exports under MOFERT supervision. MOFERT pointed to price-cutting in Hong Kong markets and drops in the price of China's exports as evidence of unhealthy competition.

Local bureaucrats also had distinctly different interests from MOFERT. The Hainan Island 1984-85 scandal was one example of a local network in foreign trade. In 1984, Hainan, an historically underdeveloped tropical island in the South China Sea, was granted special privileges along with the Special Economic Zones to use foreign exchange to promote its economy.[4] Rather than importing according to the state plan and seeking approval from Guangdong provincial authorities, local party cadres and government officials began to import autos and other consumer durables on a large scale and resell them on the mainland. Although this was against the spirit if not the letter of the law, Hainan officials continued to run a thriving gray market after repeated warnings from Guangdong and Beijing officials. At one point, even the Chinese navy joined in the scheme, bidding for the rights to ferry autos between the island and the mainland. Finally in the summer of 1985, the Party cracked down and sent several leading Hainan cadres to jail and the others to demotions. They faced a difficulty in doing so, though, as the legitimate defense of the Hainan cadres was that they had only been doing their best to raise the Hainan economy. Significantly, the cadres were indicted on the charge of disobeying the warnings from the central authorities, not of actually committing economic crimes. Apparently in the eyes of the national bureaucracy, what was good for Hainan was good for the country, as long as they had the final say in it.

Industrially, ministerial bureaucrats differed on the benefits to be gained from trade. Many Western observers have perceived heavy industry and the inland provinces to have formed a coalition benefiting from the redistributive policies of the center in prereform days. Interior industry was mostly defense-oriented as in the 1960s China mapped out three major defense lines—frontier and coastal areas being the first line, an intermediate zone as the second, and inland provinces such as Sichuan, Hunan, Guizhou, Yunnan and Shaanxi provinces as the third.[5] In this Third Zone, an emphasis on defense led to over 30,000 enterprises of some 200 billion yuan investment. These enterprises were widely scattered, far from rail facilities and lacked raw materials and sales channels. They benefited, however, from governmental diversion of resources from light industry to "take steel as the key link." Likewise, the outlying regions of China such as Guangxi and Qinghai gained from the "eating from one big pot" policy.

It might be expected that local officials in the inland provinces and bureaucrats in the heavy industry ministries would oppose the Opening. Through a combination of pork and individual incentives, however, the old inland-heavy industry coalition appears to have been swayed. In fact in 1985, the Ministry of Machine Building Industry ranked number one in the number of contracts signed for importing technology and manufacturing equipment, of which technology licensing accounted for 75.4 percent. Technology expenses accounted for over 50 percent in the Ministry, as compared to 13 percent for all industries in China.[6] Lu Dong, formerly of the Ministry of Machine Building, provided energetic leadership for the State Economic Commission's reformist efforts since 1982. The outer provinces have been some of the most aggressive in seeking out foreign investment and export opportunities. Foreign joint ventures report many sales made and paid in foreign exchange to factories from Gansu to Xinjiang. Moreover, the central government has continued to subsidize the poorest provinces such as Tibet with public works projects.

Staffers, Managers and Entrepreneurs

In the workplace, the plan to increase efficiency through trade has shifted occupational responsibilities from planning staffers to line managers. As a senior manager at the export-oriented Fujian Electronic Computer Company said in 1985, "[The state plan for computer production] will gradually wither away. . . . Although this displeases the planners, they can do nothing about it."[7] Throughout China, over 10,000 small factory managers have been allowed to lease their plants from the state with their wages tied to its performance. Financial reforms directly linked to export strategy have improved the positions of bank managers. In Shanghai, the leader in financial reform, interbank lending has increased the circulation of funds to 5 to 6 times the normal rate.[8] The newly-opened Bank of Communications staff have given Bank of China planners unusual competition. Said one senior banking reform official: "Previously banks turned depositors away because accepting their money was too much trouble. Each bank had its own monopoly."[9]

In some cases, the reforms have also "created" a new entrepreneurial interest group. Created may not be appropriate as the thriving commercial communities of Hong Kong, Monterey Park (California) and Singapore are ample evidence of "spontaneous" Chinese entrepreneurial ability. The *getihu* or self-employed have sprung up in both urban and rural areas as peasant families sold surplus products at rural markets and peddlers hawked in the cities. Reportedly over 2,000 private enterprises operated in Shenyang alone in 1987 with a total registered capital of 50 million RMB. The largest of these, "model farmer" Liu Xigui's transport company, made a 1 million RMB profit in 1987 and reportedly planned to expand into fluorescent lights and automobile repair.[10]

The Wuxi Tape Recorder Factory was another example of an entrepreneurial enterprise directly linked to trade expansion.[11] Between 1980 and 1983, the plant grew at 53 percent annually and profits realized a total increase of 120 percent. Diversification has been achieved through an agreement with a firm in the Zhuhai Special Economic Zone for six new production lines producing a new range of products including color televisions, air conditioners and VCRs, in addition to the Wuxi plant's output of recorders. Wuxi workers will own shares in the new plant. Inside the plant, bonuses based on increased productivity have increased the average salary from 814 yuan in 1983 to 1100 yuan in 1984. With the benefit of these new revenues, the enterprise would now buy foreign equipment to further expand production.[12]

The opposition to this shift away from planners toward managers has centered among mid-level cadres and threatened interested parties. In one typical instance, Xia Renfan, a reform-minded manager of Shenyang's tram company, was sacked for allegedly taking his wife on a business trip and conferring favors on subordinates, after repeated investigations by the party's transportation bureau in 1985. Remarking on his case, a *Renmin Ribao* commentator said, "The reformers are depressed because they have long been placed in the position of being the accused and being investigated."[13] In another Shenyang case, at a factory leased to its director, over 40 workers sent a petition to the municipal government demanding that the lease be terminated. Though the enterprise had made 690,000 RMB more than the year before, some of the staff saw the director's salary of 59,400 RMB as excessive.[14] Said Guan Guangmei, one of the most widely praised of the leasing directors: "The attitude seems to be 'Guan Guangmei has more than enough money, why not fine her?'"[15]

The Ideologues and the Military

Perhaps the most powerful interest group opposed to change appeared to be the "Old Guard," or those revolutionary veterans who had fought for China's liberation in 1949 and now feared a return to all they succeeded in destroying. Because of their "revolutionary legitimacy" and the high degree of public respect they commanded, they were successful in publicly emphasizing issues they considered important such as the building of "spiritual civilization," the importance of collective rule, and warnings against income inequality and materialism. Further, in opposing the winter 1986 student "democracy" protest, Hu Qiaomu, Deng Liqun and others (all key figures of the 1983 "spiritual pollution" campaign) were quoted as attacking "spreading national nihilism and denigrating China and advocating all-round Westernization," somewhat reminiscent of the Grand Secretary Wo-jen. At the provincial level, moreover, many of these leaders have been entrenched for 30 or more years and had a considerable personal stake in seeing political reforms stall. Their opposition was not so much to the direction of change as to its speed. Given their preference, many may have looked back to the 1950s as the "golden age" of China's development along the centralized statist model.[16]

Their opposition to real reform was implied in the notice of the first Central Discipline Inspection Commission (CDIC) Plenum which acknowledged that previously "the Party did not fully understand the importance of discipline inspection nor support it sufficiently."[17] And as Richard Baum notes, the Party has had a tradition of disregarding constitution and laws when these get in the way.[18] The temporary arrest of, among others, the son of ideologue Hu Qiaomu for defrauding thousands in a fraudulent correspondence school for legal education, and the indictment of the daughter of former National People's Congress head Peng Zhen for economic crimes in the Shenzhen SEZ, demonstrate a move away from the "rule by example" the Old Guard typified. The Old Guard, however, fearful of a capitalist revanche, has remained a powerful interest group opposed to quick reform. In various attacks some have criticized the Special Economic Zones as hotbeds of bourgeois liberalism. Most have been opposed to the taking up of foreign loans. At the local level conservative party secretaries have sought to minimize foreign involvement and discourage investment by mandating limits to incentive schemes in joint ventures and appropriating trade revenue by taxes. More frequent in the cultural and political than the economic spheres, campaigns against "putting money above everything" and "humanism as a science" have remained common as attested by the banning of writer Bo Yang and the expulsion of dissidents Fang Lizhi and others.

Distinct but not entirely separate from the Old Guard is the military. The People's Liberation Army (PLA) had both ideological and economic concerns about the reforms. Its factories have been turned over to civilian production. Many of these faced the loss of established sources of funds, raw materials, sales outlets as well as severe cash flow problems.[19] The PLA itself will be cut in numbers from 4.5 million to 3 million by the 1990s. Military expenditures were already cut from 17.5 percent of the budget in 1985 to 10.5 percent in 1986.[20] While an effort has been made to have jobs waiting for the hundreds of thousands of politically aware soldiers, especially in infrastructure development, they must be a source of discontent for the reformers.[21]

To assuage the army, the leadership has modernized the PLA while it shrank. NORINCO, the trade arm of the defense industry became one of China's top 5 exporters in the early 1980s, exporting approximately $5 billion between 1980 and 1985, an amount equal to the previous total exported since 1960. The newer, smaller PLA has moved away from "millet and rifle" fighting to a more professional stance. It has, moreover, been resolutely separated from politics in the backlash against the legacy of the

Cultural Revolution. On balance, as Professor Ellis Joffe notes: "The new PLA is a strong supporter of a moderate programme of economic reform."[22] This support though may be conditioned on continued military exports.

The Intellectuals

Observers of Chinese politics have also encountered both a concern for "balance" within government and the need for a "rational" economic system, perhaps the one drawn from Soviet, the other from Western intellectuals. Neither group have seemed content with *ziqiang* or *ti/yong* formulas, especially in view of China's industrialization since 1949. The influence of Soviet ideas appeared to make itself felt in the functional and industrial bureaucratic organization, although the all-inclusive power of the *danwei* or factory unit reflected a more basic "feudal" authority. Susan Shirk put it well in commenting on the differences between the State Planning Commission (SPC) and the State Economic Commission (SEC): "The SPC has an organizational ideology in which the highest value is 'balance' [*pingheng*] in the economy."[23]

Meanwhile Western-influenced managers have generally pushed for more market freedoms as the solution to China's economic problems. Lao Yuanyi, the vice-president of China Venturetech, a new investment body established specifically to fund technology-based enterprises, studied at the Harvard Business School. Liu Shaoqi's daughter was another 1980s Harvard M.B.A. These *gaoganzidi* (children of high-ranking cadres) have been among the first to promote the trade reforms. They must also share the responsibility, however, for at least some of the corruption in the field. Property offenses and economic crimes rose at about a 30 percent annual rate from 1984 to 1987. Earlier, reportedly for the period from May 1980 to December 1981, the China National Electronic Import-Export Corporation's Shenzhen branch signed $95 million worth of contracts, of which only 4.5 percent were for electronic goods! Wojtek Zafanolli has perceptively commented that such "administrative discontinuities" were the products of the conflicts between market freedoms and a planned economy. Chinese leaders said similarly: "Some unhealthy tendencies and economic crimes were carried out under the auspices of reform."[24]

INTEREST GROUP COMPETITION

China's leadership has nonetheless been able to prevent these interest groups from uniting. Instead, the policy of Opening to the Outside World has disrupted the old coalitions and increased interest group competition by an order of magnitude. Interprovincial, intraprovincial, and interbureaucracy strife have been the hallmark of China's search for foreign capital.

Interprovincial Competition

The decentralization [*xiafang*] reforms implied that all enterprises previously under direct ministerial supervision would be placed under local administrative jurisdiction. At the same time the separation of government and enterprise reform changed the role of both the ministry and its local bureaus. Combined, these directives generated an intense interprovincial competition for foreign exchange and investment.

MOFERT officially began its reform with a document presented to the State Council on August 14, 1984. The Sixth Five-year Plan in 1982 still spoke of creating central authorities wherever conflicts between departments and region appeared. In contrast Vice-Premier Tian Jiyun said on October 24th 1984: "The most important process is to decentralize the management rights to the enterprises who are directly involved in production, construction and exchange.... There should not be a middle organization which is an economic entity in name, but in reality is not separated from government administration."[25] Previously the Ministry and local bureau exercised direct supervision over the "six elements of production—" people, finance, material, production, procurement and sales. Now they exercised only "guidance," characterized as macroplanning involving investment priorities. Local bureaus were only supposed to review and coordinate long-range plans. The elements of production were the enterprise's responsibility, and whereas the bureau previously had financial responsibility for the enterprises, it no longer would.

Where these reforms were actually implemented, the national bureaucracy, however, found itself unable to control the progress of the Opening. If controls remained located in Beijing, the rewards of trade were difficult to realize as their overzealous application encouraged the restriction of imports instead of the growth of trade.[26] However, when controls were decentralized to the provinces because the foreign exchange rewards of exporting proved compelling, state control organs such as the export-licensing department of MOFERT found themselves undermanned with the flood of factories rushing to market. The old way of licensing and foreign exchange control appeared to have worked, though imperfectly, only as long as centralized control existed.

For example, the textile trade was China's top export earner accounting for approximately $6.5 billion or 25 percent of total exports in 1986. In 1987 with the transferring of license allocation to the provinces, by midyear foreign traders believed China had used up its entire yearly quota. The European Commission suspended certain imports to France of Chinese-origin textile products and one major U.S. exporter warned "a good number more [of textile quotas], if not all, will be closed by May or June."[27] MOFERT officials laid the deterioration in foreign trade management to confusion over quota allocation authority between the administrative side of MOFERT and the FTCs, the sharp recovery of the European textile market, and laxity by provincial authorities in monitoring quota levels. MOFERT officials also complained that the flood of exports by provinces eager to increase their retained share of foreign exchange had resulted in a drop in the world price of many items not only in textiles. In particular, they were sensitive to border trading between Guangdong province and Hong Kong in agricultural products. To resolve the issue, MOFERT called a national conference for mid-1987 with provincial authorities, and recentralized controls on several commodities such as bulk steel. One senior official commented that decentralized textile controls would continue however, because the major task of the textile industry was to become more responsive to world fashion trends, thereby increasing the overall volume of exports by moving more quickly into new categories without quotas. Bulk steel, on the other hand, is a business with more national economies of scale and the major consumer is domestic industry (whose demand is very high) making it more appropriate to control centrally.[28]

As might be expected, as the national bureaucracy decentralized, interprovincial competition heated up. Under the old bureaucratic redistributive mechanism, backward inland provinces such as Tibet and Guizhou shared in the wealth of the more highly industrialized coastal provinces. With the Opening, unlike the coastal factories, most isolated ill-equipped inland enterprises could not take advantage of the world market. As domestic and international trade increased, they found the protectionist barriers they had constructed were weakening. These barriers ranging from constricted distribution to direct producer subsidies ran counter to the reform policy of horizontal linkages and separation of government and trade. In Tibet, ten years after the announcement of the Opening to the Outside World policy, Doje Cering, acting chair of the regional government, noted the pervasiveness of the old mentality at a foreign trade conference: "This meeting must first tackle the issue of eliminating leftism. It is impossible to open up to the world and make a success of foreign economic relations and trade work without totally eliminating leftist ideological influence."[29] As Shanghai, Tianjin, Shenyang, Guangzhou and China's other major metropolises retained more of their own income, these other provinces found they had to be more flexible and entrepreneurial in acquiring funds. Dorothy Solinger analyzed a similar question as she looked at the impact of the industrial readjustment on individual factories in Wuhan from 1979 to 1982. She found that in China as in the West, industrial policy was inherently redistributive and that affected interests did seek to secure their own best interests. The competition was tempered however, by a general willingness to accept elite decisions on economic matters.[30]

The lure of tourism also sparked intercity competition, as between Chongqing and Chengdu in Sichuan where both vied to be the major transportation center in China's southwest. The stakes there were high as visitors to the province increased at 33 percent per year and Chongqing signed 179 contracts for $140 million to import foreign technology in 1985. Chongqing officials said that bureaucratic competition from Chengdu could stall the building of their new airport because CAAC's Chengdu-based southwest division had asked Beijing to upgrade the Chengdu airport.[31] Even in Shanghai, port authorities complained they were caught in a cash bind. Faced with increasing competition, rising costs, an old and inefficient plant, and a bad reputation, officials said they were unable to independently finance needed capital for improvements. Ironically, the port chose to put its appeal as one in the common interest of all the areas of the Yangzi River Valley, leaving Beijing to decide whether an enterprise firmly located in Shanghai could still be given preferential treatment because of its economic importance to the underdeveloped, inland areas.[32]

Enterprises versus Bureaus

As enterprises began to form networks to produce and export, the national foreign trade bureaucracies also found their traditional coordinating function coming under attack. The enterprises were often more profitable and more responsive than the national bureaucracies. The inability of bureaucracies to remain competitive was reflected in local enterprises' tendency to form joint ventures and trading relationships independently. The Guangdong branch of the Ministry of Electronics had only one joint venture (JV) to its credit in 1986, and that one was very troubled. Ministry officials said they stayed out of the JV's management because they had more experience in processing and assembly, not production.

CAAC, the national airline, after many years of debate, was gradually decentralized and sanctioned independent mini airlines formed.[33] Even before the breakup, "mavericks" such as China United Airlines appeared. Formed by the Air Force in 1985, China United used military planes landing at military airstrips. Said Hong Wenkui, deputy general director, in 1986: "China's transport needs are huge and the future is ours."[34]

In another example, Rising Sun Services of Guangzhou was one of China's first private foreign trade enterprises, providing travel and business services to mostly Hong Kong Chinese. Located on a lower floor of the New China Hotel's office block just behind the elevator, its office had no carpet, air conditioning, or much furniture for that matter, a far cry from the plush quarters favored by the Western companies around the corner. A former foreign trade official in 1984, President Wu Xiulin said he paid higher salaries than the FTCs to lure their personnel and prided himself on a quicker turnaround time to his customers. He did not, however, expect many other private trade enterprises to follow in his footsteps in the light of his perception of MOFERT's displeasure. That reaction began in early 1986 when MOFERT issued a set of regulations on the overhaul and rectification of foreign trade companies.[35] According to the MOFERT regulations, all companies must be officially approved by MOFERT and only provincial companies and higher organs can carry out foreign trade. Companies in the coastal open cities and SEZs could not trade for other areas and only state enterprises could carry out foreign trade.

As the bureaucracies lost monopolistic control in some areas, inequities in exchange power appeared. Simply put, some got rich faster than others as Deng Xiaoping observed many times. In many cases this was a progressive sign of good management bearing fruit. However, it disturbed the long-held Maoist legacy of spatially egalitarian distribution of exchange power.[36] The Ministry of Machine Building, for example, was successful by 1986 in attracting $190 million of foreign investment, which represented 15 percent of the ministry's allocated foreign exchange. The benefits of attracting investment were reflected in the difference between the average production value of 10,000 yuan per man-year in domestic enterprises and 25,000 yuan per man-year in joint ventures. Shanghai Foxboro reportedly achieved 60,000 yuan.[37] Often in a resource-scarce environment, however, a rapid gain by one province had to be at the expense of another. Tianjin received $220 million in foreign investment from 1979 to 1985. The 31 joint ventures in operation six months or longer had an average return on sales of 23 percent—27 of the 31 were profitable, 28 were exporters, and in 1984 the 31 ventures collectively generated a net $1.13 million of foreign exchange profit.[38] By contrast, inland Hunan received only $6.8 million in foreign investment by 1985, Hubei $6.4 million. There was only so much foreign investment to go around. Urban areas also benefited more than rural from the Opening. The 8 cities with more than 2 million in population accounted for 13 percent of the total population but 35 percent of exports, while the 81 cities with populations between 200,000 and 500,000 had 38 percent of the national population and only 9 percent of its exports.[39]

With the upsetting of the spatial economic applecart, an unhealthy tendency appeared perpetuating bureaucratic oligopoly and aggravating inequities.[40] Faced with threat of obsolescence, the existing state bureaucracy in some cases refused to passively fade away, the lure of foreign exchange encouraging it to ally with newly rich enterprises.[41] Numerous cases of foreign exchange speculation in state-owned units were reported nation-wide, especially in Guangdong, Sichuan, and Shandong provinces.[42] Many units attempted to overstep their authority and misspend public funds. In 1985, the Aerospace Ministry's Guangyu Company attempted to smuggle in 180,000 color TV sets, and one agricultural enterprise under the Ministry of Agriculture bought on the black market $55 million of foreign currencies, 700 automobiles, 4,600 tons of steel, and 2,000 color TV sets. Counterfeiting was widespread with blatant local government collusion. Bogus Shanghai-made cigarettes were found as far away as the Da Qing Oilfield, Hainan Island, Urumqi and Tibet. More than 2.5 million bogus wrist-watches with brand names were sold in over 20 provinces and cities, according to one investigation.[43] Among the more serious incidents prosecuted in 1986, in Heilongjiang 29 party members swindled state property; in Liaoning province 18 party cadres from state commercial and industrial organizations and the State Security Bureau were jailed for fraud; and on Hainan Island the director and deputy director of the Chanjiang Credit Bank were arrested for currency violations, illegal loans and accepting bribes.[44]

Intra-Bureaucracy Competition

With these new opportunities for gain, intra-bureaucracy strife also intensified the scramble for profits. Ministerial turf fights grew in key foreign exchange earning industries such as oil and textiles. Further, the national foreign trade bureaucracy was thrown into a state of confusion with authority unclear between administrative offices and trading branches. The bureaucracy faced an internal crisis as traditional authority relationships changed and responsibilities were redistributed.

The nonferrous metals trade was one industry which typified the bureaucratic uproar. In the past, the China National Metals and Minerals Import and Export Corporation (Minmetals), an FTC established in the 1950s with 1985 sales of $7.5 billion, controlled the entire nonferrous metals trade. But in 1979 with Dengist reforms, Minmetals lost the coal trade to the Ministry of Coal. Worse, the China National Nonferrous Metals Industry Corporation (CNNMIC) was formed in 1983 out of the Ministry of Metallurgical Industry. Now CNNMIC and Minmetals were to compete for business from nonmetals producers nationwide. This in turn led to complaints of over-eager provincial branches overstepping their authority or failing to deliver on contractual responsibilities. Price cutting ensued as there was no monopoly on either trade or production, exacerbated by the bureaucratic conflict. One Hong Kong trader noted: "There used to be one man in China buying and selling metals. Now there are a hundred. There used to be one price for Chinese tin. Now there can be a difference of 20 percent between different exporters."[45]

The issue of bureaucratic competition extended to the foreign trade sector. For example, in Guangzhou MOFERT and the SEC had overlapping responsibility for joint ventures. At MOFERT the planning section conducted feasibility studies and initiated projects. The "professional work" section reviewed and decided on JV contracts. The JV section coordinated JVs and control agencies such as the tax and import-export bureaus. The JV service section provided consulting and import export services to JVs. The SEC meanwhile had 18 bureaus overlooking 4,000 factories, and several sections dealing with specific tasks, one of which was the foreign economic section. This section coordinated between JVs and local administrative bureaus such as Material and Supply, and Labor. Thus, when a foreign venture had a problem with unreasonable fees for energy provided by a local utility under the planning commission, it found that by the rules it was supposed to work with MOFERT, the SEC and the Mayor's office to solve the problem.[46]

Sometimes these bureaucratic conflicts could be resolved by direct intervention by high-level officials. For example, for eight years Minmetals and the China Machinery Equipment Corporation (CMEC), a branch of the Ministry of Machine Building, competed to export nuts, screws and bolts, a $100 million market. Finally in 1987, both agreed to set up a "joint directing body" to work out a reasonable price for exports and to cooperate in export-production. Minmetals was spurred to the agreement because even though it dominated the market with an 80 percent share, CMEC competition forced it to cut its price by 20 percent to $500 per ton in 1986, suffering a loss of $10 million in the process. CMEC for its part was happy to gain access to Minmetals overseas distribution relationships, especially a venture with KI-KI of Britain which was scheduled to make purchases of $30 million over two years.[47]

However, when the conflicts dragged on as they usually did due to a shortage of high-level officials, bureaucracy degenerated into factionalism based on *guanxi*. Though joint ventures were willing to buy large amounts of coal from China, because different ministries with different networks were involved, most were unable to turn that into a buying credit for their foreign exchange needs. Moreover, some felt that the high expense of maintaining a selling group in China was not reciprocated with some sort of foreign exchange credit, even though they had established a trade commission with representatives of the SEC, SPC and other bodies.[48] One European venture in Shanghai encountered similar factional problems at a local level. Originally, the foreign management tried to internally control personnel and marketing policy. Now the general manager says they can't change much in management and the foreign managers do not have effective roles. The Chinese are quite capable of getting things done in their own way and time, and contractors do not report to the JV but to the Shanghai industrial "department-in-charge" of the venture.[49]

MOFERT itself has been victimized by factionalism arising from bureaucratic conflicts.[50] With rising foreign exchange expenditures for modernization, the subsidized FTC's efficiency did not keep pace and reserves continued to decline. When reformers proposed removing the subsidies to encourage greater efficiency, the FTCs protested that not only would they possibly lose money but also that the traditional career paths of FTC bureaucrats would be removed. Once independent, the FTCs would lose ministerial status and could face problems coordinating with the industrial ministries responsible for production. Access to Party documents could be restricted to them. As a result of these objections, foreign trade reform was stalled since 1984 and some officials did not expect progress until 1988 at the earliest.

Party Workstyle

At first glance, the Opening also appeared to have seriously damaged Party workstyle. In Guangdong province, the government faced problems of party cadres doing business, arbitraging foreign exchange, reselling cars, accepting money, arbitrarily imposing fees, issuing money and goods without authorization, and more recently appropriating land for private houses.[51] The leadership protested that these cadres were paying attention only to their narrow factional interests. In the long run, these practices encouraged economic stratification and the degeneration of the workers' state as smuggling and fraud disrupted the national economy in favor of factional cliques. As the higher levels of government continued to push for improved performance, the Party appeared to be finding its workstyle unsuited to respond.

Why so? During and after the revolution of 1949, internal party life had focused on the study of socialist texts. With the Opening, however, rampant personnel union resulted in what was denounced as economic crimes. Now that the party was being removed from administration, many entrenched cadres faced the possibility of losing official perquisites. This was especially galling as all could see the new possibility of wealth brought by the Opening. Ironically because the party had become so closely identified with the power structure, party recruitment efforts also suffered as some of the younger generation originally attracted by the material benefits of membership possibly came to see trade as a surer route to success. To quote Deng Liqun: "There are certain advanced elements who are actually not party members, also disinclined to join the party; some of them are children of cadres. . . . A major reason for it is the weakening of the party's ideological and political work."[52] Party organizations appeared to grope for relevance as traditional ideological appeals were vitiated by official promotion of careerism and modernization.

INTEREST GROUP ADAPTATION

With competition, more effective organizational forms have evolved during the Opening. These enterprises shared a key characteristic: an entrepreneurial ability to link Chinese conditions to domestic and foreign market needs. Their emergence could be best seen in the area where resource and demand pressures were greatest, that of finance and foreign exchange.

Foreign Exchange Regulation

Reform of trade management was and is integrally linked to foreign exchange reforms as the sources of all foreign exchange were either exports and invisible items or foreign loans and investments. As Chart 3 vastly oversimplifies, of all foreign exchange receipts, most localities were generally allowed to retain approximately 20 percent in 1986, 80 percent going to the central government which in turn banked it in the People's Bank. The percentage varied by type of export. For example, for petroleum exports, the locality handling the transaction, if involved, might retain about 3 percent of the receipts, whereas the percentage might be closer to 50 percent for electrical equipment. As late as 1984, Shanghai turned over 90 percent of its profits from both domestic and export earnings to the central government, but in 1986 it supposedly retained between 20 and 25 percent.[53] Central government foreign exchange was then disbursed first to the major FTCs and the remainder in the Import Plan to the localities. In theory the FTCs handled only products that were defined as "national priorities." The definition, as all Chinese definitions, was flexible. The Import Plan in turn was divided into mandatory and guidance plans. According to the plans, enterprises applied to local planning and provincial commissions for the foreign exchange to import at a set ratio. Officially the rate was close to 4 RMB to 1 yuan of foreign exchange in the summer of 1986. Unofficially, the rate in some areas of Guangdong went as high as 10 RMB according to Western companies.[54] These commissions also had a dollar limit on individual purchases before MOFERT needed to issue an import license. Import licenses were also needed for a variety of goods regardless of the volume ordered, e.g., computers, autos, televisions. MOFERT generally issued licenses if the imports could be justified as serving to promote exports in the future.

CHART 3
Foreign Exchange Circulation in China, 1986

☐ Key decision makers in foreign exchange circulation

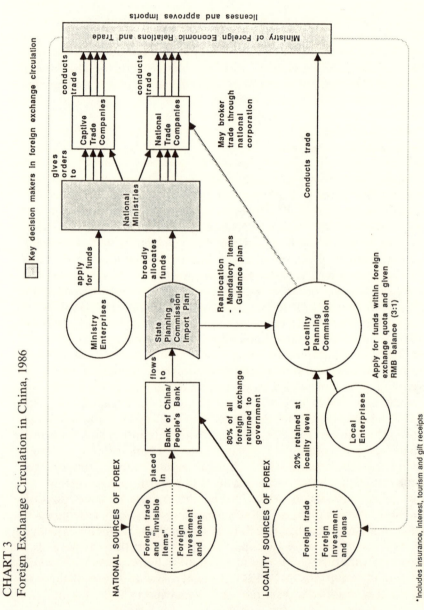

*Includes insurance, interest, tourism and gift receipts

Source: Interviews

One of the initial foreign exchange reforms was to allow lower levels of organization to retain more exchange. Beginning in 1978, provinces and then counties retained foreign exchange to give them an incentive to export. In Guangdong province, the spearhead of the Opening to the Outside World, some counties had net surpluses of foreign exchange. Individual enterprises, specially designated as export-oriented, acquired greater trading powers. Examples included the China Silk Company, Anshan Iron and Steel Company, Guangzhou Silk Company, Qingdao Textile Company, Yanshan Foreign Trade Company, and Guangda Company. These enterprises were distinctive in that they were either in industries where China had a long-standing competitive advantage internationally (e.g., textiles) or were import-substitute enterprises with substantial state investment already committed.

These enterprises and other unscrupulous individuals, however, did not hesitate to take advantage of the discrepancy between China's real and official exchange rate when possible. For example, the Liaoning Province Grain, Oil and Food Import-Export Corp., and the Shenzhen City Commerce and Trade Company, jointly known as Liaoshen Trading Company, contracted in 1985 to sell grain at a price of 3.40 yuan to the dollar to a Hong Kong company. The foreign exchange receipts from the foreign firm, however, were sold at a rate of 5.15 yuan to the dollar. The profits were then jointly divided among Liaoning, Shenzhen and the general plant producing the grain. Likewise, in the first nine months of 1986, it was discovered that over 500 enterprises had defrauded the central government of $1.7 billion in taxes, an increase of $608 million over the same period in 1985. Others, unable or unwilling to do so and compelled to export by state plan, found export prices insufficient to offset the inflexible domestic cost of materials and continuous RMB devaluations ironically undertaken to cut import levels. Thus, as Chart 4 shows, the Bank of China found itself liable for trade deficits in the billions incurred by the too slow growth of exports. The subsidies were complemented by the use of an Internal Settlement Rate (ISR) which allowed foreign trade enterprises to exchange foreign exchange at a higher rate with the state than the prevaling official rate. The ISR was, however, abolished in 1985 as the official exchange rate devalued beyond it.[55]

In turn, losses sparked a reemphasis of central control and export-orientation for factories with foreign exchange. MOFERT regulations issued on April 29, 1985, ordered provincial Foreign Economic Relations and Trade Commissions to "supervise local foreign trade enterprises in striving to improve management, strengthen financial and auditing work, and improve economic results." MOFERT also recentralized control of a number of bulk imports and exports, in particular steel and agricultural products, and enforced fixed quotas on agricultural products and textiles shipped to Hong Kong.[56]

CHART 4
Net Income of State, Non-Industrial Enterprises vs. Export Growth, 1978-1984
(RMB Billion; percent change)

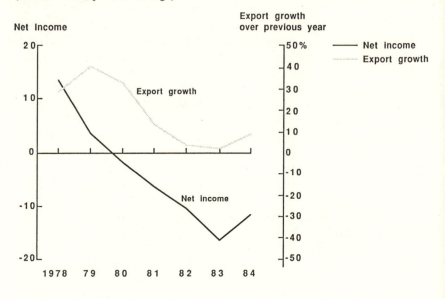

Source: SYC (1985); ACFERT (1986)

Slow export growth was aggravated by an import boom, partial blame for which could be placed on the rash decentralization of foreign exchange as well as the extension of efficiency mechanisms in the area of financial reform without corresponding pricing reforms. In 1984, credit controls were dramatically loosened. Loans expanded from 343 billion RMB in 1983 to 591 billion RMB in 1985, a net gain of 72 percent.[57] Simultaneously, local enterprises became independent accounting units able to take loans out and be responsible for their own profits and losses. This further coincided with the introduction of the trade agency system which allowed enterprises to import goods directly.[58] However, without trained personnel, too many loans were made to unreliable enterprises to import goods. Some of these enterprises took advantage of fixed higher domestic resale prices to make large profits, most notably in cars. Between January of 1984 and March of 1985, enterprises from newspapers to schools on Hainan Island spent a total of $570 million in foreign exchange to import and resell approximately 89,000 cars and vans, more than China's total planned auto imports for all of 1984.[59] Others just imported to keep up with the construction boom sparked by the release of credit. Cumulatively, imports went through the roof—rising 28 percent in 1984 and 55 percent in 1985—resulting in a $12 billion deficit in 1985.

The agricultural pesticide industry was a good example of the problems of coordinating economic reforms. The chemical industry, a late bloomer in China, by 1982 was structurally weak with mostly outdated equipment and 90 percent of its 680 factories producing less than 606 tons of gross output annually. With the 1979 to 1982 "rationalization" push, many of these factories shut down their small-scale production lines and production began to decline from 533 thousand tons in 1980 to 457 thousand tons in 1982. As production declined, however, the introduction of the responsibility system in agriculture spurred demand in the countryside and market pressure rose. With foreign exchange decentralization in 1983–84, peasants took advantage of the new source of supply to send pesticide imports skyrocketing from U.S. $99 million in 1983 to $281 million in 1984. The state foreign trade corporation, however, could not pass on the high cost of imported pesticides to the local market because of fixed domestic prices and as a result it and the Ministry of Commerce began absorbing large losses. Finally in 1984, the government removed the subsidy to farmers to buy pesticides and reduced the role of the Ministry of Commerce in pesticide sales. Prices shot up from 1423 RMB per ton in 1980 to 3934 RMB in 1985. Imports dropped from 20 percent of total use to 8 percent in 1985, as the peasants began to feel an almost ninefold price differential between imports and local production. The chemical industry was still in perilous shape, however, as production bottomed out at 211 thousand tons in 1985. Pretax return on sales was 2.7 percent, return on assets an anemic 7.4 percent. Fortunately, production began to rise again slightly in 1986, reflecting increased central investment. Ciba-Geigy, moreover, began to negotiate the first joint venture in the industry for a herbicide plant in Jilin. The painful surgery of distribution reform appeared to be mostly over and the patient still lived.

One lesson from the foreign exchange decentralization seemed to be that the feudal legacies of a self-reliant economy and unskilled personnel could not be overcome in a day. However and significantly, the trade deficits not only did not cause the cancellation of any previous policies but also brought progressive new policies focusing on the increased use of export-processing zones, credit reform, experiments in local foreign exchange markets to dampen speculation, and a cautious price reform.[60] Senior officials in an interview with the author in 1986 also continued to intimate that MOFERT had to be shaken up because of its inefficient handling of exports. Price reform appeared to be the slowest of the reforms, due to the sensitivity of the government to inflation, especially for domestic essentials. The policy for 1987 appeared to be to allow prices to fluctuate on those goods already under market regulation but to hold steady the total quantity of goods available on the open market. Foreign trade enterprises were encouraged to set up overseas subsidiaries.[61] In short, reform not retrenchment appeared to be the order of the day.[62]

Exports and Foreign Investment

As the issue of foreign exchange has illustrated, financial resources are scarce in China's modernization effort. Organizing for maximum utilization has been a major reform challenge at both the national and local level. As a People's Bank official said in 1986: "China's banking system had its Big Bang two years ago. Some complain that it was like a nuclear explosion and now we are suffering from fallout." The lack of trained personnel in provincial branches, a bureaucratic workstyle and contradictions between planned and market mechanisms have been among the factors that hindered the progress of improving organization.[63] For example, in 1987, the Ministry of Finance made one of its goals cutting administrative expenses 10 percent from the previous year's level. However, regional offices already pushed up spending by 11.6 percent in the first quarter of the year. One official from the Ministry bravely said in May: "The goal must be achieved. Even if an office has the money, it is not allowed to spend beyond the budget."[64]

On the up side, grassroots financial pressures have encouraged both local and national organizations to be entrepreneurial. For instance, after the proclamation of the Provisions for the Encouragement of Foreign Investment in October 1986, a number of state and local governments came out with their own implementing rules.[65] Inland provinces in particular made a concerted effort to attract foreign investment. Shenzhen and Zhuhai SEZs maintained their favorable investment climate with land use rates of RMB 1 to 1.6 and RMB 0.5 to 1.0 per square meter, respectively, as compared to Shanghai's RMB 2.5, and Shandong, Liaoning, and Ningbo's standard range of RMB 5 to 20. However, remote Yunnan also compared favorably with a RMB 1.5 rate. Hunan's regulations promised a 20 to 30 percent discount on labor service fees "compared with coastal areas." Hunan's 5-to 10-year local income tax exemption for foreign investment enterprises also bettered Shanghai's three year exemption and Tianjin's two year exemption.

Among the major national-level beneficiaries, the Bank of China (BoC) was favored. The 74-year-old BoC was China's foreign exchange bank. In the six years from 1978 to 1984, the BoC's assets increased from 38.7 billion yuan to 200.3 billion yuan, its domestic branches increased from 58 to 261, and its staff and workers from 4,000 to 16,000. At the end of 1984, its overseas agencies numbered 1,185 banks with 3,301 main and branch establishments in 150 countries and territories.[66] As China's need for capital to finance necessary imports and mammoth infrastructural development projects continues unabated well into the 20th century, the grassroots financial pressure for capital growth and circulation would appear to favor the BoC's expansion.[67]

Other new financial organizations have included experiments in stock, bond and foreign exchange markets under way in Shanghai, Shenyang and Shenzhen Special Economic Zone in 1985 and 1986. Also of interest, in late 1986 the Bank of Communications, China's first "genuine" commercial bank, opened in Shanghai. Western bankers commented favorably, noting that if China did not develop its own powerful financial institutions, foreign banks would inevitably dominate the market as they did prior to 1949, possible leading to a backlash.[68] The various provincial International Trust and Investment Corporations (ITICs) most notably from Shanghai, Fujian, Guangdong and Beijing, began to enter international markets. A visit by a delegation from the New York Stock Exchange in mid-November 1986 headed by Chairman John Phelan brought an agreement to train Chinese economists in New York on the finer points of trading. The four Special Economic Zones also bore mentioning as potential international players. Xiamen SEZ established the first joint venture bank in 1984. In the fall of 1985 after enjoying prolonged official support, however, the SEZs were criticized by a number of officials for their "unhealthy tendencies"—notably, foreign exchange black markets, and the failure to develop an export-oriented economy. Since that time, Shenzhen has retrenched but the SEZs no longer appeared to be the bedrock of the Opening to the Outside World.[69]

Perhaps the most successful of financial organizations, though, was China International Trust and Investment Corporation (CITIC), a $2.2 billion corporation in assets, seven years after its founding in 1980. Among its projects, it owned the most prestigious office building in Beijing, a smelter in Australia, and timber mills in the U.S. Through its Poly Technologies subsidiary it traded arms and in January 1987 it bought 12.5 percent of Cathay Pacific Airlines for nearly $250 million.[70] Both CITIC and the BoC expanded activities in Hong Kong. CITIC acquired the ailing Ka Wah bank in 1987. The BoC consolidated the operations of its seven member banks in Hong Kong and waged an aggressive campaign to capture more of Hong Kong's mass consumer market. In 1986, total deposits jumped 51 percent to reach HK $102 billion or about 18 percent of the market.[71] Provincial entities were restricted from international borrowings, by and large, although Fujian and Shanghai made offerings in the yen markets. This would undoubtedly change as they acquired more financial acumen and as their need for funds continued to mount.

With increased size, both BoC and CITIC faced new organizational issues. CITIC chose to face these head-on, by attempting to adopt a flexible organizational structure. In the last reorganization in 1986, CITIC was composed of several corporate groups with subsidiaries accountable for their own profits. BoC, on the other hand, did not move to make substantive changes in its organization despite the vastly different competitive environment it now faced.[72] Its consolidation in Hong Kong was reportedly prompted only by the embarrassing discovery that a number of its member banks, unknown to each other, had made loans to the now-defunct Carrian group. The bank also announced that, unlike CITIC, it was acutely short of funds to provide loans to joint ventures, a possible sign of bureaucratic strain.[73] In the long run, the flexible and organizationally effective CITIC appeared to be a far better advertisement for Chinese policy-makers than the slightly ossified BoC.

As CITIC has done at the national level, returning overseas Chinese have also introduced organizational innovations at the grass roots. For example, K.S. Chung, founder of Chung Cheong group—a $100 million trading company based in Thailand—fled China in 1949 with the Nationalists and most of his 13 children.[74] His oldest son Charlie and several other relatives stayed on, however. In time, K.S. built a conglomerate trading everything from tobacco to software worldwide with factories on three continents. Eventually in 1978, after several years of lobbying, K.S. succeeded in securing exit visas for his relatives in China. They in turn began to trade on their extensive personal networks in China to sell Chung Cheong products in China and distribute Chinese products internationally. Chung Cheong's Thai tobacco is now sold through Beijing to North Korea. Watches, Chung Cheong's second largest source of revenue, are made in a joint venture with Shanghai's two largest plants. China supplies a third of Chung Cheong's computer sales with major customers such as the Industrial and Commercial Bank of China. The Chungs also distribute Shanghai Silk Corporation textiles, have a taxi joint venture in Guangdong, and grow tobacco on Hainan Island.

These Cantonese traders, along with the Shanghainese financiers and Wenzhou peddlers all formed local networks that in bypassing the bureaucracy facilitated commerce and served the economy. In fact, in the long-run, such enterprises, Chinese and foreign alike, appeared to be the true beneficiaries of the foreign trade reforms.

Take for example, the Kaili telephone factory in Guizhou province.[75] For Kaili, the reality of decentralization [xiafang] was having the national ministries take those factories they wanted and handing the rest over to the provinces. Kaili, formerly under the Ministry of Posts and Telecommunications (MPT), however, found itself lacking both management resources and an export license. Moreover, the major customer for its 1500 workers had heretofore been the army (over 50 percent of sales). Sales to the army were still regulated by the MPT, which could be expected to favor its own factories in the future. Thus forced by circumstance to seek new markets, Kaili affiliated with CEIEC to develop export sales. Kaili saw CEIEC as the most knowledgeable of the import-export corporations or FTCs. CEIEC in turn was glad to take Kaili's business because it received a commission on all foreign exchange sales. CEIEC saw the competition in this case being the local Guangdong Foreign Trade Commission. They, however, were confident of keeping Kaili's business because of superior contacts and lengthier experience in foreign trade. However, both Kaili and CEIEC officials noted, the one anticipating and the other somewhat reluctantly, that as time went by Kaili would undoubtedly do more of its deals directly with Western companies.

As Kaili attests, those enterprises that achieved economies of scale and real business systems encompassing all stages of production from raw materials sourcing to trade and distribution had more potential to become profitable in China's uncertain environment. The most successful joint ventures in China were the ones with control of their own sourcing and selling mechanisms. Likewise, those few factories fortunate enough to be able to export directly had a great advantage over ordinary Chinese enterprises in that they had the freedom and the information needed to make essential resource-allocation decisions at the plant level. Thus they avoided the problems of bureaucratism and politics at the bureau level. It would be a mistake to understand by this, however, that "decentralized" enterprises uniformly benefited from the Opening. Decentralization, ignorant of economies of scale, was only a retreat to China's village economy. Modernization could not happen in a capital-intensive industry when financial resources were divided among tens of thousands of factories. For example, both Chinese and foreign executives have stated that decentralization has never really occurred in the industrial segments of the electronics industry.[76]

In a labor-intensive field such as textiles and handicrafts, however, decentralized enterprises have scored remarkable gains. For example, one provincial foreign trade enterprise, Fujian Province's Minhou County Foreign Trade Corporation reportedly achieved annual sales of 12.7 million yuan, and in the first six months of 1984, profits turned over to the state reached 76,800 yuan, a 14 percent increase over the same period in 1983. This rapid growth was made possible by instituting bonuses based on performance, cutting costs in service charges and most importantly by developing better links with its producing factories and foreign distributors. Special quality inspectors were sent to 13 leather factories resulting in a cost savings of 7,000 yuan. By encouraging rattan factories to broaden their product mix, over 1,000 new bamboo and rattan woven works were developed in 1984. Of these, 100 new products were sold in the United States and Australia for a total of 700,000 yuan. Finally, by paying attention to international competition, Minhou effectively cut prices in leather goods at the Guangzhou Trade Fair, thereby securing 3.2 million yuan worth of business or 65 percent of the county's total volume of business in certain leather goods.[77]

The existing national trade bureaucracy, like the BoC, has been too unwieldy to achieve these entrepreneurial skills. Instead it appears most likely that the entire edifice will be dismantled once again in the next few years and the FTCs revamped to link more closely with producers and domestic trade. Whether this may become another round of musical bureaucracies is another question, but with every change the bureaucracy has weakened and the enterprise culture grown stronger.

Interest group politics appear to explain how specific reform policies have been implemented. However, relying on them alone might lead one to conclude that the Opening is wholly dependent on the leadership succeeding in playing groups off each other. So far so good. Such a conclusion though, both fudges the question of leadership intent and discounts the actual change in social environment that the Opening has caused. In fact, this startling change in environs appears to point to something more profound at work than basic interest group politics. A genuine shift in horizons on the part of the individual Chinese peasant and worker, almost an empowering effect may have occurred. If this hypothesis is true, the issue is not whether the Opening continues but how the Chinese state and society will cope as it does.

NOTES

1. *BR* (30 November 1987), pp. 14-15.
2. Cited in *China's Foreign Trade* (January 1988), pp. 6-7.
3. FBIS (7 February 1986), pp. K 16-21.
4. *ACFERT* (1984), pp. 392-393.
5. *China Daily* (27 May 1987), p. 1.
6. *ACFERT* (1986), p. 481.
7. Cited in Pollack, *The Chinese Electronics Industry,* pp. 40-53, 71-85.
8. *China Daily* (25 November 1986), p. 4.
9. *International Herald Tribune* (10 February 1988), p. 11.
10. *BR* (21 March 1988), p. 14.
11. Pollack, *The Chinese Electronics Industry,* pp. 50-51.
12. Pollack also describes the Fujian Electronic Computer Company whose similarly profitable efforts include a joint venture in Hong Kong and trade and information exchanges with factories in the U.S., Japan and Western Europe.
13. FBIS (20 June 1986), p. K2.
14. *BR* (6 July 1987), p. 25.
15. *BR* (1 February 1987), p. 24.
16. Cited in *Los Angeles Times* (30 December 1986), p. 1,8. See also Schram, "Economics in Command?," pp. 437-448.
17. Cited in Graham Young, "Control and Style: Discipline Inspection Commissions Since the 11th Congress," *CQ* XXV:1, pp. 1-52.
18. Baum, "Modernization and Legal Reform," p. 13.

19. *BR* (3 August 1987), pp. 14-16.
20. FBIS (1 August 1986), p. K 29.
21. Carol Hamrin notes: "There is considerable evidence that strong pressures from the military eventually forced the civilian planners to modify their program, in both its domestic and foreign policy aspects, producing compromise positions," Hamrin, "Competing 'Policy Packages,'" p. 493.
22. See, generally, Ellis Joffe, *The Chinese Army After Mao* (Cambridge: Harvard University Press, 1987).
23. Shirk, "The Central Economic Bureaucracy in China," in Cady (ed.), *American Economist Study Team,* pp. 28-31.
24. Wojtek Zafanolli, "A Brief Outline of China's Second Economy," *AS* XXV:7 (July 1985), pp. 715-736; *FEER* (18 September 1986), pp. 46-59; FBIS (8 April 1986), pp. K4-5.
25. *ACFERT* (1983), p. 389; *ACFERT* (1985), p. 395.
26. Whiting, *Chinese Domestic Politics,* pp. 74-75.
27. *SCMP* (20 March 1987), p. 1.
28. Interviews with China International Trust and Investment Corporation and MOFERT, Beijing, January 1987.
29. FBIS (8 April 1986), p. Q2.
30. Dorothy Solinger, "The Politics of Redistribution and the Chinese Industrial Readjustment, 1979-1982", paper presented at the Southern California China Colloquium, University of Southern California (16 May 1987).
31. *AWSJ* (30 December 1986), p. 10.
32. *China Daily* (20 March 1987), p. 4.
33. In 1987, six new airlines were to be spun off from CAAC's six main administrative regions in Beijing, Shanghai, Guangzhou, Shenyang, Lanzhou and Chengdu. *SCMP* (26 November 1985), pp. 1-2.
34. *SCMP* (3 June 1986), p. 3.
35. FBIS (7 February 1986), pp. K16-21.
36. Y.L. Wu, *The Spatial Economy of Communist China* (New York: Praeger, 1967), p. 200.
37. Interview at the Ministry of Machine Building, Beijing, August 1986.
38. Interview at Tianjin Foreign Economic Relations and Trade Commission, Tianjin, June 1986.
39. *China's Urban Statistics* (Beijing: China Statistical Information and Consultancy Service Centre, 1985), pp. 191-192.
40. Joyce Kallgren, "China in 1983: The Turmoil of Modernization," *AS* XXIV:1 (January 1984), p. 79.
41. *Zhongguo Faxue* in JPRS-CPS (12 March 1987), pp. 59-64.
42. *Zhongguo Xinwen She* in JPRS-CEA (9 August 1985), p. 10.
43. *Zhongguo Xinwen She* in JPRS-CEA (9 August 1985), p. 116.
44. *AWSJW* (23 June 1986), p. 12.
45. *SCMP* (20 November 1986), p. B1.
46. Interviews with Guangzhou Municipal Economic Commission and Guangzhou Foreign Trade and Economic Relations Commission, Guangzhou, July 1986.
47. *China Daily Business Weekly* (13 May 1987), p. 4.
48. Interviews with the author, Beijing, August 1986.

49. Interview with the author, Shanghai, 13 July 1986.
50. *AWSJ* (6 February 1987), p. 1.
51. FBIS (13 June 1986), pp. P1-5.
52. FBIS (1 May 1987), pp. K6-7; *Sixiang Zhengzhi Gongzuo Yanjiu* in JPRS-CPS (12 March 1987), pp. 19-31; *Jiushi Niendai* in JPRS-CPS (4 April 1987), pp. 31-48.
53. From interviews with Yao Nienqing, President, Guangzhou Institute of Foreign Trade, Guangzhou, June 1986.
54. Interviews in Guangzhou, July 1986.
55. *Asian Perspectives* (May 1986), pp. 7-11.
56. *Guoji Shangbao* in JPRS-CEA (16 July 1985), pp. 67-68; *Intertrade* (March 1986), p. 18.
57. *China: A Statistical Survey in 1986,* p. 122.
58. *Guoji Maoyi Wenti* in JPRS-CEA (23 September 1985), pp. 66-70.
59. *Zhongguo Xinwen She* in JPRS-CEA (9 August 1985), p. 10; FBIS (22 October 1985), pp. K3-13; *Wall Street Journal* (1 October 1985), p. 38.
60. Huan Guocang, "China's Opening to the Outside World," *Problems of Communism* XXXV:6 (November-December 1986), pp. 63-64.
61. *China Daily* (21 August 1987), p. 4.
62. Interview with Chinese pricing officials, Beijing, January 1987.
63. *Euromoney* (June 1986), pp. 40-53.
64. *China Daily Business Weekly* (13 May 1987), p. 1.
65. *East Asian Executive Reports* (February 1987), pp. 9-19.
66. *Intertrade* (27 July 1985), pp. 5-6.
67. To quote Lu Peijian, former President of the People's Bank: "It [the banking system] could not be adapted to the requirements of national economic development and monetary expansion." *BR* (9 April 1984), pp. 16-18.
68. *Euromoney* (April 1985), pp. 49-70; *AWSJ* (18 November 1986), p. 1, 15.
69. *Asian Wall Street Journal Weekly* (28 October 1985), p. 17; *BR* (30 September 1985), pp. 405; *Fujian Luntan* in JPRS-CEA (15 May 1986), pp. 104-109; *Ming Pao* in JPRS-CEA (16 July 1985), p. 122.
70. *NYT* (4 May 1987), p. B1.
71. *SCMP* (20 March 1987), p. B1.
72. One Chinese analyst suggested foreign investment in an "offshore financial center" in Shanghai for "teaching Chinese banks advanced management experience." *Guoji Maoyi Wenti* in JPRS-CEA (19 September 1985), pp. 86-89.
73. *China Daily* (18 August 1986), p. 2.
74. *Inc.* (June 1987), pp. 66-70.
75. The following is based on interviews with officials of the Kaili Telecommunications Factory and CEIEC Guangdong, Guangdong, June 1986.
76. Interviews with Wang Computers, Beijing, June 1986; Gould, Beijing, June 1986; CEIEC, Beijing, June 1986.
77. *ACFERT* (1985), pp. 662-663.

7

The Trend to Individual Empowerment

A GRASSROOTS CHANGE

The hypothesis of "empowering change" begins with the fundamental revolution in the ability of the Chinese individual to change his environment through the elimination of imperialism and the redistribution of wealth. This in turn has led to increased demands from the grassroots for degrees of political and economic freedom. The political leadership may be able to respond to this challenge in the short term with "slowdowns" and other repressive actions. But only by developing better ways of managing growth can reformist leadership hope to prevail over a longer period.

Wealth Redistribution

By the 1940s, only 4 percent of China's industrial output was mechanized, and industrial output itself formed a mere 5.6 percent of the gross national product. Compared to Japan and Russia, which had started to industrialize in the same period, China's record was deplorable. For example, the Hanyeping foundry, originally started by viceroy Zhang Zhidong to supply iron and coal for China's defense, found coal and coke distribution so inadequate inside China that in 1896 it undertook to exchange local iron ores for coal and coke from Japan's Yawata Iron and Steel Works. A victim of overstaffing, bureaucratic infighting, management incompetence and the lack of funds, the foundry was further compelled in 1903 to borrow 3 million yuan from Yawata at 6 percent interest, to be repaid over thirty years in terms of 60,000 tons of iron ore per year at 3 yuan per ton. These arrangements paid the interest annually but left the principal untouched. By 1934 (after several further large loans) 64 percent of the 11,767,241 tons of iron ore processed went to Yawata. In short, Hanyeping, China's mightiest industrial complex, was reduced to little more than a raw materials supplier for Japan.[1]

On top of the existing decay, the turmoil of first the Japanese invasion and then the civil war accompanied by the venality of the Nationalist government left most of China a smoking wreck by 1949.[2] Inflation had made the yuan worthless in 1948 and by 1949 the new "gold yuan" was also worthless. In the 12 years from 1937 to May 1949, the Kuomintang government increased banknote circulation by a factor of over 140 billion. Commodity prices rose by over 8.5 million times.[3] Total output of steel amounted to only 900,000 tons and coal only 60 million tons. In 1949 real wages in Chongqing were 50 to 60 percent below what they were in 1936.

With Communist victory a new stage arrived. Many acknowledged successes were made under Chairman Mao's rule. Most importantly, the social revolution achieved one of the most equal redistributions of wealth in history. The extremes of ostentation and starvation common under previous regimes were virtually wiped out. In the three years of reconstruction from 1949 to 1952, state-owned industry rose from 34.7 percent of production to 56 percent, and wages in the lower income brackets were raised by 30 to 60 percent. The average pay of workers and staff continued to rise by some 30 percent from 1953 to 1957. From 1952 to 1976, China was also one of the few countries in the world that sustained an industrial growth rate of over 10 percent. By contrast, for this period India and other low-income countries expanded their industrial sectors at 5 percent. Middle-income countries grew at about 7.5 percent.[4] Resources, particularly in heavy industry, rapidly expanded. Except for the aftermath of the Great Leap Forward in 1960, agriculture also largely succeeded in feeding a quarter of the world's population on approximately 7 percent of its arable land. The top-down expansion, however, came at a cost and failed to change China's "feudal" economy as well.

This "feudal" economy limited economic horizons, prevented the economic application of funds and blocked capital and goods from freely circulating. While providing full employment, it stunted the growth of exchange and encouraged a policy of wasteful and inefficient local self-sufficiency. During the Cultural Revolution, restrictions on exchange went so far as to mandate that all enterprise transactions of more than 30 yuan could be done only directly through the People's Bank, officially to prevent fraud.[5] Consumer goods production was neglected as personal incomes rose at only 3.5 percent annually after inflation from 1952 to 1978, and almost not at all from 1966 to 1976. Efficiency was at an all-time low following the Cultural Revolution as 25 percent of state enterprises operated at a loss in 1978. The very strong barriers to horizontal information and goods flows made it difficult to achieve any economies of scale. The relative weakness of central planning as practiced in China hampered the ability of the central bureaucracy to act as resource allocators. In fact as time went by, resource allocation appeared to occur generally as a function of personal connections among local bosses, each with a mandate for a small faction, none for the whole people. Contrary to expectations, the Cultural Revolution encouraged this trend by pushing more power into the hands of one man in the factory, destroying incentives, and nurturing a cult of leadership.[6]

Eliminating Imperialism

Politically, old China's Confucian bureaucratic reformers were bankrupt. In 1885, Chinese statesman Li Hongzhang had met with Japan's great reformer Ito Hirobumi to stabilize Sino-Japanese rivalry in Korea. Ten years later they met again after China's crashing defeat in the Sino-Japanese War to negotiate the Treaty of Shimonoseki. Said Ito then: "Ten years ago when I was at Tianjin, I talked about reform with the grand secretary [Li Hongzhang]. Why is it that up to now not a single thing has been changed or reformed?"[7]

With the Communist victory in 1949, Confucian China's bureaucracy appeared to be turned on its head. The Party declared the institution of private property to be at the root of the economic oppression of the Chinese people. Landlords and rich peasants made up less than 10 percent of the population but owned over 70 percent of the cultivated land. Because foreigners controlled China's industrial production and siphoned off its foreign revenues into their own pockets, they particularly benefited from a property-based political economy. In 1937, 91 percent of China's railways were under foreign control and, between 1913 and 1930, the average annual capital outflow from China was $56 million.[8] Said reformer Kang Youwei in 1900: "Although China is nominally an independent country, its territory, railways, shipping, trade and banks are all under the control of its enemies who can grab whatever they like."[9] As the Qing court and the bureaucrat-capitalists had so compromised themselves with their foreign friends, they, too, came under the label of foreign exploiters. Mao added in 1927: "The big bourgeoisie and big comprador classes in particular always side with imperialism and constitute an extreme counterrevolutionary group."[10] Communists thought that only by eliminating property rights, especially those of foreigners, the basis of the institutionalized inequities of haves and have-nots, could China even have the chance to modernize. Said Chen Duxiu, an early Marxist and founder of the Party though later purged: "We believe that only objective material causes can change society, can explain history, and can determine one's philosphy of life."[11]

The Marxist attack on foreign property appeared to coincide with the nationalist desires of much of the Chinese peasantry. Anti-Christian riots had always marked a tendency towards violence against proselytizing foreigners. By recruiting young peasant leaders and during the Yan'an period "penetrating the natural village," the party built a cadre of young, politically motivated and militarily active peasant leaders, who succeeded in launching something akin to a generational revolution against their conservative village elders.[12] After the Long March in 1934-35, foreign journalists first visited areas formerly under communist control and found peasants talking nostalgically of Red rule without interest, rents and rapacious landlords.[13] Understandably so, as peasants generally paid half of their crop to landlords and the amount could go as high as 80 percent. With the fall of the village elders and the crystallization of communist ideology in the revolutionary base areas, as one foreign observer put it: "The parallel movements of foreign communism and Chinese nationalism were suddenly joined, and, like the guilty lovers in Dante's *Inferno*, were condemned to journey to the end together."[14]

Despite the intentions of 1949 reformers though, the repudiation of imperialism did not prove to be a panacea for "feudal" China. Politically, "conservative thinking" [*baoshou sixiang*] and its repressive influence appeared to continue to dominate Chinese life. The leadership seldom if ever assumed that the peasants could act as responsible citizens who would want well-defined political rights and responsibilities according to a legal code. Though Mao often made end-runs around the bureaucracy to talk directly to the people, such events were always one-way movements pushed from the top down. The peasants, circumscribed by their world of personal relationships, ancestor worship, and superstition, also remained basically unquestioning of Mao and the party's paternalistic, absolute power. The phenomenon existed at all levels of society and grew most acute at the local village and county. There, the local party cadre often was also the mayor and factory chief as well, in reality the de facto warlord of an economically self-sufficient area.

The failure of Mao's most utopian efforts at change, the Great Leap Forward and the Cultural Revolution, may have come from his fundamentally flawed perception of this political problem. On the eve of the Great Leap, Mao reiterated his famous 1956 statement that the Chinese people were both poor and blank, and therefore they were inclined to revolution and new things could be written on them with ease.[15] The revolution "to touch men's souls" in fact did no such thing. By removing traditional authority constraints during the first two years of the Cultural Revolution, the leadership succeeded only in revealing the factional and lawless side of Chinese politics. Likewise, in destroying overnight entire levels of economic organization in the Great Leap Forward, Mao succeeded in creating large labor-intensive communes and small labor-intensive "backyard factories," both hopelessly uneconomic without adequate raw materials, distribution or sales channels. In both cases, the destruction of the old order did not in and of itself bring in a new one. Rather, in the absence of new ideas, "feudal" habits remained in the vacuum.

The Leadership Challenge

With the dramatic redistribution of wealth and the elimination of imperialism, the Communists had removed two of the great stumbling blocks to individual empowerment in China. However, the limitations of a feudal economy and political structure remained. These in turn sparked an apparent resurgence of popular dissatisfaction with the leadership. The economic malaise had made itself felt already in 1972 when China resumed complete plant imports from the West. These imports would wax and wane with domestic power struggles, reaching a peak in 1975 just before the unfolding of the last radical campaign to criticize Deng Xiaoping. A startling break with the rhetoric of the so-called Gang of Four about self-reliance and Third World solidarity, the very fact of their existence confirmed a deep insecurity among some in the Chinese leadership about the path China was on. As poor harvests and the Tangshan earthquake disrupted 1976, economic unrest also reappeared for the first time in many years. In inland provinces such as Sichuan, meat and vegetables were often unavailable. In the factories old workers had already grown disgruntled at the laxity in production and increasing accident rates.[16]

Political unrest also appeared to be increasing. In 1974, Li Yizhe, a pseudonymous poster-writing group, criticized Maoist policies under the guise of the Lin Biao system, calling instead for "revolutionary supervision by the masses of people over the leadership at various levels in the Party and the state."[17] Dissatisfaction boiled over into the Tiananmen Square Incident in 1976, the most dramatic expression of popular disapproval of political developments since 1949. Hundreds of thousands of Chinese students, peasants, and workers came in the face of official disapproval to pay their respects to the late Zhou Enlai and listen to dissident speakers, only to be dispersed by the Beijing police in a bloody riot. As Deng Xiaoping said, partly in warning to his Party colleagues, in 1977: "At this time, the political consciousness of the whole Party, army and people has risen remarkably, as has their ability to distinguish right from wrong. *People are using their heads,* thinking problems over and showing concern for the state and the Party [italics added]."[18]

THE LEADERSHIP DILEMMA

In 1976, then, the classic ingredients of a Chinese reform movement appeared to exist—dissatisfied populace, discredited leadership, economic crisis. Why though should this reform movement have been any more successful than the previous ones? How could the Opening succeed where the Great Leap Forward and "self-strengthening" had not?

Opening as Objective

For Deng and his fellow reformers, the choice to open China drew directly from the lessons of the past century. The downfall of both the so-called Gang of Four and of the reactionary 19th century court was a warning of the danger of cutting oneself off from the outside world. Liang Qichao had rejected those Chinese who would "say that merely embracing the several thousand years of our own morals, academic learning, and customs will be sufficient to enable us to stand up on the great earth."[19] Half a century later Mao, the greatest Chinese nationalist of all, still condemned the isolationist past. As he said: "Some people advocate 'Chinese learning as the substance, Western learning for practical application.' Is this right or wrong? It is wrong."[20]

In announcing the Opening to the Outside World, Deng's step-by-step pragmatism was abundantly in evidence. The goals, extent and content of this "great thaw" were clearly delineated by the leadership at every turn. Deng realized that China's industrial apparatus was in dire need of renovation.[21] Some industries, such as chemicals, were particularly worse off compared to a relatively stronger machine-building sector. Technological imports were the focus of the Opening and to pay for them Deng resolved to also expand exports, first of natural resources and then those products where China might have a competitive advantage, principally textiles. At first the leadership also studied the examples of Eastern European economic reforms to find certain benchmarks.[22] In 1979, however, they stepped forward independently with the passage of the Joint Venture Law, a significant advance in Sino-foreign cooperation. The introduction of Special Economic Zones and the use of model cities and factories to promote foreign economic relations also enabled the leadership to experiment and hedge its bets at the same time. If the Opening brought beneficial economic results, it could be extended. If not, the affected area was relatively small and the damage could be controlled.

The political ramifications of the Opening to the Outside World were subject to even greater leadership control. By the late 1970s, reformers were acknowledging that much of the stagnation of the Cultural Revolution was due to repressive grassroots political phenomena. They hypothesized that "mountain strongholds" and *guanxi*-based networks would prove more vulnerable to the forces of international exchange than to domestic "renovation" movements. They also gambled however, that the party could divorce itself from its "feudal" past yet maintain its dominance of China's political system. To safeguard socialist China, not even the most ardent state reformer was prepared to do away with the Party. At the same time they officially promoted the development of law, cultural and academic exchanges, and learning from other countries' experiences, all of which appeared to threaten the party's existing control mechanisms. The reformers seemed to present the party with a dilemma: even though its political dominance remained a sine qua non for reform, it too would have to improve its workstyle or face obsolescence as the Chinese people continued to expand their abilities.

These abilities were basically increased by the Opening. The opportunities for export earnings and foreign investment could dramatically enhance the fortunes of those able to seize them. With new transportation, communication and power networks, the peasant in Anhui could for the first time do business in Liaoning. In 1985 alone, the World Bank financed water-supply facilities in Beijing, thousands of kilometres of railway lines, transmission lines in Jiangsu, mine development in Shanxi, gas exploration in Sichuan, seed production nationwide, afforestation in ninety-two state farms, and technical assistance to engineering and economic university departments.[23] Export revenues soared from $8 billion in 1977 to $31 billion in 1986. Chinese students learned how to do business at Western schools of management, both in China (such as the Dalian program run by SUNY-Binghampton or the joint State Economic Commission-EEC program in Beijing) and abroad at Harvard, Stanford and other business schools. In the decade from 1977 to 1987, some 7,900 U.S. students and scholars went to China, while 28,000 Chinese went to the U.S.[24]

The threat posed to state control mechanisms by this increase in exchange came both from disgruntled local powerholders and from individuals with too high expectations. Serious incidents occurred domestically as "10,000 yuan households" were on occasion attacked by mobs of poor peasants, sometimes led by the local party secretary. Farmers protested bureaucratic incompetence by sacking office buildings. A layoff by a Chinese oil company in the South China Sea prompted a well-reported sit-down strike. Crime waves hit several major cities, including Beijing, as peasants, sometimes with the cooperation of local police, robbed vendors of entire goods shipments. The turbulence appeared to be testing the reformers' traditional interest group skills to the limit. To quote Yan Jiaqi, director of the Institute of Politics: "First of all, we must solve the incompatibilities of the political system with economic reforms."[25]

Slowdowns Temporarily Effective

With the increased conflict, the leadership became increasingly prone to slow down the pace of reform at intervals. These "slow-downs" generally consisted of a tightening of central credit controls, reregulation of prices, and the extensive use of informal negotiators to defuse political situations—such as the winter 1986 democracy protests. More controversially, certain reformers came under attack during these "slowdowns." The leadership, faced with the problem of maintaining its preeminence while modernizing, placed a premium on peace and order. Thus, to assure the ongoing train of reform, some specific reformers may have become scapegoats. Political activists were particular targets. Wei Jingsheng received fifteen years for his posters in 1979. Editors Xu Wenli and Liu Qing received fifteen and ten years, respectively, as well. Likewise in 1987, playwright Wu Guang, astrophysicist Fang Lizhi, and ideologian Su Shaozhi all lost their posts for excessive liberalism.

Unfortunately, by repressing the most dynamic elements of the society, the "slowdowns" retarded economic and political growth. For example, faced with an outbreak of inflation, central authorities had two choices.[26] One, they could cut off the import of expensive goods, fix domestic prices and centralize all credit in the People's Bank—in short "slowdown" and return to the statist development policy. Or, second, they could make importing enterprises responsible for the trading losses the state currently bore, allow nonessential goods to fluctuate, and reform and expand both the credit and audit functions of the nation's provincial and central financial institutions. The former might stanch the oubreak faster but by depriving the economy of needed economic and information inputs it prevented growth. Farmers could not raise yields without pesticides, expensive or not. Managers could not produce cost competitively without price benchmarks. Geographic and bureaucratic barriers could not be breached without capital.

The implication of the "slowdown" was increasing dispute over distribution. If the pie grew more slowly, the eaters would compete all the more fiercely for their share of it. They would also make scapegoats of the newcomers. For example, in the backlash of the deficits of 1983 to 1985, caused by overrapid foreign exchange decentralization, the central government unilaterally voided millions of dollars of contracts. Some interest groups were so compelling that their needs had to be met. Reportedly to supply needed foreign exchange to one heavy industry venture with very high-level connections over 25 projects had to be dropped from the 1986 annual plan. Meanwhile in Hong Kong, many smaller suppliers to Chinese consumers went bankrupt. Even giant Matsushita with reduced demand, cut production by 10 percent at its Ibaraki color television plant. The "briefcase" companies went underground. Deng Xiaoping criticized the Special Economic Zones, warning that the "blood transfusions" from the mainland could not go on much longer.

"Slowdowns," moreover, not only increased interest group competition but also appeared to deepen, not diminish, grassroots pressure for change. Popular expectations were still high for reforms and the pressure for positive developments seemed to be intensified by a growth failure. According to one poll in May-June 1987, 66 percent of respondents said economic reforms were going in the right direction. Also, however, 43 percent said they were dissatisfied with their current financial situation.[27] At one joint venture, workers compared the venture to an apple. With every day, a little more was bitten out of it until soon there would be nothing left.

The political forecasts of reformers were the ones farthest from being met under 1986 conditions. Student protestors for "democracy" appeared much in the vanguard of popular opinion. Law was still practiced with great irregularity. The Party still dominated the government. Economic decisions at the local level were usually motivated in the interests of the local elite. Reformers often said that reform was never easy and the obstacles would be many. The longer the delay though, the greater the grassroots pressure for change. In one 1987 poll, 94 percent of respondents thought it was necessary for political reforms to be carried out.[28] The legacy of the Cultural Revolution appeared to have left many in the younger generation unwilling to wait indefinitely.

TOWARDS A GROWTH SOLUTION

The challenge for the Opening to the Outside World then is to promote change without turbulence. Too much turbulence and "slowdowns" will ensue. Too little change and interest group coalitions will fossilize. It is a delicate line between promoting change and fostering instability but it is the essence of good management. As has been noted there are a number of key elements that have to be achieved for change to be successfully managed. Among them are—the rule of law to replace the rule of man, indirect economic controls to supercede direct appropriation, separation of authority versus personnel-union (e.g., Party-state), and most importantly an emphasis on national growth as compared to the sterile conservation of past glories.

One way to avoid factional infighting and consequent "slowdowns" is to distribute the pie fairly. Here the Chinese leadership has a good deal of experience and has been quite successful at keeping relatively powerful interest groups happy. For example, though the military found its numbers cut by 20 percent and its budget substantially reduced, export opportunities afforded by foreign trade reforms have made it very prosperous. Military factories now being turned over to civilian production are reportedly among the best managed due to their long service to one of the few scale-volume customers in China. The centralized state, moreover, has also made sure that its traditional heavy industry clients have remained adequately financed.

If the economy is to become self-sustaining, though, China's resource base must continue to grow. The Opening should give the greatest economic rewards to entrepreneurial enterprises such as the Kaili telephone factory and flexible bureaucracies such as CITIC. Bureaucrats must learn they should be good managers to survive. Party officials for the first time need to make a distinction between their charismatic function and the administrative sphere which is government terrain. To do so, more flexible and more universal regulations are needed. The FTC model is too rigid, with authority resting in Beijing and personally delegated to the ministerial branch in the provinces. Because authority is both personal and centralized in any given region, bureaucrats rely not on rules but on *guanxi* to make decisions. The multiplication of decisions presented by the Opening, however, demands a change to multiple centers of authority. Traditional authorities will be broken up to be replaced either by chaos or a new order. Either China will fragment into cliques paying "feudal" allegiance to Beijing or patrimonial bureaucracy will be replaced by rational-legal authority. The message appears clear in the short-term: either factionalism and low profits confined to a cliquish elite, or the development of a rational trade authority with greater revenues for all.

In the longer run, the Opening's growth and its incumbent tensions should also contribute to developing the individual in Chinese society and resolving the grassroots pressure for reform. When tendencies in the leadership conflict, the individual's political power grows, just as his or her social power grew with the elimination of the institutionalized inequities of capitalist distribution. Mao predicted that these contradictions would remain for at least a thousand years to come. But by resolving them democratically and without factional strife, human emancipation can increase and a more perfect socialism may result. As Deng said in 1975: " . . . the people cannot dictate to themselves and a section of the people should not be allowed to suppress another."[29] In a genuine socialist society, the individual's social and political power are reconciled. From a Marxist ideological point of view, the policies of China's socialist leadership should in fact lead to the development of an advanced, socialist political and economic democracy without compromising the original achievements of independence and equity.

As the political structure may expand, so too definitely must the economy. The new and more vital organizations that have been created by the Opening to the Outside World must become the engines of growth. For example, Shenzhen SEZ illustrated how mainland enterprises could use geography to their benefit through Shenzhen branches of mainland enterprises, joint ventures, and profits from mainland institutions such as banks, railways and customs. According to one set of figures, Shenzhen generated total sales of 519.4 million yuan for the mainland from 1979 to 1984, of which 131 million fell in commerce, 71 million in industry, 61 million in agriculture, 120 million in construction, 40 million in transportation, 59 million in banking, and 169 million from the sale of construction materials.[30] From 1980 to 1984, Shenzhen also acquired 51 percent of its rolled steel, 55 percent of its cement and 30 percent of its timber through enterprises contracting throughout China for materials and supplies.[31]

Reform though, does not mean wholesale decentralization of authority. Some businesses are better managed locally than nationally. Decentralizing without attention to economies of scale, at worst, encourages already present inefficiencies in the provincial structure. What enterprise autonomy does entail is the ability to make integrative decisions. Chinese factories must move from being stand-alone manufacturing centers to include sourcing and sales functions as well, if they are to be economically viable over the long-term. Recently the reformers have been encouraging "horizontal linkages" between enterprises to bridge business system gaps, especially in export industries. Likewise, the more successful foreign companies in China have helped their own economics by establishing multiple ventures to develop a national sales and sourcing infrastructure for their products.[32]

On balance the Opening to the Outside World has greatly expanded the horizons of the individual Chinese. In this sense, it represents a "great thaw." For the first time in the history of Chinese reform attempts, the leadership has actively challenged individuals (not bureaucrats) to improve their own conditions. The challenge has now moved from how to start change to how to best manage it. In the future new and greater external challenges will arise as China comes into its own as a global trading power. Domestically, factionalism and change will continue to play out their dialectic. The "key facts" of reform, however, appear promising—increased trade and exchange, increased individual income, increased use of law, and a perceived increased willingness to reform.

NOTES

1. Ch'en, *China and the West*, pp. 355-359.
2. See, generally, Sterling Seagrave, *The Soong Dynasty* (London: Sidgwick & Jackson, 1985).
3. Xu Dixin, "Transformation of China's Economy," in Xu Dixin (ed.), *China's Search*, p. 3.
4. World Bank, *China: Socialist Economic Development*, Volume II (Washington D.C.: World Bank, 1983), p. 119.

5. D. Solinger, "Marxism and the Market in Socialist China," in Nee and Mozingo (eds.), *State and Society,* p. 201.
6. Walder, "Some Ironies of the Maoist Legacy," in Selden and Lippit (eds.), *The Transition to Socialism,* pp. 234-235.
7. Cited in Teng and Fairbank (eds.), *China's Response to the West,* p. 126.
8. C.F. Remer, *Foreign Investment in China* (New York: MacMillan, 1923), p. 160.
9. Cited in Hu Sheng, *Imperialism and Chinese Politics,* p. 165.
10. Mao Zedong, *Selected Readings,* p. 12.
11. Cited in Teng and Fairbank (eds.), *China's Response to the West,* p. 250.
12. Schurmann, *Ideology and Organization,* p. 437.
13. Ch'en, *China and the West,* p. 54.
14. Cited in Ch'en, *China and the West,* p. 52.
15. Cited in Stuart Schram, "A Historical Perspective on the Cultural Revolution," in Schram (ed.), *Authority, Participation and Cultural Change in China,* p. 55.
16. Chi Hsin, *The Case of the Gang of Four,* p. 134.
17. Cited in Nathan, *Chinese Democracy,* p. 74.
18. Deng Xiaoping, *Selected Works,* p. 60.
19. Cited in Teng and Fairbank (eds.), *China's Response to the West,* p. 223.
20. Cited in Schram, "A Historical Perspective," p. 6.
21. Cited in Lotta (ed.), *And Mao Makes Five,* pp. 460-464.
22. Halpern, "Learning from Abroad," pp. 77-110.
23. The World Bank, *Annual Report 1985,* pp. 125-144.
24. *China Daily* (5 June 1987), p. 1.
25. Cited in *Jiushi Niendai* in JPRS-CPS (13 February 1987), p. 36.
26. *BR* (20 May 1985), pp. 6-10.
27. *SCMP* (10 September 1987), p. 10.
28. *BR* (31 August 1987), pp. 6-7.
29. Deng Xiaoping, *Selected Works,* p. 60.
30. *Jingni Daobao* in JPRS-CEA (3 September 1985), pp. 85-88.
31. *Jingji Guanli* in JPRS-CEA (30 July 1985), pp. 141-148.
32. Universal Matchbox, a $260 million Hong Kong company, has about 60 percent of its manufacturing based in China. The company owns a 35 percent interest in Shanghai Universal Toys and a 55 percent interest in Guangzhou Unitoys Tooling. Jay Forcelledo, vice chairman, predicted that it would continue to acquire toy companies in China and would be entering a more aggressive marketing phase in China.

Selected Bibliography

As is the case with most works on China, a great debt is owed to the Foreign Broadcast Information Service and the Joint Publications Research Service. Their transcriptions have been used extensively throughout this book. Among other Western periodicals, *China Trade Report, East Asian Executive Reports, China Business Review, China's Foreign Trade, China Quarterly, Intertrade, Journal of Asian Studies, Euromoney, Modern China, Australian Journal of Chinese Affairs, Asian Perspectives, Nihon Keizai Shimbun, Studies in Comparative Communism,* and *Nomura Securities* have been most useful. I have also relied on several Chinese source magazines including *Jingji Yanjiu, Jingji Wenti Tansuo, Hong Qi, Caimao Jingji, Shijie Jingji, Zhongguo Shehui Kexue* (both the national and Shanghai versions), as well as the daily and weekly editions of *Renmin Ribao, Jingji Ribao, Beijing Ribao, Guangming Ribao, China Daily* and *Liaowang*.

PERIODICALS

ACE	Almanac of China's Economy
ACFERT	Almanac of China's Foreign Economic Relations and Trade
APSR	American Political Science Review
AS	Asian Survey
AWSJ(W)	Asian Wall Street Journal (Weekly)
BR	Beijing Review
CBR	China Business Review
CQ	China Quarterly

FBIS   Foreign Broadcast Information Service
IS   Issues and Studies
ISQ   International Studies Quarterly
JAS   Journal of Asian Studies
JCS   Journal of Chinese Studies
JPRS-CPS Joint Publications Research Service—Chinese Political Studies
JPRS-CEA Joint Publications Research Service—Chinese Economic Affairs
MC   Modern China
NYT   New York Times
SCMP   South China Morning Post
SICC   Studies in Comparative Communism
SSC   Social Sciences in China
SYC   Statistical Yearbook of China
WP   World Politics

What follows is a summary of the books and articles I found most useful in the analysis of the politics of China's foreign economic relations.

Afanasyev, Victor, *Scientific Communism,* Moscow: Progress Publishers, 1967.

Bachman, David, *Chen Yun and the Political System,* Berkeley: Center for East Asian Studies, 1985.

Barnett, A. Doak, *Cadres, Bureaucracy and Political Power in Communist China,* New York: Columbia University Press, 1967.

Baum, Richard, "Modernization and Legal Reform in China: The Rebirth of Socialist Legality," paper presented at the Regional Seminar in Chinese Studies (Berkeley: University of California, 1986)

Beale, Louis, Pelham G., and Hutchison J., *Trade and Economic Conditions in China, 1931-33,* London: H.M. Stationery Office, 1933 (reprint San Francisco: Chinese Materials Center 1975).

Bedeski, Robert, "Leadership Roles in Modern China: The KMT and Communist Experiences," *Studies in Comparative Communism,* VII:1 (Spring/Summer 1974), 53-63.

Bernard, Elizabeth, "Post-1976 Drama: Institutional Authority Versus the Inherent Dignity of the Individual," *Journal of Chinese Studies,* I:1 (October 1984), 299-312.

Brodsgaard, Kjeld, "Paradigmatic Change: Readjustment and Reform in the Chinese Economy, 1953-1981," *Modern China,* IX:1,2 (January, April, 1983).

Cady, Janet (ed.), *Economic Reform in China: Report of the American Economists Study Team to the PRC,* Washington D.C.: National Committee on U.S.-China Relations, 1985.

Ch'en, Jerome, *China and the West,* London: Hutchinson Press, 1979.

Chen Jiyuan, "Technological Renovation and Restoration of the Economy," *Social Sciences in China,* VI:2 (June 1985), 27-43.

Cheng Chuyuan, *China's Economic Development: Growth and Structural Change,* Boulder, CO: Westview Press, 1982.

Cheng Hung-Sheng, "Historical Factors of China's Economic Underdevelopment, *Journal of Chinese Studies,* I:1 (June 1984), 221-234.

Chi Hsin (ed.), *The Case of the Gang of Four,* Hong Kong: Cosmos Books, 1978.

Chu Baotai, *Foreign Investment in China: Questions and Answers,* Beijing: Foreign Languages Press, 1986.

Collier, John and Elsie, *China's Socialist Revolution,* New York: Monthly Review Press, 1973.

Communist Party of China, *Uphold Reform and Strive for the Realization of Socialist Modernization,* Beijing: Foreign Languages Press, 1985.

Communist Party of China, *The Twelfth National Congress of the CPC,* Beijing: Foreign Languages Press, 1982.

Communist Party of China, *China's Economic Structure Reform,* Beijing: Foreign Languages Press, 1984.

Communist Party of China, *Resolution on CPC History (1949-1981),* Beijing: Foreign Languages Press, 1981.

Communist Party of the Soviet Union, *The Programme of the Communist Party of the Soviet Union,* Moscow: Novosti Press Agency, 1986.

Conroy, Richard, "Laissez-Faire Socialism? Prosperity, Peasants and China's Current Rural Development Strategy," *Australian Journal of Chinese Affairs,* 12 (July 1984), 1-35.

Creel, Herrlee G., *Chinese Thought: From Confucius to Mao Tse-tung,* Chicago: University of Chicago Press, 1953.

de Bary, Theodore (ed.), *Sources of Chinese Tradition* (2 vols.), New York: Columbia University Press, 1960.

Deng Xiaoping, *Selected Works (1975-1982),* Beijing: Foreign Languages Press, 1984.

Deng Xiaoping, *Fundamental Issues in Present-Day China,* Beijing: Foreign Languages Press, 1987.

Dittmer, Lowell, "Ideology and Organization in Post-Mao China," *Asian Survey,* XXIV:3 (March 1984), 349-369.

Dittmer, Lowell, "Chinese Communist Revisionism in Comparative Perspective," *Studies in Comparative Communism,* XIII:1 (Spring 1980), 3-40.

Dittmer, Lowell, "Power and Personality in China: Mao Tse-tung, Liu Shao-ch'i, and the Politics of Charismatic Succession," *Studies in Comparative Communism,* VII:1 (Spring/Summer 1974), 21-52.

Donnithorne, Audrey, *Centre-Provincial Economic Relations in China,* Canberra: Australian National University, 1981.

Douglass, Bruce and Terrill, Ross (eds.), *China and Ourselves: Explorations and Revisions by a New Generation,* Boston: Beacon Press, 1970.

Eckstein, Alexander, *China's Economic Development,* Cambridge: Cambridge University Press, 1977.

Elliott, David W.P., "Training Revolutionary Successors in Vietnam and China, 1958-1976: The Role of Education, Science and Technology in Development," *Studies in Comparative Communism,* XV:1 (Spring/Summer 1982), 31-70.

Elliott, John E., (ed.), *Marx and Engels on Economics, Politics and Society,* Santa Monica: Goodyear Publishing, 1981.

Etzioni, Amitai, *A Comparative Analysis of Complex Organizations*, Glencoe, IL: The Free Press, 1961.

Fairbank, John K., and May, Ernest R. (eds.), *America's China Trade in Historical Perspective: The Chinese and American Performance*, Cambridge: Harvard University Press, 1986.

Falkenheim, Victor, "Bureaucracy, Factions and Political Change in China," *Pacific Affairs*, LVII:3 (Fall 1985), 471-80.

Fine, Ben, and Harris, Laurence, *Rereading Capital*, New York: Columbia University Press, 1979.

Ghosh, Partha, *Sino-Soviet Relations: U.S. Perceptions and Policy Responses 1949-59*, New Delhi: Uppal Publishers, 1981.

Gorbachev, Mikhail, *Political Report of the CPSU Central Committee*, Moscow: Novosti Press Agency, 1986.

Gray, Jack, and White, Gordon (eds.), *China's New Development Strategy*, London: Academic Press, 1982.

Greene, Felix, *A Curtain of Ignorance*, New York: Doubleday & Company, 1964.

Griffith, William E., *The Sino-Soviet Rift*, Cambridge: M.I.T. Press, 1964.

Halpern, Nina, "Learning from Abroad: Chinese Views of the Eastern European Economic Experiments, January 1977 to June 1981," *Modern China*, XI:1 (January 1985), 77-110.

Halpern, Nina P., "China's Industrial Economic Reforms: The Question of Strategy," *Asian Survey*, XXV:10 (October 1985), 998-1012.

Hamrin, Carol Lee, "Competing Policy Packages in Post-Mao China," *Asian Survey*, XXIV:5 (May 1984), 487-518.

Hao, Yen-p'ing, *The Commercial Revolution in Nineteenth-Century China*, Berkeley: University of California Press, 1986.

Harding, Harry, *Organizing China: The Problem of Bureaucracy*, Stanford: Stanford University Press, 1981.

Harding, Harry (ed.), *China's Foreign Relations in the 1980s*, New Haven: Yale University Press, 1984.

Hayhoe, Ruth E.S., "A Comparative Approach to the Cultural Dynamics of Sino-Western Educational Cooperation," *China Quarterly*, 104 (December 1985), 676-699.

Ho, Alfred, "Trade and Economic Development of the PRC," *Journal of Chinese Studies*, I:1 (June 1984), 203-219.

Horsley, Jamie, "Comments on Law and Legal Development Affecting Foreign Investment in China," *China Law Reporter*, III:2 (Summer 1986), 3-15.

Hou Chi-ming, *Foreign Investment and Economic Development in China, 1840-1937*, Cambridge: Harvard University Press, 1965.

Howard, M.C., and King, J.E., *The Political Economy of Marx*, New York: Longman, Inc., 1985.

Hsia Tao-tai, "The New Constitution of the PRC: Implications for Reunification with Taiwan," *Journal of Chinese Studies*, I:1 (February 1984), 105-119.

Hu Sheng, *Imperialism and Chinese Politics*, Beijing: Foreign Languages Press, 1981.

Huan Guocang, "China's Opening to the Outside World," *Problems of Communism*, XXXV (November 1986), 40-71.

Huan Xiang, "The New Technological Revolution and China's Response," *Social Sciences in China,* VI:1 (March 1985), 64-77.

Johnson, Chalmers (ed.), *Change in Communist Systems,* Stanford: Stanford University Press, 1970.

Kallgren, Joyce, "China in 1983: The Turmoil of Modernization," *Asian Survey,* XXIV:1 (January 1984), 60-80.

Kapur, Haresh (ed.), *The End of Isolation: China After Mao,* The Hague: Martinus Nijhoff Publishers 1985.

King, Wunsz (ed.), *V.K. Wellington Koo's Foreign Policy: Some Selected Documents,* Shanghai: Kelly & Walsh, 1931 (reprint, University Publications of America 1976).

Kueh, Y.Y., and Howe, Christopher, "China's International Trade Policy and Organization Change and Their Place in the 'Economic Readjustment,'" *China Quarterly,* 100 (December 1984), 813-849.

Lampton, David, "Policy Arenas and the Study of Chinese Politics," *Studies in Comparative Communism,* VII:4 (Winter 1974), 409-413.

Lane, David, *The End of Social Inequality?,* London: George Allen & Unwin, 1982.

Lasswell, H., and Lerner, D. (eds.), *World Revolutionary Elites: Studies in Coercive Ideological Movements,* Cambridge: M.I.T. Press, 1966, 319-455.

Lee, Rensselaer W., III, "Political Absorption of Western Technology: The Soviet and Chinese Cases," *Studies in Comparative Communism,* XV:1 (Spring/Summer 1982), 9-33.

Levenson, Joseph R., *Confucian China and Its Modern Fate,* Berkeley: University of California Press, 1972.

Li Fan, "Are Concepts and Mentality Changing? An Explanatory Discussion on the New Technological Revolution and the Modernization of Mentality," *Chinese Sociology and Anthropology,* XVII:3, 107-115.

Lieberthal, Kenneth, "The Foreign Policy Debate in Peking as Seen Through Allegorical Articles," *China Quarterly,* 71 (September 1977), 528-554.

Lin Fang, "Comments on Western Humanistic Psychology with a Discussion of Certain Psychological Problems in Economic Reform," *Social Sciences in China,* VI:3 (August 1985), 21-35.

Lotta, Raymond (ed.), *And Mao Makes Five,* Chicago: Banner Press, 1978.

Ma Hong (ed.), *New Strategy for China's Economy,* Beijing: New World Press, 1983.

Mancall, Mark, *China at the Center: 300 Years of Foreign Policy,* New York: Free Press, 1986.

Mao Zedong, *Selected Works,* Beijing: Foreign Languages Press, 1956.

Ministry of Electronic Industries, *Mechanical and Electronic Industries Yearbook of China,* Hong Kong: Economic and Information Agency, 1985.

Ministry of Foreign Economic Relations and Trade, *Collection of Laws and Regulations of the People's Republic of China Concerning Foreign Economic Affairs* (3 vols.), Beijing: China Development Press, 1985.

Ministry of Foreign Economic Relations and Trade (ed.), *Almanac of China's Foreign Economic Relations and Trade,* Hong Kong: China Resources Trade Consultancy, 1984 to 1986.

Moser, Michael (ed.), *Foreign Trade, Investment and the Law,* Hong Kong: Oxford University Press, 1984.

Myers, Henry (ed.), *Western Views of China and the Far East,* (2 vols.), Hong Kong: Asian Research Service, 1982.

Myers, James T., "China—The 'Germs' of Modernization," *Asian Survey,* XXV:10 (October 1985), 981-997.

Nathan, Andrew, "A Factionalism Model for CCP Politics," *China Quarterly,* 53 (Spring 1973), 34-66.

Nathan, Andrew J., *Chinese Democracy,* Berkeley: University of California Press, 1985.

National People's Congress, *Fifth Session of the Fifth National People's Congress,* Beijing: Foreign Languages Press, 1983.

National People's Congress, *The Third Session of the Sixth National People's Congress,* Beijing: Foreign Languages Press, 1985.

Nee, Victor, and Mozingo, David, (eds.), *State and Society in Contemporary China,* Ithaca: Cornell University Press, 1983.

Nove, Alec, *The Economics of Feasible Socialism,* London: George Allen & Unwin, 1983.

Oi, Jean, "Communism and Clientelism: Rural Politics in China," *World Politics,* (January 1985), 238-266.

Oksenberg, Michel, "Economic Policy-making in China, Summer 1981," *China Quarterly,* 90 (June 1981), 165-194.

Osterhammel, Jurgen, "Imperialism in Transition: British Business and the Chinese Authorities, 1931-1937," *China Quarterly,* 98 (June 1984), 260-287.

Pfennig, Werner, "Political Aspects of Modernization and Judicial Reform in the PRC," *Journal of Chinese Studies,* I:1 (February 1984), 79-103.

Pollack, Jonathan, *The Chinese Electronics Industry in Transition,* Santa Monica: Rand Corporation, 1985.

Prybyla, Jan S., "The Chinese Economy: Adjustment of the System or Systemic Reform?" *Asian Survey,* XXV:5 (May 1985), 553-586.

Pye, Lucian, *Chinese Commercial Negotiating Behavior,* Cambridge: Oelgeschlager, Gunn & Hain, 1982.

Pye, Lucian, *The Dynamics of Chinese Politics,* Cambridge: Oelgeschlager, Gunn & Hain, 1981.

Rice, Edward E., *Mao's Way,* Berkeley: University of California Press, 1972.

Rosenau, James N., *The Study of Global Interdependence,* London: Frances Pinter, 1980.

Rosenau, James N., (ed.), *International Politics and Foreign Policy,* New York: The Free Press, 1969.

Rubin, I.I., *Essays on Marx's Theory of Value,* Detroit: Black & Red Press, 1972.

Ryzhkov, Nikolai, *Guidelines for the Economic and Social Development of the USSR,* Moscow: Novosti Press Agency, 1986.

Schram, Stuart, "Economics in Command? Ideology and Policy since the Third Plenum, 1978-84," *China Quarterly,* 99 (Summer 1985), 417-461.

Schram, Stuart (ed.), *Authority, Participation and Cultural Change in China,* Cambridge: Cambridge University Press, 1973.

Schurmann, Franz, *Ideology and Organization in Communist China,* Berkeley: University of California Press, 1966.

Selden, Mark, and Lippit, Victor (eds.), *The Transition to Socialism in China*, Armonk, NY: M.E. Sharpe, 1981.

Shaw, Yu-Ming (ed.), *Power and Policy in the People's Republic of China*, Boulder, CO: Westview Press, 1985.

Sheahan, John, *Alternative International Economic Strategies and Their Relevance for China*, Washington D.C.: World Bank, 1986.

Skilling, H. Gordon, "Interest Groups and Communist Political Revolutions," *World Politics*, (October 1983), 1-27.

Solinger, Dorothy, *Chinese Business Under Socialism*, Berkeley: University of California Press, 1984.

Solinger, Dorothy (ed.), *Three Views of Chinese Socialism*, Boulder, CO: Westview Press, 1984.

Statistical Yearbook of China, Hong Kong: Economic Information & Agency, 1984 to 1986.

Stoltenberg, Clyde D., "China's Special Economic Zones: Their Development and Prospects," *Asian Survey*, XXIV:6 (June 1984), 637-654.

Sullivan, Lawrence R., "The Role of the Control Organs in the CCP, 1977-1983," *Asian Survey*, XXIV:6 (June 1984), 597-617.

Sun Xiangjian, "The Question of the Profitability of China's Foreign Trade to the National Economy," *Social Sciences in China*, II:1 (Spring 1981), 35-60.

Sweezy, Paul M., and Bettelheim, Charles, *On the Transition to Socialism*, New York: Monthly Review Press, 1971.

Tai Chun-Kuo, and Myers, Ramon, *Understanding Communist China: Communist China Studies in the U.S. and the Republic of China 1949-1978*, Stanford: Hoover Institute Press, 1986.

Teng Ssu-yu, and Fairbank, John K. (eds.), *China's Response to the West: A Documentary Survey, 1839-1923*, Cambridge: Harvard University Press, 1979.

U.S. Congress, Joint Economic Committee, *China Under the Four Modernizations*, U.S. 97th Congress, 2d session, Washington D.C.: GPO, 1982, p. 24.

Van Ness, Peter, *Revolution and Chinese Foreign Policy*, Berkeley: University of California Press, 1970.

Walder, Andrew, "Organized Dependency and Cultures of Authority in Chinese Industry, *Journal of Asian Studies*, November 1983, 51-76.

Wang, Nora, "Deng Xiaoping: The Years in France," *China Quarterly*, 92 (December 1982), 698-706.

Weber, Max, *The Theory of Social and Economic Organization*, New York: The Free Press, 1964.

Wei Yung, "Elite Conflicts in Chinese Politics: A Comparative Note," *Studies in Comparative Communism*, VII:1 (Spring/Summer 1974), 64-72.

Whiting, Allen, *Chinese Domestic Politics and Foreign Policy in the 1970s*, Ann Arbor: University of Michigan Papers in Chinese Studies, No. 36, 1979.

Wiarda, Howard, *Ethnocentrism in Foreign Policy: Can We Understand the Third World?*, Washington D.C.: American Enterprise Institute for Public Policy Research, 1985.

Wilhelm, Alfred D., Jr., "Chinese Elites and Comparative Elite Studies: A Progress Report," *Studies in Comparative Communism*, XIII:1 (Spring 1980), 63-81.

Womack, Brantly, "Modernization and Democratic Reform in China," *Journal of Asian Studies*, XLIII:3 (May 1984), 417-439.

World Bank, *China: Long-term Development Issues and Options,* Baltimore: Johns Hopkins University Press, 1985.

World Bank, *China: Economic Structure in International Perspective,* Washington D.C.: World Bank, 1985.

Wu, Friedrich, "Explanatory Approaches to Chinese Foreign Policy: A Critique of the Western Literature," *Studies in Comparative Communism,* XIII:1 (Spring 1980), 41-62.

Xu Dixin (ed.), *China's Search for Economic Growth,* Beijing: New World Press, 1982.

Xue Muqiao, *China's Socialist Economy,* Beijing: Foreign Languages Press, 1986.

Yahuda, Michael, *Towards the End of Isolation—China's Foreign Policy After Mao,* Hong Kong: MacMillan Press, 1983.

Yang Liqiang, and Shen Weibin, "Symposium on Modern China's Bourgeoisie," *Social Sciences in China,* V:2 (June 1984), 9-27.

Youngson, A.J. (ed.), *China and Hong Kong: The Economic Nexus,* Hong Kong: Oxford University Press, 1983.

Yuan Wenqi, Dai Lunzhang, and Wang Linsheng, "International Division of Labor and China's Economic Relations with Foreign Countries," *Social Sciences in China,* I:1 (March 1980), 22-48.

Zafanolli, Wojtek, "A Brief Outline of China's Second Economy," *Asian Survey,* XXV:7 (July 1985), 715-736.

Zhongguo Jingwei Jingji Guanli Yanjiusuobian, *Zhongguo Gudai Sixiang Yu Guanli Xiandaihua,* Yunnan: Yunnan Renmin Chubanshe, 1985.

Zhou Guo (ed.), *China and the World,* Beijing: Beijing Review, 1986.

Zhou Xiuluan, "Development of China's Native Industries During World War One," *Chinese Sociology and Anthropology,* XVII:1 (Fall 1984), 35-67.

Zi Zhongyun, "Zhongguo de Meiguo Yanjiu," *Meiguo Yanjiu,* I:1 (Summer 1987), 7-21.

Most primary source material was gathered during interviews conducted from 1984 to 1987. In the summer of 1984, under a grant from the Department of Education administered by the University of Southern California, I conducted a series of interviews mostly with provincial foreign trade organizations and joint ventures in Guangdong and Shanghai. In 1986, I returned to conduct further interviews from April until September, again initially on a grant from the Department of Education administered by Universtiy of Southern California. These interviews covered a wide spectrum of Chinese government officials and domestic and foreign businessmen. From September 1986 until September 1987, I continued intermittently travelling to China to conduct further research. In most cases, the interviewees were visited more than once. In the case of Chinese government organizations, both provincial and national personnel were seen. Among those whom I interviewed are the following:

Enterprises with Foreign Investment
Amtech
ARCO
Beijing Jeep
Beijing Nabisco
Cable and Wireless
China Hewlett-Packard (CH P)
China Hotel–Guangzhou
Data General
Fluor
General Electric
Gould China
Heinz UFE
IBM-China
Intel
Jardines China
Jin Rong Electronics
Pepsi
Pilkington Glass
Sanyo Huaqiang
Shanghai Bell
Shanghai Ekchor Motorcycle
Shanghai Foxboro
Shanghai Schindler
Shanghai Squibb
Shanghai Volkswagen
Siemens
Swire Pacific
Tianjin Otis
Tianjin Otsuka
Tianjin Wella
Wang Computer
White Swan Hotel–Guangzhou
Xerox

Government Organizations
Beijing Foreign Economic Relations and Trade Commission
Beijing Economic Commission
China National Chemicals Import/Export Corporation (SINOCHEM)
China National Electronics Import/Export Corporation (CEIEC)
China National Technical Import Corporation (CNTIC)
Guangzhou Foreign Economic Relations and Trade Commission

Guangzhou Economic Commission
Ministry of Electronics Industry (MEI)
Ministry of Foreign Economic Relations and Trade (MOFERT)
Ministry of Light Industry (MOLI)
Ministry of Machine Building (MMB)
Ministry of Posts and Telecommunications (MPT)
Shanghai Foreign Economic Relations and Trade Commission
Shanghai Economic Commission
Shenzhen Industrial Development Committee
State Administration of Exchange Control (SAEC)
State Economic Commission (SEC)
State Planning Commission (SPC)
Tianjin Foreign Economic Relations and Trade Commission
Tianjin Economic Commission

Other Organizations
Baoshan Steel
Beijing Institute of Foreign Trade
Beijing University, Department of Law
China Academy of Social Sciences, Institute of Politics
China Academy of Social Sciences, Institute of American Studies
China Business News
China Enterprise Management Association (CEMA)
Guangzhou Bottle Factory
Guangzhou Institute of Foreign Trade
Kaili Electronics Factory
National Committee on U.S. China Relations
Tianjin Bicycle Factory

Index

ABOUT THE AUTHOR

Jonathan R. Woetzel holds a Ph.D. in Chinese political economy from the University of Southern California and has been the recipient of a National Resource Fellowship for studies in China. He has lived and worked in Hong Kong and China for several years and speaks Mandarin Chinese. He is currently a consultant in the Hong Kong office of McKinsey & Co., the general management consulting firm.